ORGANIZATION MODELING

INNOVATIVE ARCHITECTURES FOR THE 21ST CENTURY

Joseph Morabito
Ira Sack
Anilkumar Bhate

ISBN 0-13-257552-3

Prentice Hall PTR
Upper Saddle River, NJ 07458
www.phptr.com

Editorial/production supervision: *Kathleen M. Caren*
Acquisitions editor: *Jeffrey M. Pepper*
Cover design director: *Jerry Votta*
Cover designer: *Talar Agasyan*
Manufacturing manager: *Alexis R. Heydt*
Marketing manager: *Dan Rush*
Editorial assistant: *Linda Ramagnano*
Compositor: *Pine Tree Composition, Inc.*

ISBN 0-13-257552-3

Prentice-Hall International (UK) Limited, *London*
Prentice-Hall of Australia Pty. Limited, *Sydney*
Prentice-Hall Canada Inc., *Toronto*
Prentice-Hall Hispanoamericana, S.A., *Mexico*
Prentice-Hall of India Private Limited, *New Delhi*
Prentice-Hall of Japan, Inc., *Tokyo*
Prentice-Hall (Singapore) Pte. Ltd., *Singapore*
Editora Prentice-Hall do Brasil, Ltda., *Rio de Janeiro*

To
Betty, Jeff, and Charlie

To
Jeanette, Alex, and Kenny

To
Priya, Soniya, Manjiri, and Chinmoy

TABLE OF CONTENTS

PREFACE   vii

CHAPTER 1
ORGANIZATION MODELING   1

PART 1
ORGANIZING OM   9

CHAPTER 2
AN INTRODUCTION AND CRITIQUE OF ORGANIZATION THEORY   14

CHAPTER 3
DESIGNING ORGANIZATIONS   26

CHAPTER 4
A NEW APPROACH TO ORGANIZATION MODELING   43

CHAPTER 5
THE LAYERED ORGANIZATION   62

CHAPTER 6
ORGANIZATION MOLECULES   78

CHAPTER 7
ALIGNING ORGANIZATION MOLECULES   94

CHAPTER 8
THE OM DESIGN PROCESS   109

CHAPTER 9
ORGANIZATIONAL PATTERNS   124

PART 2
BUILDING A 21ST CENTURY ORGANIZATIONAL ARCHITECTURE   155

CHAPTER 10
DIRECTIONALITY AND CULTURE   158

CHAPTER 11
PROCESS FORMULATION   169

CHAPTER 12
DATA, KNOWLEDGE, AND INFORMATION   199

CHAPTER 13
KNOWLEDGE FORMULATION   230

CHAPTER 14
THE 21ST CENTURY LEARNING ORGANIZATION   248

APPENDIX
A BRIEF REVIEW OF INFORMATION MODELING   275

BIBLIOGRAPHY   281

INDEX   286

PREFACE

Organization Modeling (OM) is all about architecting organizations. Architecting the organization entails understanding, analyzing, designing, and communicating the most relevant parts of the organization and how they fit together. In this book, we provide an innovative framework that models organizational constructs with analytical discipline. We draw on organization theory (OT) to identify organizational components and their relationships, and use information modeling (borrowed from the computer software field) as a structuring mechanism. The result is a revolutionary, yet simple and effective, paradigm for crafting organizational architecture.

Organizations succeed, or fail, as a whole. No single ingredient—strategy, information, process, people, structure, or culture—is solely accountable for organizational success or failure. Competitive advantage accrues to those corporations whose managers analyze and shape their respective organizations: the whole, each of its parts, the relationships of the parts, and how the whole and its parts change. This book gives managers a language to structure and change organizations. This is the first work of its kind.

Managers are becoming architects. Their new roles include *designing* structure, *engineering* processes, *developing* people, *leveraging* information technology, *facilitating* learning, and *changing* the whole. The *manager-architect* has an arduous task: He or she must design across organizational boundaries, engineer processes into strategic capabilities, develop individual competencies into a learning organization, align information technology with business strategy, and integrate the disparate pieces that constitute the organization so that the "theory of the business" is practiced every day. Successful organizations have manager-architects who practice a disciplined approach to both analysis and design. This book guides managers in developing the art and skill of architecting organizations.

Our fundamental premise is that the wealth of organizational research and literature may be given the structure required for creating architecture. We start with organization theory (OT) and identify core organizational constructs: environment, power, strategy, process, information, human, structure, and tool. We further identify derivative management philosophies (e.g., learning and culture) in terms of the core constructs. Both core organizational constructs and derivative management philosophies are the *materials* with which we create an organization model. We shall refer to these materials collectively as *organizational constructs*.

Our second premise is that organizational constructs may be framed with *behavior*. By specifying behavior among constructs, we arrive at a semantic understanding of their relationships. Behavior is specified with a design mechanism known as a *contract*. Using behavior for understanding organizations resolves the problem of associating constructs with dissimilar structural properties, such as organizational structure and business processes. It is only during implementation that behavior is operationalized in the form of structure. The semantic association between organizational constructs is the *glue* of organization modeling.

WHY THIS BOOK IS NEEDED

This book brings together what previously have been the unrelated domains of OT and information modeling. Organizations are extraordinarily complex, yet disappointingly, their analysis is undisciplined. By undisciplined, we mean that no formal framework exists by which individual research efforts may be consistently integrated. Organizational problems are more easily understood with an architecture framed with a disciplined approach to modeling.

Another motivation for this book is the need to provide a meaningful alternative to the current – *incorrect and damaging* – trend to think of information technology (IT) related models as business models. For example, a business class is an object-oriented software element whose advantage over a traditional software element is the greater organizational alignment it produces. However, the business class is unrelated to the models required for organizational analysis. For example, business process transformation requires a business process model, whose specifications derive from organizational, and not IT, literature. Therefore, for correct and meaningful analysis and design, a formal framework for organizational research is required. OM is our choice for that framework.

SCOPE OF THE BOOK

Because it is likely that the reader will be familiar with either OT or information modeling, but not both, we present a brief overview of each. However, we assume a certain level of familiarity with organizational literature. In contrast, information modeling is relatively new. Though we present a dense modeling tutorial in the *Appendix*, the novice is referred to several books: in particular, *Information Modeling* by Kilov and Ross, and the more recent *Business Specifications* by Kilov.

Organization Modeling: Innovative Architectures for the 21st Century is intended for students of business, management, and information management. This includes graduate students and faculty in business, management, and information management programs. The intended business audience consists of managers and practitioners involved in organizational analysis and design. It is expected that the reader is interested in something more than a mere overview of organizations. The material we present is concept-rich and requires more than a casual interest. To facilitate understanding, we include many examples and, of course, a fair number of diagrams that illustrate the concepts. We believe professionals want and require a sufficient level of detail to solve organizational problems.

THE FEATURES OF OM

OM provides *business professionals* with a road map which assists them to arrive at an architectural prescription for their organizations. We introduce the concept of an architectural building block known as an *organization molecule*. Molecules are arrangements of organizational constructs that facilitate focused analysis of a specific class of business problem. For the manager engaged in a given business-level activity, we provide a corresponding organization molecule. For example, business process change is supported with the molecule known as a *process molecule*.

Molecules are derived from organizational research but framed with information modeling concepts to facilitate understanding, analysis, and design. Representative molecules are introduced: process, information, and culture, among others. We provide guidelines for managers to design an architecture and corresponding molecules that best fit their organizational needs. Molecules have the property of *abstraction*, facilitating varying levels of analysis. Accordingly, OM uniformizes – as opposed to standardizes – the organizational processes of strategic planning, process change (e.g., business transformation and improvement), structural design, knowledge management, and organizational learning, among others.

Similarly, to the *IT professional*, we provide a framework for analyzing and implementing data, information, and knowledge in a particular context, such as a business process. In our framework, IT and business strategy are complementary concepts – IT is crafted to *fit* a particular organization's strategy, process, and culture. This means that business analysis in the 21st century will be very different from what is currently the case. It must include several domains, such as business process analysis, data and knowledge, culture, learning, and so on.

This is the first book to create a coherent formalism for the manager-architect. OM is a rich tapestry that weaves together organizational and IT concepts.

CHAPTER 1

ORGANIZATION MODELING

1.1 GROPING IN THE DARK

Change is everywhere—global competition, mergers and acquisitions, strategic alignment, teams, knowledge management, the Web. How about decision making with seemingly insufficient information—or is it too much of the wrong information? And let's not forget young knowledge workers who know more than their managers—about work *and* management. Oh, yes, how about innovative culture—what's that, anyway? And what is the manager with an MBA to make of Michael Porter's strategic positioning concepts—low cost, differentiation, and niche—when Japanese manufacturers do all three at once? And what is the relationship between culture, information, competitiveness, and all the rest? The questions never end.

It seems bewildering. Organizations respond to these management philosophies of position with yet other management philosophies of action: business process transformation, organizational learning, downsizing, object-oriented development, restructuring, and so on. A few initiatives may work for a time with certain companies, still others for other companies. Most will only marginally improve an organization's effectiveness.

Change is seldom coordinated. Management rewards people as individuals, yet expects teams to flourish. Management introduces a quality or learning initiative, and then deliberately staffs its organizations with disaffected, short-term employees. And why does management expect a healthy culture when the only *real* stakeholders are they and the shareholders? Each of us has observed this random and inconsistent approach to management—a great deal of activity with little progress and almost no chance for success.

SEARCHING FOR DISCIPLINE

To avoid the pitfalls associated with haphazard decision making, management sometimes systematizes its approach to change. There are "change" models, "decision-making" models, and so on—each a step-by-step procedure leading the manager through the "process of change." The results are questionable. In practice, such procedures provide only a tactical focus, producing little of enduring value.

1

Other organizations try a more strategic approach—they seek to provide a framework or architecture that gives coherence to decision making. But which architecture? Is there a modeling framework of the organization to which management may refer? Every day we see another "business," "enterprise," or "organization" model put on the auction block. Why has none claimed victory?

As an example, let us examine the primary force behind organizational change: information technology (IT). At one time, management had tremendous faith in the IT professional to produce architectures that would really work. Remember information engineering and all those "enterprise models" that cost millions of dollars and took months, sometimes years, to construct? Have they produced effective information systems?

In a classic paper, "Experiences in Strategic Information Systems Planning," Earl (1993) has shown that technology-driven (e.g., information engineering) and methodology-driven (e.g., Method/1) approaches to information systems (IS) planning confer relatively little competitive advantage. These weak approaches are formalized in the sense that they impose a structure and a degree of rigor. They use highly technical constructs such as data flow diagrams, and, not surprisingly, are popular with IT professionals. In contrast, the most successful approaches to IS planning are those that make IT professionals uncomfortable: They are the "soft" organizational approaches that emphasize teams and learning in place of technical artifacts.

Perhaps our expectations are misplaced. Why should IT professionals have a model of the organization? After all, their information architectures seldom work. Furthermore, organizations are much more than information; in fact, they are characterized by many *organizational domains*: information, culture, people, business processes, learning, decision making, organizational structure, business strategy, power, and so on. Each of us intuitively knows this.

An organization model must answer a variety of questions, not merely those concerning IT: "Competition . . . is ultimately driven by ideas, not technology . . . ideas come to life in the form of business models and ultimately become the soul of the business, what Peter Drucker has called the 'theory of the business' . . . a successful business model must provide the right answers to a key set of questions" (Stahlman 1993).

1.2 ARCHITECTURE AND MODELING

Seemingly, every day a new management philosophy is introduced: business engineering, total quality management, organizational learning, culture change, knowledge management, and so on. Management is confronted with new ideas, but has no organizational framework in which they may be neatly placed and integrated. Furthermore, the failure of traditional IT frameworks has created the impression among senior managers that modeling, and to some extent architecture, does not deliver value to organizations.

But what do managers currently do? Don't they design, or "craft" strategy? How do they formulate new business processes and integrate them into their organization—their information systems, their culture, and so on?

Invariably, the artifacts of organizational design are little more than *lists* of things to be done, or *pictures* showing arrangements of things. These illustrations regularly appear in executive summaries, and eventually become "blueprints" by which plans are formulated, organizations designed, and work performed. And when the plans produce only marginal results, another study is initiated, there is another reorganization, and the process repeats itself.

For example, we have all seen "vision" statements, strategic goals, charts showing information flows, "maps" of business processes, culture change initiatives, new talk of organizational learning, and so on. Are these change efforts ever coordinated? Do they ever materialize into something concrete and integrated that actually improves performance?

Of course, if management is negligent and finds that it must institute change—for example, *reengineer* its business processes—some improvement will occur. But this argument negates itself. Successful reengineering efforts are testimonies to past management failures.

These artifacts of management are analogous to those of the early days of information technology—people have an idea of what they want, then implement something that supposedly corresponds to their intentions, adjust it when it fails, and hope for the best.

A FRESH LOOK AT ORGANIZATION MODELING

The missing ingredient in all this is a well-defined, yet practical framework by which the organization may be designed and changed. Such a framework is much more than the picturesque presentations that have become the trademark of modern management. And it is certainly *not* another IT enterprise model. But then, what constitutes such a framework? Can it be made convenient, suitable, and effective?

Successful organizations are driven by a consistent set of principles and constructs—organizational pieces, their interconnections, and their behaviors that collectively may be thought of as *organizational architecture*. Effective organizations are characterized by an ability to understand, interrelate, and leverage each of these pieces.

What are these organizational pieces? They are *organizational domains*: areas of interest to the organization that are distinct, yet interrelated. A list of domains includes strategy, information, organizational structure, business processes, products, people, knowledge, learning, technology, quality, culture—and much more. Furthermore, though information technology has become the primary change agent in modern organizations, no single domain (i.e., organizational piece) can work without each of the others. Their interconnections are as important as the pieces themselves, perhaps more so.

For example, a racecar may win or lose on the basis of its engine, but it's going nowhere without a driver and the lowly tire. Furthermore, a *particular* driver and a *particular* set of tires may leverage the power of the engine more so than another driver or set of tires. And the same may be said of the pit crew. Motivation, commitment, mutual respect, and teamwork are as much the components of victory as is engine power.

So too an organization, no matter how IT-driven it may be, is going to be at a competitive disadvantage unless it knows how to associate and leverage each of its parts. This can be accomplished only with an organizational architecture—an architecture sufficiently rich in its modeling schema so that it may be used to define the intent of the planner, is implementable, and provides a mechanism for that implementation! And it must do so for the organization as a whole, for each of its pieces, and for their associations.

Applying Information Modeling

Managers require a new *language* to design organizations. The first element of a new language is a *vocabulary* to prescribe the behavior of organizational domains. The second ingredient is a *grammar* in which to model the associations among domains. Finally, managers require a new manner of *discourse* by which to implement their intentions.

This book presents a new language for organizational design. We draw on the discipline of information modeling to structure organizational pieces, and therefore, advance an organizational architecture and modeling approach called *organization modeling (OM)*. A vocabulary for organizational planning and analysis, a grammar for design, a discourse for implementation—all in all, this is OM.

In addition, OM is strongly anchored in a philosophical foundation that supports the social sciences. It is therefore expected that in the future, not only managers and business executives, but also social science researchers will find OM to be a convenient approach that complements many of their modeling requirements.

You may ask, "Doesn't your new approach use the information modeling paradigm, and therefore, isn't this yet another IT business or enterprise model? What makes OM so special? Isn't it another IT model that you just argued against?" The answer is not so simple. We argue throughout this book that the answer to one technology approach is emphatically not another technology approach. The artifacts of one domain (e.g., IT) do not necessarily lend themselves to the specification of another (e.g., strategy)—not without a great deal of compromise.

For example, an article in a popular IT magazine actually suggests a new organizational structure built around object-oriented "classes" (Newman 1996). No doubt, this has a certain appeal to the IT professional. On the other hand, to a line manager this must sound preposterous, and only serves to underscore past IT failures at creating useful models. Information objects (i.e., classes) do not necessarily address the way value is added in an organization. They address neither the knowledge of people nor how they learn. Nor how strategy is formed. Nor how culture affects organizational behavior. And so on and so forth. And each of these domains impacts the design of structure—IT being only one dimension of organizational design.

1.3 WHY OM?

Why are we using OM for developing organization models, and claiming that this is a revolutionary way of building such models? Are there not many business or organizational models already present? Are not these models already giving us enough information about organizations? In any case, why create another way of modeling? What is so special about OM that qualifies it as a revolutionary approach?

Such questions and many other ones will be raised by each of you. Obviously, as the innovators of OM, we must answer these questions.

The point is that we are not claiming any originality in developing a new discipline as such. What we *are* claiming is that we are trying to take an entirely fresh look at the whole game of organizational architecture. With this new approach to architecture, we advance new ways of designing cultures, strategies, structures, processes, and information systems that are supposedly suitable and useful to these organizations.

In doing this, we have to get to the bottom of the whole endeavor. We need to ask some very basic questions, including the famous one, "What is an organization in the first place?" The next question is "How do we go about building an organization that satisfies our requirements?" The question that arises further is "How do we implement these ideas that we formed in our minds while designing the organization in a manner that is convenient, suitable, realizable, and hence realistic in every sense of the word?"

To do this, we had to break new ground. The result of this quest is OM. OM provides a universal path that anyone—in particular, the manager-architect—can follow with reasonable assurance of reaching his or her goal. Such an assurance can come only if we can introduce precision into our thinking. If our thinking is nebulous, how can we make sure that we are on the right path?

Bringing precision requires specification. Precision may provide correct, legitimate, provable ways of implementation. Essentially, OM is a way of *channeling* and *crystallizing* our thoughts into something tangible. The word crystallization is very meaningful here. Before crystallization, everything is in a fluid state, in a state of flux. It is only during crystallization in nature that atoms (1) come together, (2) align themselves in an orderly fashion, (3) make the order repeat further throughout the entire structure, (4) make these atoms settle down in their respective positions gradually, first rather loosely in the form of a jelly, and (5) subsequently settle into well-organized fixed positions.

What is the result of all this? A beautiful, appealing crystalline structure. But it is not just beauty that is available here; the crystal structure also brings strength. The orderliness, the organization, the bonding, the repeatability—all lead to strength. That is something very desirable in organizations consisting of humans as well. Is it not?

1.4 THE EXPANSE OF OM

The width and breadth of OM include several foundational principles:

1. *Architecture-in-the-large and architecture-in-the-small.*
2. *Capturing the creative and informal aspects of organizations.*
3. *Harnessing tacit knowledge and learning.*
4. *Weaving the tapestry that contains all of the above.*

This book is adaptable as an advanced college text in both management and MIS curricula. It is also suitable as a reference book for managers and IT professionals. We discuss several concepts with which most students of management are familiar. This includes strategy models, the value chain, competence, tacit and explicit knowledge, etc. We give structure to the relationships between these concepts, thus giving added value and utility to each. Each concept has become popular because of its local application, whether in strategy, structure, etc. We show how these different relationships culminate in the development of a scalable architecture.

At a low level of analysis, we talk of the nitty-gritty. The *organization molecule* represents the building block of architecture. It may be used to formulate the internal constitution of a given domain, thus creating an architecture-in-the-small. This may include business process design, culture, knowledge, information, learning, and so on. Naturally, we may align these microconstituents for a proper placement into an architecture-in-the-large.

In the process of developing an architecture—whether in-the-large or in-the-small—we refer to several well-known management and organization concepts and disciplines. Some of these are very formal, such as data and information systems. Others are much more slippery, such as culture and learning. Managers have developed formal processes for the former, while either ignoring or merely separating the latter from the larger organization. In our approach, the two (formal and not so formal) are aligned, and thus a real-world architecture emerges.

One such example of a slippery concept is tacit knowledge. We provide a certain formalization of tacit knowledge. We illustrate the relationship between tacit knowledge and the culture model proposed by Edgar Schein. Furthermore, we propose a "formal" scheme that gives structure to tacit knowledge—the *knowledge contract* discussed in Chapter 14.

The most important and the most difficult aspect of organization modeling, though, is answering the question, "How do we capture the innate processes that occur inside the mind of a gifted and intelligent manager, which enable him or her to architect an organization that is bound to be successful in practice?" This requires an ability to somehow "express" the unformalizable, that is, to appropriately and explicitly reference what is tacit in the vision of the designer. This includes not only the individual components of the architecture, but also their interrelationships, and putting together all the pieces of the jigsaw puzzle.

1.5 ORGANIZATION OF THE BOOK

Part 1 introduces the structure and organization of OM. *Chapter 2* gives a brief review of organization theory (OT). OT is the discipline of structuring organizations, and provides us with the *materials* of OM. *Chapter 3* discusses several well-known concepts and issues associated with organizational design. This chapter includes contingency theory, Mintzberg's generic structure model, the employment relation, and so on. Although the content of Chapter 2 and Chapter 3 is a review to students of management, we intersperse value-added commentary.

Chapter 4 lays out the rationale and structure of OM. Three views of modeling are proposed for organizations: *the richness of modeling concepts, the level of granularity,* and *the refinement approach.* In OM, the refinement levels include a philosophy of organizations, the meta-framework in which to model the organization, the establishment of an organizational perspective, the creation and specification of architectural building blocks, the realization of the building blocks in which organizations find themselves, and finally, execution.

In *Chapter 5,* we develop a *layered model of the organization.* Layers of abstraction may be used to think about a variety of organizational characteristics. The layered model is used to represent an organization in an historical OT context. Examples of the Max Weber functional view of an organization, the size view of the Aston group from Great Britain, and so on, are each illustrated. Finally, a new way of thinking about organizations, and then crystallizing thoughts into orderly patterns, is presented. *Crystallization* involves the formulation and integration of thought patterns into concrete notions, making up a holistic representation of organizational reality. These pave the way for the development of a radically new building block of organizational design.

Chapter 6 introduces this new building block of OM: the *organization molecule.* A molecule represents the crystalline formations of generic modeling ideas as they pertain to an organization. Generic organization molecules are introduced for business processes, information, and organizational culture. The importance of imprecision to an organization's competitive distinctiveness (John Kay 1995) is also discussed. Examples of imprecise specifications known as *relational contracts* are reviewed. The importance of an organizational architecture composed of interrelated precise and imprecise contracts is advanced.

Chapter 7 introduces architecture and *alignment patterns.* Examples of alignment patterns and techniques include consistent, compatible, and dynamic alignment. The competitive advantage afforded an organization with both a hard (i.e., precise) and soft (i.e., imprecise) architecture is discussed. An example of cultural alignment described by John Kay is used to illustrate OM alignment patterns.

In *Chapter 8,* refinement and its relationship to managerial choice are discussed. Implementing OM through the *OM refinement model* is introduced. The OM stages of implementation are baseline, scoping and elaboration, specification, alignment, realization, and execution layers. The OM paradigm may be used with existing approaches to organizational design. Accordingly, we illustrate the correspondences between the OM refinement model and Tom Davenport's approach to business process reengineering (BPR), and Jay Galbraith's approach to designing an organization, respectively.

Chapter 9 discusses *patterns* as products of *crystallization* and *manifest representation.* A variety of organizational patterns, and their relationships to each other, are advanced. Organizational patterns and their formation are associated with molecules. A new high-level pattern, the *lattice,* is introduced. Lattices are patterns of molecules with specific organizational characteristics or properties. These properties include competitiveness, inventiveness, and adaptability. Finally, the importance of visualization in the design process is discussed.

Part 2 develops the notion of a 21st century organizational architecture. Its core principles include the relationships among culture, people, information, process, and learning.

Chapter 10 discusses culture and the culture model advanced by Edgar Schein. Also discussed are the idea of *directionality* and the importance of culture as its anchor.

Chapter 11 discusses the notion of *process formulation.* Process formulation is the development of all the artifacts of a business process: its characterization, transformation, specification, and design and implementation.

Chapter 12 discusses *data, knowledge,* and *information.* Information is characterized in terms of data (syntax) and knowledge (semantic) characteristics. Data and knowledge are each characterized. Knowledge is detailed in terms of several dimensions: *explicit* and *tacit* (Nonaka and Takeuchi 1995), *individual* and *social* (Spender 1993), *industry* and *organization* (Leonard-Barton 1995), and *distributed* and *common* (Sack and Thalissinidis 1998). Alignment contexts—*automating, informating,* and *knowledging*—are discussed. We update the *information continuum* introduced by Tom Davenport (1997), and discuss the various dimensions of *business rules: knowledge rules, relational rules, explicit rules,* and *data rules.*

Chapter 13 discusses *knowledge formulation.* Knowledge formulation includes a *knowledge world* framework, *layered knowledge models,* the *knowledge spiral* and its *conversion modes* (introduced by Nonaka and Takeuchi 1995), and *knowledge binding.* Also discussed are various *knowledge system models.* Finally, we illustrate the application of our knowledge system models by using them to characterize the ten strategy approaches described by Mintzberg, Ahlstrand, and Lampel (1998).

Chapter 14 discusses the emergence of a 21st century learning organization. The implications of *individual value* as well as *organizational value* in relation to learning are discussed. *Contract analogs* are introduced as constructs to explain the working of both the formal and informal aspects of organizations. There are two types of contract analogs: *complete* (i.e., *precise, relativized*), and *open* (i.e., *relational, knowledge*). The issues associated with both *system* and *organizational dynamicity* are discussed. An example of a *federated structure* for IS & IT is proposed as a mechanism to leverage the benefits of both centralized and decentralized decision making. *Knowledge management* is briefly reviewed, and a new system that implements an *integrated knowledge architecture* is presented. Finally, a framework for the *business designer of the 21st century* is advanced.

The *Appendix* contains an overview of information modeling. In the same way that organization and management literature provide us with the materials of OM, information modeling provides the glue to construct an architecture.

PART 1

ORGANIZING OM

Part 1 contains the core concepts of OM. We apply the "layered model" technique to OT, and thus illustrate certain generalizations of the organization in terms of commonly discussed constructs, such as technology and structure. We create an *architecture-in-the-small* by defining and elaborating the *organization molecule:* a new type of building block for specific domains such as process and information. We also discuss the elaboration and implementation of molecules. Next, we introduce the notion of patterns as composites of aligned molecules—information, service, business, and organization. This takes us to a level of modeling that is still higher, thus developing an *architecture-in-the-large.*

Structuring OM

The artifacts of traditional organizational design are of uneven quality, often applied at varying levels of analysis—formulation, implementation—without any distinction. For example, popular techniques of business process reengineering often use simple process diagrams without distinguishing specification from implementation. Furthermore, designing each domain of the organization involves a different knowledge area, using different techniques. After all, designing organizational structure, instituting culture change, transforming business processes, developing new information systems, and so on, are very different. And once constructed, do they work effectively together? Attempts at integration certainly exist—for example, the strategic alignment model (Henderson and Venkatraman 1993). Unfortunately, most such frameworks tend to be specific pair-wise associations (e.g., business and IT strategy), and do not provide a comprehensive organization model for integration among many domains, such as culture, IS, structure, strategy, process, etc.

Currently, there is no single, integrating framework or architecture that leads the manager from formulation through execution across domains. There is no method of assuring that the intentions of the designer have been met during execution, nor a mechanism by which either the intentions or results may be mutually adjusted through learning. Moreover, there is no systematic approach for aligning and adjusting organizational domains—e.g., strategy, information, business processes, and culture. Finally, there is no framework by which the peculiarities of an organization may be accounted. Indeed, the artifacts of traditional design used by managers today leave them groping in the dark!

OM is structured to address these very issues. We accept the proposition of John Kay (1995) that the real world of business is too complex to be fully modeled. OM is a minimalist approach. OM *enriches* existing methods of organizational design, e.g., designing organizations with Jay Galbraith's techniques (1995), or reengineering business processes following the Tom Davenport approach (1993). In each of these areas, or in areas not yet fully explored, such as understanding the effects of information technology on culture, OM may be used to *organize and implement ideas.*

OM is an *organizing* framework by which concepts and goals may be formulated, extended, synthesized, and actually implemented with some sense of assurance. These ideas may be merely framed, as with culture, or precisely specified, as with a business process or an information system. Moreover, each nebulous understanding or precise specification may be fully aligned. OM, then, is a framework for understanding and designing real-world organizations.

The OM Design Process

First, we recognize that organizations do not exist in isolation, but are products of their social context and history. Though managers recognize this, there has never been a systematic approach for inclusion of culture and history into a design framework. We identify and account for the *social and historical context* in which organizations operate—the *cultural invariant* that defines and constrains what is, and what is not, possible to design in an organization.

Second, OM is distinguished from other frameworks in that OM contains *assumptions* and a *deductive structure* that serve to guide the manager from formulation through implementation. OM structures its assumptions around organization, management, and information modeling paradigms. Organization paradigms center on OT, while management paradigms include existing "models" or frameworks that managers currently employ. Henry Mintzberg's generic organizational structures and Michael Porter's competitive strategy framework are common examples of organization and management paradigms, respectively. These paradigms motivate the *constructs* with which an organization must deal to form its *baseline*.

Third, OM represents a paradigm shift for organizational design. We take the vague assumptions created by sociologists and practicing managers, both of which have uneven, narrow, and non-scientific perspectives, and make organizational design *disciplined*. OM creates "molecules" by which each domain of the organization may be comprehensively analyzed and operationalized. OM specifies molecules with artifacts sufficiently rich to capture the *dynamic* as well as the *static*, and *emergent* as well as *deliberate* properties of the organization. For this purpose, we borrow the techniques of specification from information modeling.

Fourth, we create a systematic framework for *aligning* domains of the organization. "Alignment" is becoming a new management buzzword, and for good reason. It often means the difference between success and failure. In OM, for example, business process change (e.g., business process transformation, continuous improvement) is systematically addressed from planning through implementation, and aligned with people, organizational structure, information, and technology.

Fifth, OM provides a mechanism for *realizing* the design in concrete terms. Where possible, we integrate with existing artifacts, such as the popular process diagrams, "IS-maps," and "SHOULD-maps" used during business process reengineering. Realization makes a design specific by identifying and integrating specifications with structural properties. Furthermore, the structural properties will be different for each domain; again, implementing an information system is very different than implementing a change in culture or organizational structure. Moreover, the difference in structural properties among domains only highlights the need for an effective framework for both alignment and realization.

Sixth, OM accounts for design performance and "organizational effectiveness." This is effected by linking, and mutually adjusting each of the "deliverables" associated with the OM stages of organizational design: baseline (i.e., invariant), specification, alignment, realization, and execution.

Seventh, OM facilitates learning about organizational issues and concerns. One of the benefits of OM is that it provides an organizing framework at all stages of design so that new ways of formulating domains are possible. We illustrate this in subsequent chapters by enriching the notions of culture, business processes, and information.

DISCOVERING A NEW PATH

Our quest for a new understanding of organizations began with information modeling and our study of organization theory and management. Concepts associated with the new approach of information modeling clearly applied, at least in some cases, to organizations. The notion of emergent characteristics, for example, is associated not only with the information modeling concept known as a *composition,* but also with theories on the formation of strategy advanced by Henry Mintzberg. The constructs associated with reengineering business processes advanced by Hammer and Champy may be precisely specified with the precise contracts associated with information modeling. Similarly, business process workflows and enterprise resource planning (ERP) specifications may be so specified. Other contracts—relational contracts advanced by John Kay—are incorporated in OM, and may be used to account for more slippery constructs such as culture. Still other contracts advanced in OM—knowledge contracts—may be used to describe knowledge work. And so on and so forth.

As our understanding grew, we discovered one important caveat. The correspondence between information modeling concepts, and organization theory and management is not one-to-one, nor even very clear at times. For example, generic information modeling concepts cannot *prescribe* generic organizational structures, or generic strategies. These organizational constructs exist on the one hand, but require a reconfiguration if modeling is to be employed.

There are vast differences in the perspectives of organizational researchers, business managers, organizational planners and designers, strategic planners, and IT professionals. The knowledge and viewpoints of each of these professionals or researchers are very different. Furthermore, each requires a model for a *different purpose,* and therefore each expects to find very different characteristics in the thing called an organization model.

Our new understanding emerged as we extended and combined the best of all worlds. We discovered that one cannot simply apply information modeling concepts to organizational constructs and expect that they will be useful in the design of an organization. If information is so important to the culture of an organization, what IT architectural principle will be used to facilitate cultural transformation? For such questions to be asked, and for meaningful answers to be given, a reconciliation between the many different, but interconnected, perspectives is needed. A *new formulation* is required if the organization and information perspectives are to be reconciled. This formulation—a new way of thinking about organizations—is OM.

Our search, then, led us to consider the purposes and expectations of various interested parties, including researchers in a university, organizational planners and designers, line managers, and IT professionals. A single, common organization architecture has been created to satisfy the viewpoint of each of these professionals.

The OM approach is to reformulate the "materials of organizations" with the "glue of specification." We gather the organizational materials from OT and management literature and similarly the "glue of specification" from IT literature. Their interconnection and reconfiguration are fundamental to formulating a new approach to organization modeling.

A single construct for each domain is defined based on the literature from that domain. For example, *process* is defined in terms of the literature on business processes, *culture* on culture literature, *information* on IT literature, *knowledge* on knowledge literature, and so on and so forth. Each domain of the organization may be architected, modeled, and interconnected. A truly organization level architecture and modeling approach is crafted from the *materials* of organizational literature.

Efforts at formulating an organizational perspective using information modeling concepts began in 1993. Strategy formulations and contracts, and a contract approach to an enterprise architecture, were introduced in various papers. A more robust architecture—the organization building block of organization architecture and design called an *organization molecule*—was first introduced in a paper submitted to the Society for Information Management (SIM)–New Jersey Chapter, in 1993 (Morabito 1993). This paper was a submittal in a contest and subsequently earned the Academic Excellence Award (first place). With these initial papers as a framework, other papers were published that represented refinements of the original architecture (Morabito 1994, Morabito 1995, Morabito and Bhate 1995, Morabito and Bhate 1997, Morabito, Bhate, and Sack 1996, Sack and Thalassinidis 1998). With each paper, our understanding grew and our approach to organizational architecture was enriched. This book is the result of that journey, and marks the beginning of a new journey whose purpose is to establish the foundation of 21st century organizational architecture.

CHAPTER 2

An Introduction and Critique of Organization Theory

2.1 THE FOUNDATION OF ORGANIZATIONAL DESIGN

Human beings are social creatures. Since their existence, people have been designing, participating, and sharing in the burdens and rewards of organizations. Armed with primitive technologies, they planned and executed strategies to accomplish well-understood goals: acquiring food, securing shelter, and providing for the common defense. How these families and hunting groups were organized can only be inferred from anthropological evidence. But of course, all depends on how far back you trace human evolution. We will leave such concerns to the anthropologist.

The early organizations of which there *is* a record were primarily military or governmental in nature. It is said that Moses delegated his administrative authority along hierarchical lines. In *The Art of War*, Sun Tzu describes the need for hierarchical structure, communications, and strategy. Aristotle wrote of administrative power and its association with culture. Ibn Taymiyyah used the "scientific method" to outline Islamic principles of administration. To the would-be leader, Machiavelli advocated power over morality (see Shafritz and Ott 1996).

The roots of organization theory, then, may be traced to antiquity, covering writers from around the world. Each has grappled with some aspect of the organization to improve its workings, in whatever manner "improvement" may have been defined.

The Factory System and the Division of Labor

The emergence of the Industrial Age in Great Britain marked the beginning of relatively complex economic organizations. The advent of power and transportation technologies transformed the market from one of provincial, small-scale production to centralized, large-scale production with widespread product distribution. This became known as the factory system.

14

With the factory system came the requirement for more sophisticated organizing and management skills, and hence a systematic logic to the workings of organizations. Adam Smith provided that framework. In 1776, *The Wealth of Nations* described the workings of a pin factory. Throughout the world, this book soon became the most influential rationale for the factory system and the *division of labor*. Furthermore, Smith gave credence to an exclusively economic rationale for organizations, and narrowed the definition of "organizing" to the production *specialization* inherent in division of labor.

The division of labor is the single most important concept that may be used to describe an organization. In 1776, Adam Smith set the stage: "I have seen a small factory of this kind where ten men only were employed, and where some of them consequently performed two or three distinct operations. . . . Those ten persons, therefore, could make among them upwards of forty-eight thousand pins in a day. Each person, therefore, making a tenth part of forty-eight thousand pins, might be considered as making four thousand eight hundred pins in a day. But if they had all wrought separately and independently, and without any of them having been educated to this peculiar business, they certainly could not each of them have made twenty, perhaps not one pin in a day; that is, certainly, not the two hundred and fortieth, perhaps not the four thousand eight hundredth part of what they are at present capable of performing, in consequence of a proper division and combination of their different operations."

The serious study of economic organizations known as organization theory (OT) may be traced back to the introduction of the factory system and the division of labor. The body of thinking and writing termed classical OT represents the *culture of the industrial age*. Its assumptions are still largely held today by most managers:

- Organizations make economically rational decisions.
- The most efficient form of organizing production is the division of labor.

The factory system was characterized by centralized production, newly contrived machines, the new technologies of power and transportation, and large concentrations of workers. Classical OT thus concerned itself with the management of this new form of production.

Today, a new form of technology has begun to change society and organizations. Information is revolutionizing the nature of work as strongly as power and transportation fostered the factory system. The effects are beginning to take shape—for example, reengineered business processes, flattening hierarchies, electronic commerce, virtual organizations, learning, and knowledge management, etc. We shall see in what new directions this second revolution will take us.

2.2 WHAT IS AN ORGANIZATION?

The textbook definition of *organization* given by Robbins (1990) states the following: "An organization is a consciously coordinated social entity, with a relatively identifiable boundary, that functions on a relatively continuous basis to achieve a common goal or a set of goals." Let us examine this definition in some detail.

In the above definition, the words "consciously coordinated" imply *management*. The words "social entity" indicate a composition of people. These people interact with each other and with the outside world, both individually as well as in groups. The interaction patterns determine the "culture" of the organization.

Commentary: Things in organizations are not random, but form patterns, such as culture. As we will see later, a pattern is what we call a "managed collection." A managed collection is subject to generalization and a certain formalism, and therefore, we may use it to construct an "architecture-in-the-small" for a particular area of interest, such as culture, structure, or strategy. When we align these individual pieces, an "architecture-in-the-large" takes shape—the organization.

The "relatively identifiable boundary" of the organization distinguishes the members of the organization from nonmembers. It differentiates who is and who is not part of the organization. In practice, it serves as a kind of "binding" force. This binding is in the form of either an *explicit* or *implicit* "contract" among the individual members as well as among the members and the organization.

Commentary: There are two important issues here—contract arrangements and explicit and implicit agreements. As we shall see, the domains of organizations are such that not all contracts may be specified "precisely." That is, while designing organizations, we maintain the notion of a "specification," but we will have to be more flexible and careful in using the term "precise." This may stun those of you who are IT professionals. Certainly, there are domains of an organization that may, and should, be precisely specified, such as information systems and routine workflows. However, other domains such as culture and human relationships cannot be precisely prescribed. Still others—structure, for instance—are somewhere between precise and imprecise.

Furthermore, the noted economist John Kay has asserted that it is the imprecise contracts that confer enduring competitive advantage. This may sound strange in the information era, where IT is assumed to be a source of advantage and where precision is a requirement. In fact, both views are correct. Successful organizations are designed with contracts of varying precision, at varying levels of abstraction, aligned in a network of managed collections, each of which represents a domain of the organization. Welcome to OM!

2.3 STUDYING ORGANIZATIONS

Most of us have some intuitive understanding of what organizations are, how they function, and how they ought to be functioning. We carry opinions about whether private organizations are more efficient than government bureaucracies. Some of us wonder why the organizations that we deal with in our day-to-day lives operate the way they do. Eventually, however, we may want to replace our intuitive understanding with more systematized knowledge about organizations.

Organization theory (OT) deals with issues related to the structure, design, and performance of organizations. It tries to find answers to such questions as:

- How does the size of an organization affect its performance?
- What factors are important for the survival and success of an organization?
- What is the best way to manage an organization?
- What is the effect of IT on the performance of an organization?
- How do we manage knowledge resources?

And of course, there are many other such questions. Unfortunately, there are no simple and straightforward answers to these questions. Yet, finding answers is important because they pave the way towards improvement, and increase an organization's "effectiveness."

Thus, OT is the discipline that studies both structure and design in organizations. Structure deals with the descriptive aspect while design refers to the prescriptive aspect of the discipline. OT describes how practical organizations are actually structured. Additionally, OT offers suggestions on how new organizations can be constructed, and how old ones can change in order to improve effectiveness.

2.4 SCHOOLS OF ORGANIZATION THEORY

We will *never* understand an organization or a particular situation completely. Accordingly, it is useful to look at organizations through a variety of lenses. We therefore examine organizations in different contexts to better understand the forces that confront them. This serves to better assess a given situation, a firm's culture, its history, and the options available to us as organizational designers. The resulting descriptions are forms of "organization models."

Since Adam Smith, there has been an explosion of thinking on the design and workings of organizations. Each writer has concentrated on some dimension of the organization: its culture, production methods, job roles, administration, etc.

A writer's perspective is naturally formed by his or her cultural context. Society's value system, the market, the technologies, the political system, the social movements—all come into play. Certain characteristics of organizations may be emphasized while others are ignored; as the social climate changes, others are given more weight.

There is no approach or theory that fits all situations. Each approach is a school of OT that carries with it assumptions about what an organization should be, how it should be structured, its place in society, the value accorded people and technology, and so on. A school, then, embodies a particular set of assumptions and principles about organizations. Each carries with it an idea of what an organization should be, and what managers and employees are supposed to do.

A SAMPLING OF THINKING ON ORGANIZATIONS

For example, one relatively simple way of understanding organizations in terms of "schools of thought" is as follows:

1. Classical theory—this typically represents the culture of the Industrial Age. Its tenets are normally associated with the view of the *owner*. The underlying premise is that the organization should be operated as a machine.

2. Neo-classical theory—in response to the owner's view, neo-classical theory advances the position of the *employee*. This is the so-called "humanistic school" and emphasizes motivation and employee involvement.

3. Information theory—the classical and neo-classical theories have been framed in terms of the division of labor. With the advent of the new technology of information, we have seen a variety of models that portray the organization and decision making in terms of information flows.

The first two notions have come to represent contrasting poles: the machine vs. the human. Classical theory is sometimes known as the mechanistic model, and emphasizes such things as hierarchical structures and vertical communication channels. In contrast, the neo-classical model has been termed a humanistic view. In this model, the organization is more sensitive to the needs of employees. It places great emphasis on motivation.

We may refine this simple classification. Charles Handy (1993) describes the schools of OT as follows:

1. *Scientific Management.* This school is premised on the work of Frederick Winslow Taylor (*Principles of Scientific Management*, 1911), and emphasizes the detailed, scientific design of tasks, the scientific selection and training of workers, and the separation of planning (management) and execution (labor). In 1914, Henri Fayol published *Administration Industrielle et Generale*, in which he sought to develop general principles applicable to all managers at all levels of the organization. He elaborated upon 14 universal management principles, including the division of labor, authority, centralization, equity, and *esprit de corps*. While Taylor applied science to the shop floor, Fayol depended on extensive experience. Even today, the principles of both Taylor and Fayol are widely followed by managers. This is generally considered the beginning of contemporary thought on OT, and serves to advance the machine view of organizations.

2. *Human Relations.* In response to the mechanistic views of scientific management, Chester Barnard introduced the notion of an organization as a *cooperative system*. A cooperative system involves equal attention to job tasks and the people who perform them. Additionally, this school believes that authority does not flow from the top, but is accorded the manager by employees. In this framework, the major role of a manager is to motivate employees. Building on the Hawthorne Studies, Barnard advanced the notion of the informal organization (e.g., group pressure and acceptance) and its effect on productivity. Another important contribution came from Douglas McGregor, who proposed two distinct views of human beings: *Theory X* and *Theory Y*. Theory X holds that people inherently dislike work, while Theory Y states that people view work positively. Theory Y states that everyone, not just the managers, has creativity and decision-making ability (Robbins 1990).

In practice, however, the human relations model never advanced the individual as a *knowledge-creating* member of the organization, and people became little more than "stimulus-response mechanisms" (Nonaka and Takeuchi 1995). The humanistic school was eventually swallowed by the machine perspective advocated by the school of Scientific Management.

3. *Bureaucracy.* In 1922, Max Weber described the *ideal* structure of an organization—the *bureaucracy*. It is characterized by a division of labor, hierarchical decision making, a high degree of formal procedures and regulations, and impersonal relationships. It is the latter quality that has given bureaucracy an unpleasant connotation. It should be noted that an "ideal type" is a metaphor for an ideal state, and should be not be confused with reality. Nevertheless, the bureaucracy is the archetype for the structure of today's large organizations.

Commentary: Before we assume bureaucracies are "bad," we should reflect on their benefits. A bureaucracy is respectful of an employee's privacy, and protects workers from arbitrary behavior on the part of management. This is operationalized through the very mechanism that is often blamed for the bureaucracy's indifference towards its customers—impersonal relationships. Recently, however, the tradeoff has been reversed. U.S. firms have begun to undo bureaucracy through flattened hierarchies, lateral relationships, increased availability of information, and less formalization. One consequence has been an increase in customer focus, and, as we would expect, a rise in arbitrary decision-making and political activity.

4. *Power, Conflict, and Decisions.* This school challenges the notion that organizations make rational decisions. Organizations are best understood by looking at power, conflict, and the way decisions are *actually* made (as opposed to the way they *should* be made). This has given rise to the observation that managers rarely make optimal decisions, but instead make ones that are "good enough" and that serve their *self-interest*. According to this view, the power-grabbing political coalitions are the controlling factor determining organizational structure. The coalition in power at any particular moment is known as the *dominant coalition*.

5. *Technology.* The notions of *mechanistic* and *organic* forms of work were introduced by Burns and Stalker in 1961. The mix of task complexity, communications, control, and authority were used to explain the appropriate structure and environment in which organizations should operate. In 1965, Joan Woodward published *Industrial Organization: Theory and Practice*. Based on research in the south of England, Woodward described the connection between the type of technology an organization used and the type of structure it employed. She classified manufacturing technology into three categories—unit, mass, and process production—and found a correlation between the type of technology employed and the structure chosen.

Whereas Woodward studied manufacturing technology, Perrow looked at knowledge technology. Using the dimensions of *task variability* and *problem analyzability*, Perrow identified four types of task technologies:

routine, craft, engineering, and *nonroutine.* Perrow characterized each technology classification according to the control and coordination methods employed. Thus, characteristics of a given process task are related to such control and coordination mechanisms as *formalization* and *centralization*—each a dimension of structure.

Thompson put a slightly different twist into the technology equation. Rather than claiming a relationship between technology and structure, he demonstrated a relationship between technology and the strategy selected to reduce *uncertainty.* Thompson identified three types of technologies: *long-linked, mediating,* and *intensive.* Each class of technology represents a collection of tasks, and is related to task dependencies: long-linked is characterized by *sequential,* mediating by *pooled,* and intensive by *reciprocal interdependence* among tasks. Each type of interdependence, in turn, is related to the coordinating mechanisms associated with structure—*complexity and formalization.* (See Robbins 1990.)

6. *Systems.* In response to increasingly complex theories, this school sees the organization as an open system. But as Handy points out, the systems perspective is somewhat like economics: It asserts that everything is related to everything, explains everything based on this assumption, but predicts nothing. However, Peter Senge's writings on the learning organization, and modern business process reengineering techniques, are serving to make the systems view more applicable in the real world.

7. *Institutional.* This school advocates the importance of culture and a given organization's history and particular circumstances. Rather than rejecting the other schools, it seeks to encompass them in a *contingency* framework where all schools of thought apply to some degree, based on a particular situation.

2.5 DIMENSIONS OF ORGANIZATIONAL STRUCTURE

An organization's *structure* defines how it is organized, usually by means of some "formal" coordination mechanism. According to OT literature, structure consists of three primary component characteristics: *complexity, formalization,* and *centralization.*

It is important to note that all of these structural characteristics have only a relative significance in that they do not have an absolute measure. In general, they are only concepts or *logical constructs* used mainly for the purpose of description. They are not "variables" which are measured in terms of some unit of measurement. When we are looking at a particular organization or a given set of organizations, however, they are sometimes treated as *variables* purely for the purpose of convenience in analysis. This makes them amenable to statistical analysis and enables the OT expert to see how they correlate with other variables that affect the behavior of the organization.

Commentary: As we shall argue in subsequent chapters, such an ambiguity often leads to the problem of precise specification. As we shall see, associations leading to specification, statistical, and cause-and-effect relationships are different. In IT, only the first is employed; in OT, it is the latter two; in OM, it is all three.

Complexity deals with the extent of differentiation among the various tasks performed within the organization. This is based on the degree of specialization present in the work of its members. It also indicates the number of levels in the organization's hierarchy. Occasionally, the term complexity is also used in the current OT literature to denote the extent to which the various departmental units present in the organization are geographically dispersed.

Commentary: Does this mean that the flatter an organization, the lesser is its complexity? Not necessarily so, in our opinion. In the age of "teamwork," work is performed through a multiplicity of teams. Each team contains people drawn from various departments so that each member is a specialist in a given field. Obviously, the degree of specialization that is present has a large variation which, by definition, should lead to higher complexity. Do we, therefore, say that teams are complex? Also, if the different work-units, sections, or departments within an organization are geographically dispersed, does this really have any effect on its complexity? In classical OT, the answer is "yes"—but certainly not in the age of the information highway.

Formalization indicates the degree to which the day-to-day work in an organization relies on specific rules and regulations. In practice, this gets reflected in the behavior of employees and hence is a determinant of the culture of the organization.

Commentary: In a knowledge worker society, what is the value of formalization as a dimension of the organization? As information becomes more readily available, does formalization decrease or is it simply communicated more effectively?

Centralization deals with the way decisions are taken. In centralized organizations, decision making is the prerogative of senior executives; issues or problems may surface anywhere in the organization, but only senior managers choose the appropriate actions. In other organizations, decision making is decentralized. Authority is distributed downward in the hierarchy, and employees are "empowered" to make work-related decisions. In practice, centralization and decentralization represent two extremes. Most real-life organizations contain both of these characteristics. The difference lies only in the extent of centralization or decentralization.

Commentary: There is a catch here! Senior management can take undue advantage of decentralization in the following way: Don't promote employees, empower them and give them more responsibilities, more risk, and little reward. Finally, management can promote legitimacy under the guise of business process reengineering and culture change.

2.6 ORGANIZATIONAL LIFE-CYCLE

In current literature, organizations are often compared to biological systems. Thinking of organizations as living organisms has certain advantages. It serves to highlight two important characteristics of organizations: their systems and life-cycle dimensions. The metaphor, of course, is not exact, since all organisms eventually die while presumably, organizations may be renewed and continue for some time.

Commentary: We advance an improved metaphor which compares an organization to a species rather than an individual member of a species. Species outlive their members, as organizations customarily do. Species "fit" their environment through the behavior of individuals. This is analogous to an organization competing through its technology—the collective behavior of business processes, people, and information systems. Furthermore, through environmental pressure and the need to adapt, a species will change its gene pool, changing the behaviors of each of its members. This is analogous to an organization's redefining its business scope or changing its culture. The evolutionary pressure comes from the environment, while an organization's gene pool is enriched through new members.

The five stages in an organization's "life" generally follow the pattern advanced by Robbins (1990): (1) entrepreneurial, (2) collectivity, (3) formalization-and-control (4) elaboration-of-structure, and finally the (5) decline stage. It is important to note that not all organizations go through all five stages. Many attempt to remain in stage 2. Several of America's largest organizations find themselves in stage 3, 4, or even 5, and are desperately trying to figure out how to get into stage 2. Hence, we see downsizing, process reengineering efforts, restructuring, and so on.

Commentary: As with the biological metaphor from which it is derived, an organization, like a species, cannot undo its history. What it can do is return to the same circumstances, but with a different culture and technology. We see such a situation in the improved biological metaphor (species): Whales returned to the water and became sea creatures for a second time in their history; however, they will never again become fish.

2.7 ORGANIZATIONAL EFFECTIVENESS

Organizational effectiveness (OE) is *the* central theme in OT. Unfortunately, experts differ considerably among themselves in defining OE. The belief that OE defies a precise definition has been widely accepted. There is no dearth of either constructs or variables that could be used or have been used for measurement of OE. These include items such as effectiveness, productivity, efficiency, profit, quality, growth, turnover, stability, flexibility, adaptability, and so on and so forth, just to name a few. It is also possible to use not just one but a combination of these variables for measuring OE.

There are many different approaches to OE. For example, Stanley Seashore (1965) has come up with several criteria, among them *means vs. ends*, and *long vs. short run*. Robbins (1990) describes a *competing values approach*, where different criteria (e.g., means vs. ends) compete with each other. In this approach, the competing values form a three-dimensional model of OE as follows: *flexibility vs. control, organization vs. people*, and *means vs. ends*.

These values may be combined to produce a particular perspective of OE. Robbins describes various models such as:

1. *Open-systems model.* Emphasizes the organization and flexibility.
2. *Rational-goal model.* Emphasizes the organization and control.
3. *Internal-process.* Emphasizes people and control.
4. *Human-relations model.* Emphasizes people and flexibility.

Robbins then combines his life-cycle model with his OE model. The choice of an OE approach is not an isolated strategy: It is governed by the philosophy to which an organization adheres (i.e., OT school) and its life-cycle stage. Table 2–1 illustrates a combination of an organization's life-cycle and the OE model it is likely to adopt (adapted from Robbins).

TABLE 2–1 LIFE-CYCLE STAGE AND MODELS OF OE ADAPTED FROM ROBBINS (1990)

Life-Cycle Stage	OE Model
Entrepreneurial	Open-systems
Collectivity	Human-relations
Formalization/control	Internal-process & rational-goals
Elaboration-of-structure	Open-systems
Decline	Open-systems

2.8 ORGANIZATIONAL MATERIALS

This leads us once again to the issue of "organizational materials." This also highlights our rationale for selecting OT as the discipline from which to acquire these materials. There are a large number of management philosophies available. However, OT deals explicitly with the study of organizations and identifies a set of stable constructs. Theory building requires a situation which may be characterized as follows: (1) a discipline broad enough to cover a wide range of organizational ideas, yet (2) sufficiently constrained to address only those that change little over time, and (3) found to some degree in all organizations.

As we have seen in this chapter, organizational researchers maintain that organizations have been structured in a relatively stable fashion with a constant set of building blocks, or constructs. It is these constructs which are the subject of study in OT. We term these constructs the *core organizational constructs.* We define these fundamental units of the organization as those constructs that *change infrequently.* These include constructs such as strategy and structure.

These relatively stable set of constructs are not immutable. Global competition and computer technology have recently changed the mix of core constructs. In this new context, certain constructs, such as *function* (i.e., the division of labor) are much less important. Others, such as *process* and *information,* have emerged as critical to the success of the organization. The authors consider process and information to be sufficiently consequential and stable to be considered "core," and added to the list of more "traditional" OT constructs. Figure 2–1 illustrates what we consider to be the current list of core organizational constructs, from which

```
┌─────────────────────┐
│     Environment      │
│   Power & Control    │
│      Strategy        │
│        Size          │
│      Process         │
│      Function        │
│      Structure       │
│       People         │
│     Information       │
│        Tool          │
└─────────────────────┘
```

FIGURE 2–1   Core Organizational Constructs

organizations are designed and managed, and thus are the fundamental "materials" of OM.

Reviewing the list, please observe that we have not explicitly included the construct *technology*. Technology is the transformation of inputs into outputs, and therefore overlaps with several of the above constructs, such as *process, structure, people, information*, and non-human artifacts called *tool*.

Derivative Management Philosophies

As the reader is no doubt aware, in addition to these fundamental units, many other management notions are advanced every day. Several relatively new management philosophies, such as organizational learning, derive from the systems school of OT. Still others, such as culture, have long been acknowledged as important to the organization. Some, such as teams, are variations of existing constructs (e.g., structure) that operationalize an information processing mechanism—horizontal information linkages. In OM, we propose a framework to *specify* and *implement* each of these *derivative management philosophies* in terms of the core organizational constructs.

Hence, OM divides constructs into two categories: the stable core constructs which form the foundation of OT, and derivative management philosophies. Together, they represent the *domains* of an organization. In classical OT literature, an organization's domain is the suite of products and services it chooses to provide in a specific market or environment. Here, we take liberty and use the term "domain" in the very specific context of organization modeling. *An organizational domain, then, is a principle area of the organization that forms a distinct but integral part of an organization's overall architecture.*

The core organizational constructs and the derivative management philosophies are the materials of OM. From these organizational constructs, a meta-architecture is created from which *specific* organizational designs, from strategy, business processes, and information, to power, learning, and culture may be *instantiated* and *implemented*. Accordingly, we advance OM as an architecture from which the entire organization may be formulated, designed, and implemented.

MODELING CONSTRUCTS FOR ORGANIZATIONAL DESIGN

A question that naturally arises from the IT professional is "Well what's so special about organizational materials? We can model them with IT paradigms." The answer is, you can, if you are building an information system (IS). The "business objects" with which the IT professional is typically concerned are those that fit neatly into an information system, such as *customer* or *product.*

An information system describes the information content of an existing domain; it does not embody other characteristics of a domain. Designing real organizations, of course, is both more complex and unclear than designing an information system. An organization model must provide answers to questions that are not asked of an information model. As our brief review of OT has demonstrated, an organization model must deal with both the precision of information and workflow processes, as well as the vagaries of power, culture, and learning. Moreover, aligning and implementing these constructs is at least as important, perhaps more so, as formulating them in the first place. And of course, let us not forget an organization's social context and history. Indeed, organization modeling is challenging!

2.9 CORE CONCEPTS

Organizations	Organization theory
Factory system	Rational decisions
Division of labor	Schools of organization theory
Scientific management school	Human relations school
Bureaucracy school	Power school
Technology school	Institutional school
Systems school	Complexity
Formalization	Centralization
Organizational life-cycle	Organizational effectiveness
Organizational materials	Core organizational constructs
Derivative management philosophies	Organizational domain
Life-cycle stages	OE model

CHAPTER 3

DESIGNING ORGANIZATIONS

3.1 WHEN IN DOUBT, REORGANIZE

Sounds familiar. Managers reorganize structure all the time. Why do managers spend such effort on structure, and so little on, say, culture? Even core business processes receive so little attention that they eventually break, and suddenly need to be "reengineered." The great change technology of our time, information technology, is increasingly being outsourced. What does management think it's doing anyway—design?

Modern day managers largely see organizational design as did industrial era managers: refining the division of labor and hierarchical structure, job design, and managing (i.e., controlling) people. Of course, within the core belief system in which they operate, managers view both organizations and people as machines. They may not articulate such a belief, but as Drucker (1992) states, most truly believe it: "All organizations now say routinely, 'People are our greatest asset.' Yet few practice what they preach, let alone truly believe it. Most still believe, though perhaps not consciously, what nineteenth-century employers believed: people need us more than we need them. But, in fact, organizations have to market membership as much as they market products and services—and perhaps more. They have to attract people, hold people, recognize and reward people, motivate people, and serve and satisfy people."

Popular management philosophies such as business process reengineering, culture change, and organizational learning, have joined more "traditional" initiatives such as quality management, concurrent engineering, and competitive advantage information systems as something different, and separate, from organizational design. As if acknowledging the illogic of this separation, managers often engage in separate initiatives, followed by subsequent "alignment" efforts.

If a thoughtful manager were to attempt an integrated design, how would he or she go about it? What framework or methodology would this manager rely upon? And what would an integrated organizational design framework look like?

This chapter continues our discussion of OT by focusing on organizational design. We highlight standard design practice, current organizational trends, particularly as they pertain to IT, and thereby bring forth the rationale for this book.

3.2 A BRIEF HISTORY OF WORK

Pre-Factory System

Prior to the 1700s, workers operated in proprietorships where they owned their own equipment, and worked for themselves, often with their families. A regulated work schedule was unknown. Basic decisions about the production process were made by the people who performed the process.

By the late 1700s, a production method known as the *putting out* system emerged. Under this system, the workers owned their production technology (e.g., looms), but not the raw material, and did not sell their product. "Instead, raw material was supplied to, and the product removed from, the worker by a merchant putter out" (Pfeffer 1994). The workers did not necessarily understand the entire process, only that each worker was between various levels of producers (other workers), the final product, and the market.

Commentary: The putting out system is remarkably similar to the network or virtual organization.

The putting out system was eventually replaced with another "market mechanism" known as *inside contracting.* Inside contracting is distinguished from putting out in that the former requires that work be performed in a central location, the factory. Those who worked in the factory still were separate from the factory owner.

Commentary: This form of arrangement is similar to independent subcontracting today.

Both putting out and inside contracting are market driven in that individuals sell by some variation of the "piece." Pfeffer maintains that there is no need for managers in market-driven arrangements. In contrast, with the *employment relation* that has been the standard since inside contracting disappeared, the buyer buys "the power of labor over an agreed period of time." It is the employment relation that necessitates the task of management.

The putting out and inside contracting systems organized work on the basis of *markets.* In contrast, the employment relation organized work around *control.* Pfeffer states that there is no single reason why the employment relationship replaced the market systems. One reason, however, according to Pfeffer, is that the individual-centered market systems had little access to capital, and therefore could not invest in equipment or expansion.

(For an in-depth discussion of putting out, inside contracting, and the employment relation, see Jeffrey Pfeffer 1994.)

Commentary: The one exception, relevant today, is the knowledge worker and knowledge work. Knowledge workers sell their knowledge and their interdependence with the task they bid on. They are neither technology intensive nor in need of large capital investments. Any required access to data is relatively easy and inexpensive.

THE FACTORY SYSTEM

The division of labor and large numbers of workers that characterize the factory system necessitated the employment relationship discussed above. The employment relation shifted the "metric" of production from the "piece" to new notions associated with the purchase of time and labor, such as productivity.

Recall that the basic tenets of classical OT, premised on the factory system and the employment relation, are that (1) organizations make economically rational decisions, and (2) the division of labor is the most efficient form of production. Building on these principles, designing organizations has been traditionally seen as tailoring the hierarchy to a specific organization. This includes the following:

1. Design of an organizational structure in accordance with the division of labor.
2. Transformation of tasks into job roles (called job design).
3. Management of the people in those roles.

Industrial engineers assumed prominent positions in the new production system known as the factory system. It was implicitly understood that the organization as a whole—its mechanical devices and workers—should be run as machines. Looking through the front windshield, managers concerned themselves with the development of new products. Looking inward, managers were interested in controlling the technologies, the machines, and the people—as if there were no differences among them.

After World War II, U.S. organizations found that they had essentially no competition. The focus of managing thus shifted from one of forward-looking innovation to one of optimizing existing production. This resulted in a decline in the authority of engineers and scientists in most organizations. A new form of manager was created to fill the void—the *professional manager*.

Professional managers use financial techniques to optimize the organization of work. They look through the rear window by comparing today's performance to yesterday's. Wealth is created by optimizing such comparisons, or through investment in *other* organizations rather than one's own.

Uncertain how to respond to turbulent environments, professional managers often avoid looking through the front windshield. The tenants of professional management have joined those of classical OT as the framework by which most managers operate today. To this day, most U.S. managers search for high profitability through low wages strategies, as opposed to investing in technology and people (Thurow 1992).

POST-FACTORY SYSTEM

In "The New Society of Organizations," Peter Drucker (1992) describes the forces shaping a new organization model. According to Drucker, Western society changes radically every few hundred years. The change, when it occurs, is rapid, usually taking no more than 50 years. Our society is currently undergoing such a transformation, which, if history is a guide, will be complete by 2010 or so.

What are the dimensions of the current transformation? For one thing, the change is no longer confined to the West, but is global in extent. The new source of wealth—indeed, the primary agent of competitive advantage—is *information* and *knowledge*. This is in sharp contrast to traditional economics, where the primary factors have been land, labor, and capital. It is not that these factors are no longer important, only that they are now secondary.

One word of caution here. The notion of a knowledge-based organization has become quite popular. Recall, however, that there is a vast difference between the way organizations *should* operate and the way they *actually* operate. High-end service organizations suffer from this dual characteristic: Knowledge is certainly a source of wealth, but capital often buys knowledge. Also, knowledge is more likely to be realized in an organization given proper context. The *patterns* associated with power and social affiliations (the way organizations actually operate) often act as a *constraint* on knowledge creation and application.

Charles Savage (1990) has described the transformation of organizations through four historical eras. This is illustrated in Table 3–1 below (adapted from Savage 1990).

Observe the close association between the elements of Savage's framework and those of Pfeffer. The early industrial era is based on market arrangements, while the late industrial era is representative of the employment relation.

In the current transformation from late industrial to early knowledge, we are moving from a principle of automation to one of integrative processes. This is somewhat analogous to the principle of *informating* advanced by Zuboff (1988). While automation involves the removal of the individual from a process, informating is a form of process abstraction and integration between the individual and a computer system. Through IT, an individual manipulates the inputs and outputs of several tasks, sees beyond his or her immediate work, and is able to perceive the entire process.

**TABLE 3–1   ORGANIZATIONAL TRANSFORMATION—
ADAPTED FROM CHARLES SAVAGE (1990)**

Era	Source of Wealth	Type of Organization	Conceptual Principles
Late Agricultural	Land	Feudal	—
Early Industrial	Labor	Proprietorships	Division of labor Self-interest Pay for task
Late Industrial	Capital	Steep hierarchies	Division of management Separate owner/manager Separate thinking/doing One person/one boss Automate
Early Knowledge	Knowledge	Human networking	Peer-to-peer networking Integrative processes Work as dialogue Human time and timing Virtual task-focusing teams

A third form of process integration is an extension of informating, known as *knowledging*. Savage (1990) refers to knowledging as "an active and continual process of interrelating patterns. It is more than the accumulation of and access to information, because it looks at both the known (information) and the visionary (what could be)." As we will see in subsequent chapters, knowledging involves both explicit (i.e., the known) and tacit (i.e., the vision) forms of knowledge. Thus, knowledging depends on people—for interpreting the known and for embodying the vision. For example, an organization that is focused on knowledging is more likely to anticipate shifts in market patterns than a traditional bureaucratic one. *Thus, knowledging is focused on learning*, and is characterized by the content and process of *knowledge creation*, individual *motivation*, and the active *involvement* of the individual with his or her work. We refer to such a knowledging environment as a *culture of engagement*.

Each successive transformation, from automating to informating to knowledging, requires *higher levels of process abstraction and a broader range of process integration*. For knowledge integration to work, individuals in an organization will play several roles: operational (early industrial era), tactical (late industrial era), and strategic (knowledge era). Finally, organizational learning may be thought of as organizational knowledging. This includes the collective development and awareness of business and organizational patterns, particularly as they pertain to processes, people, markets, and strategies.

3.3 ORGANIZATIONAL DESIGN AND IT

Information technology effects the organization in ways that far surpass any other form of technology. For example, Michael Porter's value chain (Porter 1985) represents the generic activities of an organization. It is a standard analytical mechanism for assessing the internal environment during strategic planning. Perhaps the most important dimension of the value chain is that IT is the only technology involved with *every* value activity. As such, IT has the potential to introduce both dramatic change and integration throughout the organization.

Popular applications of IT-organizational interconnectivity include structure and process redesign. This manifests itself in flattening hierarchies and all sorts of business process reengineering efforts. Other forms of interconnectivity are less obvious, but sometimes more enduring. For example, IT may facilitate innovative culture types in organizations that require adaptive change in turbulent environments (Schein 1994).

SHIFTING BACK TO MARKET ARRANGEMENTS

Malone and Rockart (1993) have described an economic rationale for the current change in organizational structure. The crux of their argument is that IT is moving the organization from a hierarchical (i.e., employment relation) to a market-driven decision-making process to manage economic activity.

In a market-driven structure, *coordination costs* are higher than in the traditional hierarchy because of the need to compare suppliers, negotiate contracts, and actually transfer assets. On the other hand, *production costs* are relatively lower because the organization can benefit from a specialist's economies of scale. Furthermore, the organization is able to choose the best product available, and to rapidly change its selection as the market changes.

The declining costs of coordinating implementation technologies (i.e., computers and telecommunications) facilitate the emergence of market-driven decision making. That is to say, technology has driven down coordinating costs, thus making market arrangements economically more desirable than a traditional employment relation-based hierarchy. The result is likely to be more "buy" decisions, fewer "make" decisions, and the continued rise of networked organizations. The result will be a shift from an economy based on effort and time (i.e., the employment relation), to one based on the production of products and services (i.e., market arrangements).

Please note that the network structures which are such an integral part of market arrangements may or may not be structures of very small organizations, as some writers have predicted. For example, Malone and Rockart (1993) see the possibility of a return to pre-Industrial Revolution era organizations that operate as independent contractors (i.e., "putting out"). This was previously predicted by Peter Drucker (1988). Organizations could be assembled overnight to solve a problem or produce a product. This is sometimes known as a *virtual organization.*

In contrast, we see a network of a variety of structures—small organizations and large. We see evidence of smaller, but not vastly smaller organizations, with flattened, but not very flat hierarchies in a web of relationships with truly small, entrepreneurial independent contractors or organizations.

COORDINATING MECHANISMS

Two different types of coordinating mechanisms characterize modern organizations. The first is a vertical coordinating mechanism that derives from the employment relation that has developed since the factory system. The second is a horizontal coordinating mechanism across departments or organizations (i.e., market arrangements).

The first type of coordinating mechanism is known as a *vertical information linkage.* This type of linkage concerns itself with vertical information flows. In practice, it usually functions as a control mechanism, and reinforces both the hierarchy and employment relation. This coordination type includes mechanisms such as hierarchical referral, rules and standardized work plans, and vertical information systems (Daft 1998).

In contrast, *horizontal information linkages* coordinate tasks across the functional silos imposed by the division of labor. This includes everything from e-mail to direct contact, task forces, and teams. An information system designed around a business process model, as opposed to a functional model, would be an example of a horizontal information system that functions to coordinate business process tasks. Since traditional information systems are developed around functional/vertical models (e.g., information engineering), these high impact, integrative process-based information systems are rare!

Of course, organizations have both forms of linkage. In practice, vertical forms are more formal and exist for control—they represent reporting relationships and reinforce the presence of the hierarchy. In contrast, horizontal linkages concern the *business* of the organization. They represent the coordination within and between business processes that are cross-functional, and may even cross organizational boundaries.

One important observation: According to Daft (1998), as the requirement for vertical coordination and control increases, the most effective (i.e., *information carrying capacity*) vertical information linkages are, in increasing order: hierarchical referral, rules and plans, additional slots in the hierarchy, and IS. Similarly, as the requirement for the horizontal coordination of work increases, the most effective (again, the information carrying capacity) horizontal information linkages are, in increasing order: IS, direct control, task forces, integrators (a person), and teams.

Observe that a computer information system is the *most* effective mechanism for control, but the *least* effective for coordination. *This concerns the different character of the information required for control and coordination.* Control is satisfied with simple, well-understood threads of data and explicit knowledge (even routine knowledge). A computer system often functions as a *lean information channel*. In contrast, task coordination requires *richer* forms of information, knowledge not necessarily well understood. The most effective *information channel* for *rich communications* is the interactive communications between people. In Part 2 of this book, we more fully develop the notion of quantitative and rich information in terms of data and various forms of knowledge.

TRANSFORMATION

A great deal has been written on how to exploit IT for business advantage. Managers are assessing the impact of IT on the organization in a global environment that demands low-cost, high-quality products, and fast and flexible response to customer needs. Below is a brief summary of all five levels of IT-enabled business transformation, according to Venkatraman (1994):

1. *Localized Exploitation.* The focused application of IT to address functional requirements of high-value business operations. This is the standard IT application with little, if any, change in business processes.
2. *Internal Integration.* A systematic approach to leverage IT throughout an enterprise. In principle, this involves technical interconnectivity and business process interdependence. In practice, the emphasis is on the former rather than the latter, resulting in automated, but antiquated, business processes.
3. *Business Process Redesign.* The IT-enabled redesign of critical business processes. The emphasis is on shifting the business paradigm to achieve competitive advantage, and not on "fixing" current weaknesses. IT is used

as an enabler in support of the larger goal of improved organizational capabilities and competencies.

4. *Business Network Redesign*. The redesign, and concomitant redistribution, of business activities across different firms. This extends business process redesign to a firm's value system. The rationale is improved efficiency (transaction processing, inventory movement) and differentiation (through interdependent process linkages and knowledge networks). This facilitates organizational flexibility to respond to customer needs by exploiting core competencies in the entire business network.

5. *Business Scope Redefinition*. Business scope redefinition implies a change in business scope and external relationships. It also supports the "virtual business network" and the move toward corporate flexibility. This involves the fundamental reorganization of activities in a firm's value chain.

Venkatraman refers to the first two levels as evolutionary, and the last three as revolutionary. Our analysis of the literature on information management suggests that problems may stem from a technology-focused rather than an organization-driven architecture (Goodhue, Quillard, and Rockart 1988, Lederer and Sethi 1988, Goodhue, Kirsch, Quillard, and Wybo 1992, Earl 1993). In other words, the failure to move from technical to business process interdependence—to fully exploit level two, and to move from level two to level three—is largely responsible for the failure of the traditional approaches to move out of the evolutionary phase into the revolutionary stage. IT professionals have been largely driven by the technology of information, and not the *interconnectivity* of information with other domains of the organization, notably its business processes and knowledge workers.

Naturally, firms are leveraging the revolutionary capabilities of IT (e.g., business process reengineering); but they are doing so *apart from* traditional IT architectures. There is no current IT "architecture" or "approach" that facilitates movement toward revolutionary business transformation. Recall, for example, that Davenport (1993) maintains that information engineering does not support business process reengineering, or more generally process change, because of its focus on the stove-pipe, functional model characteristic of industrial era organizations. A systematic approach to revolutionary business transformation requires a move from a 19th century organizational model to one appropriate for the 21st century!

PRODUCT AND SERVICE COMPLEXITY

Driven by power and transportation technologies, the Industrial Revolution brought forth the factory system *and* the capability to produce substantially more complex products than otherwise. Similarly, IT has changed the organization of work, and has fostered the creation of products and services of still greater complexity.

The development of complex products, particularly through IT, may be characterized by the notion of capabilities and competencies discussed later in this chapter. As we will subsequently see, the development of a *core technological capability* is one where an organization's knowledge-based competitiveness is sustained through its technical competencies (Leonard-Barton 1995).

This leads to a second consideration in organizational design: *the network organization*. Despite all the talk of network structures, the most successful, and popular, implementations have been with organizations that manufacture relatively simple, pre-factory-system classes of products—footwear, for example. But what of complex products, say, automobiles or airplanes? To build complex products in a network structure requires a different form of market arrangement. This arrangement goes well beyond the notion of simply comparing suppliers to locate the most cost-effective. Rather, the network is composed of organizations with *long-term* relationships. In this way, the economies of scale associated with market arrangements may be leveraged, while benefiting from the stability of an organizational arrangement of committed stakeholders. A network designed to build complex products requires a sharing of product designs, and integrative processes and knowledge areas—one that requires a commitment that comes from the expectation of long-term relationships. *In effect, the network is an arrangement among several organizations that leverages their separate competencies and capabilities.*

UNCERTAINTY

Uncertainty is typically defined as the *absence of information*. Hence, sufficient information reduces uncertainty, while insufficient information increases uncertainty. Note, too, that information may be delivered in various forms or *channels*—computer systems or lateral relations (e.g., direct contact), for example. Since organizations seek to reduce uncertainty, the different forms of information technologies (e.g., computers, lateral relations), then, become options in organizational design.

Information processing theory attempts to identify organizational design options in terms of uncertainty. Tushman and Nadler (1978) have identified the sources of uncertainty (inputs) as interdependence among subunits, nonroutine tasks, and unstable environments. Similarly, Galbraith (1973) has categorized the design options (outputs) as those that reduce the need for information, and those that increase the information processing capability of the organization.

Goodhue, Wybo, and Kirsch (1992) have created an "updated" organization information processing theory by combining the works of Galbraith, and Tushman and Nadler. This is illustrated in Figure 3–1, taken from Goodhue *et al.* (1992).

As illustrated, the degree of uncertainty is determined by the interdependence of subunits, complexity or nonroutineness of subunit tasks, and stability of task environment. One organizational design strategy is to reduce the need for information processing, through creation of slack resources (i.e., reduce level of performance) or creation of self-contained tasks (e.g., employ a non-functional structure, such as one based on product lines). A second design strategy is to increase the capacity to process information. This may be accomplished through creation of lateral relations (e.g., teams), or investment in computerized information systems. Goodhue *et al.* (1992) elaborate on this model, which we briefly summarize in the next section.

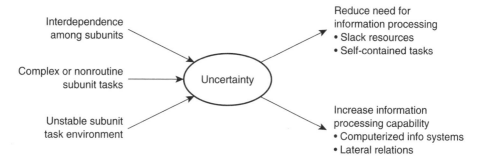

FIGURE 3–1   Uncertainty and an Updated Information Processing Model—Goodhue et al. (1992)

INFORMATION RICHNESS

Recall from Chapter 2 that the Perrow model characterized knowledge tasks in terms of task variability and problem analyzability. This resulted in four types of task technologies: routine, craft, engineering, and nonroutine. Each of these tasks is associated with a *pattern* of organizational design: the more routine the task, the higher the level of formalization and centralization, the "deeper" the hierarchy, and the greater reliance on vertical information linkages. In contrast, the more nonroutine the task technology, the lower the level of formalization and centralization, the "flatter" the hierarchy, and the greater reliance on horizontal information linkages (Daft 1998).

The Perrow model is a good example of the concept of uncertainty and another concept, that of *ambiguity*. While uncertainty is defined as the absence of information, ambiguity (or the term *equivocality* used by Goodhue *et al.* 1992) is the presence of multiple, conflicting interpretations of a situation.

Low levels of uncertainty characterize routine technology, and therefore, its information requirements are characterized by *small* amounts of *quantitative* information, usually in the form of standardized work procedures and reports. High levels of uncertainty characterize engineering technologies, and therefore, their information requirements are characterized by *large* amounts of *quantitative* information, usually in the form of computer information systems. In each case (routine and engineering), the technology is characterized by clearly defined tasks, differing only in the level of uncertainty. *Uncertainty* is thus reduced by sufficient *amounts* of information. Computer information systems are good sources of large amounts of quantitative information.

In contrast, craft and nonroutine technologies also differ in the degree of uncertainty, but these technologies are characterized by equivocality—ambiguous situations without clearly defined solutions. Accordingly, craft technologies (low uncertainty, high equivocality) are satisfied with *small* amounts of *rich* information, usually a consequence of experience and observation. Nonroutine technologies (high uncertainty, high equivocality) are satisfied with *large* amounts of *rich* information, usually in the form of lateral relations (e.g., teams). Generally, *equivocality* is reduced by sufficiently *rich* information. Knowledge workers and lateral relations are good sources of rich information. (See both Goodhue *et al.* 1992 and Daft 1998 for details.)

Rich information is that which carries with it something beyond manifest data, a deep understanding born of human experience and knowledge. Information richness is associated with the *information carrying capacity of data* and is a function of its *communications channel*. Lean forms of communications (e.g., written) contain a low carrying capacity, while rich channels (e.g., face-to-face meeting) contain a high carrying capacity. It is the rich channels that are the vehicles for rich information.

Design Fit

We refer to the patterns described above as design fit—desired associations. For example, a routine process task is one with low levels of uncertainty and ambiguity, and therefore, requires the processing of small amounts of quantitative information. The design with the best fit, then, would utilize lean communication channels and vertical information linkages (e.g., a hierarchy). Transaction computer systems and a high level of formalization may also be expected. In contrast, a nonroutine task is characterized by high levels of uncertainty and ambiguity, and requires the processing of high amounts of quantitative and rich information. Therefore, we would expect to see rich communication channels and horizontal linkages, possibly in the form of a team or some other form of lateral relationship. While teams address the requirement for rich information, we may satisfy the requirement for large amounts of quantitative information with decision support systems, such as data warehouses and technical reference manuals.

As an example of "misfit," Davenport (1994) has reported on the failure of technology architectures and enterprise information models. Davenport claims the cause of failure is an exclusive focus on technology, and the failure to address how people actually use information: "since people are important sources and integrators of information, any maps or models of information should include people."

The lesson is obvious: Whether you are designing an information system, a new organizational structure, or engaging in a process or quality improvement effort, the effective designer is aware that each construct is intertwined with the design of the others. Designs must "fit" and reinforce each other in a consistent and compatible pattern.

3.4   ORGANIZATIONAL CONTEXTS AND STRUCTURE

Traditional OT defines organizational design in terms of organizational structure. This is a consequence of its history: Classical OT has perceived organizations to be mechanical devices, and hence, has considered design as transforming structure. This structure perspective has governed organizational design research.

THE VARIED CONTEXTS OF OT AND ORGANIZATIONAL DESIGN

Design has historically been framed as series of interactions between organizational constructs and structure. Figure 3–2 illustrates several approaches to design.

The upper left portion of Figure 3–2 represents classical contingency theory. In contingency theory, structure is said to be determined by contexts: technology, size, environment, and strategy. In Chapter 2, we introduced a short sampling: Recall, for example, that routine process tasks (i.e., technology) are best operationalized with high levels of formalization and centralization (i.e., structure).

The strategy imperative is more complicated. (The strategy oval in Figure 3–2 represents the content of strategy, not the mechanism by which it comes into existence.) Beginning with the classical work of Alfred Chandler in the 1960s, it has been argued that strategy determines structure (moving right-to-left along the strategy-structure imperative arrow in Figure 3–2). Michael Porter's work on generic strategies supports the "structure follows strategy" logic; for example, a low-cost strategy would indicate high complexity, centralization, and formalization; a differentiation strategy indicates the reverse. Miles and Snow demonstrated a relationship between environmental uncertainty and strategic types of organizations (the arrow labeled strategy formulation). Robbins (1990) reports that still other researchers suggest that the imperative be reversed—perhaps strategy follows structure (moving left-to-right along the strategy-structure imperative arrow).

More recently, work by Prahalad and Hamel (1990), Stalk, Evans, and Shulman (1992), and others, suggests that strategy and the organization as a whole are best supported through core capabilities (i.e., strategic processes) and core competencies (i.e., knowledge areas applied to the capabilities). It is suggested that because environmental uncertainty is a given, the best management and design philosophy is one that develops and enriches competencies and capabilities.

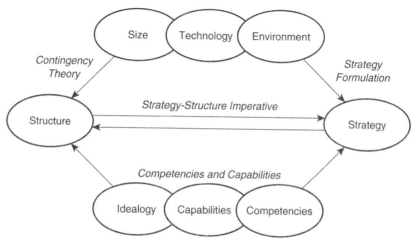

FIGURE 3–2   Organizational Contexts and Design

To the deep-seated competencies and capabilities, Collins and Porras (1996) have described how success depends on an organization's vision framework: its *core ideology* (i.e., core values and purpose) and its *envisioned future*. This is illustrated in the lower portion of Figure 3–2.

GENERIC COMPONENTS OF ORGANIZATIONAL STRUCTURE

Each organizational construct is, of course, an area which has received a great deal of attention. In fact, many constructs such as strategy, power, process, information, and structure, have themselves become disciplines.

Among the more interesting endeavors has been the attempt to create *generic* formulations of constructs. For example, in 1985 Michael Porter defined three generic types of strategy: low cost, differentiation, and niche strategies (1985). Roger Harrison proposes four generic types of culture: power, role, task/achievement, and person/support (in Handy 1993).

A great deal of attention has also been given to the study of structure. Henry Mintzberg has been something of a trendsetter in many areas. In 1983, he defined both generic components of structure and generic types (1983).

The generic components of structure are portrayed visually by Mintzberg. Figure 3–3 is taken from Mintzberg, and some form of this illustration appears in numerous texts.

The five generic areas of the organization are as follows (see Mintzberg 1983 for an in-depth discussion):

1. *Strategic apex.* The senior managers who direct the overall organization. Their interests lie in *centralizing decision making.*
2. *Operating core.* The people who perform the work (i.e., technology) of the organization. The emphasis on work results in their promotion of skills and *professionalism.*

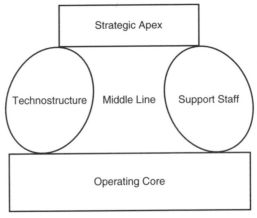

FIGURE 3.3   Mintzberg's Generic Structural Components

3. *Middle line.* Middle level managers who "connect" the strategic apex and the operating core. Middle managers are motivated to *balkanize* the organization by drawing power from both the strategic apex and the operating core.

4. *Technostructure.* Analysts who formulate standards. Their power derives from *standardization*, particularly of work processes.

5. *Support staff.* The people who perform staff functions. Their interests are to *collaborate* in decision making with other members of the organization, owing to their expertise.

Observe the effects of history on OT thinking. As mentioned in Chapter 2, since Adam Smith's time, designing and managing have been closely linked to defining structure and the tasks people perform, almost always along a division of labor. Accordingly, Mintzberg has defined the common elements of structure in terms of the *roles* people play in an organization.

Note also that Mintzberg describes each generic component of structure with the notion of another construct: power. The motivation of each member of the organization is identical—to increase his or her power. Depending on where in the organization each is located, a different technique is employed. The senior manager seeks to *centralize* power; the people in the operating core must rely on *knowledge* and *skill* (i.e., professionalism); middle managers on controlling the flow of information and creating *friction* between members of the other generic parts; technical analysts on *standardizing* work; and staff analysts or specialists on their *expertise* so that they may be involved in decision making by *collaborating* with other members of the organization (Mintzberg 1983).

GENERIC ORGANIZATIONAL STRUCTURES

Figure 3–4 illustrates the generic organizational structure with information modeling concepts. Organizational structure is a composite of the five generic substructures. As with all compositions, the composite—in this case, organizational structure—has certain emergent properties that correspond to its components. The emergent character of an organization's structure depends on which component predominates, and thus defines a generic structure type.

The five generic structures, with a sampling of some of their emergent characteristics, are as follows (Mintzberg 1983):

1. *Simple structure*—emphasizes the strategic apex. The simple structure is characterized by an organic form (i.e., low formalization), young age, small in size, centralized decision making, a simple and dynamic environment, and centralized power in the strategic apex. The primary coordinating mechanism is direct supervision.

2. *Machine bureaucracy*—emphasizes the technostructure. The machine bureaucracy is characterized by high formalization and bureaucracy, old age, large size, limited horizontal decentralized decision making, a simple and stable environment, and technocratic power. The primary coordinating mechanism is standardization of work processes.

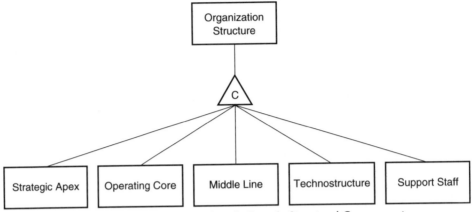

Figure 3–4   Information Model of Mintzberg's Generic Structural Components

3. *Professional bureaucracy*—emphasizes the operating core. The professional bureaucracy is characterized by low formalization and bureaucracy, varies in age and size, horizontal and vertical decentralization, a complex and stable environment, and a professional power base. The primary coordinating mechanism is standardization of skills.

4. *Divisionalized form*—emphasizes the middle line. The divisionalized form is characterized by high formalization and bureaucracy, old age, very large size, limited vertical decentralization, a simple and stable environment with diversified markets, and middle line control. The primary coordinating mechanism is standardization of outputs.

5. *Adhocracy*—emphasizes the support staff. The adhocracy is characterized by an organic form (i.e., low formalization), young age, selective decentralization, a complex and dynamic environment, and expert control. The primary coordinating mechanism is mutual adjustment.

3.5   FUTURE ISSUES

Each of us has witnessed the rapid change in societies and organizations during the past 20 years. If Peter Drucker is correct, we can expect another decade or two of such turbulence. What will organizations, and our lives, look like in the "calmer" future?

Predicting the future is always risky. Below are listed several ideas. A good source for further reading is Charles Handy (1993). We have supplemented his thoughts with ours, with the caveat that there is, no doubt, a major storm brewing, the effects of which no one has yet anticipated.

- The continued integration of business processes, information, people, and knowledge.

- The rise of the individual who possesses an internal source of wealth (i.e., knowledge), and whose values and requirements will now have to be reconciled with those of the organization.

- The continued emergence of networked structures, with the caveat mentioned above: Existing organizations will become flatter, but not very flat, and smaller, but not very small. However, these existing organizations will increasingly depend on a growing number of smaller, knowledge-based ones. The network, then, will consist of organizations of assorted sizes, small groups of people, and even individuals.

- The professionalization of people. The knowledge era will continue the shift back to market arrangements. The employment relation will never disappear, but will become less important. There will be an increase in certification, as knowledge becomes the construct around which people and organizations form relationships. Finally, there will be an increase in the number of contractual relationships (needed to support the network form): short-term, transactional contracts, and more long-term contracts based on trust and experience among the parties to a contract.

- Greater social and political instability. This will result from the growing balkanization in our society as the rewards associated with work grow even more inequitable—a consequence of the division between those who can market their knowledge and those who cannot.

- Charles Handy (1997) has observed that shareholders are no longer an organization's sole source of wealth, but increasingly, the people who work in an organization are its principle assets. Furthermore, the *social* rationale of Eastern organizations will challenge the *economic* rationale of Western ones. From this will emerge new theories on the social purpose of organizations. An organization will no longer be seen as a "property" owned by financial investors (i.e., shareholders), but as a community where the concept of ownership has little meaning, and each of its stakeholders shares in its risks and rewards.

- Discontinuous change will make an understanding of organizational patterns and architecture the key to improved effectiveness. Architectural models that portray patterns of behavior among organizational components will replace existing models. Design by architecture will be a new source of competitive advantage,

The central theme for the future will be greater *meaning* for people, organizations, and societies. The role of both managers and professionals will be to bring coherence to such a *web* of relationships. Organizational architecture and modeling will move to center stage as one approach to achieving common purpose.

3.6 DESIGN BY ARCHITECTURE

We complete our discussion of traditional design, and mark the beginning of our new approach, by building on the conclusion that noted economist John Kay makes in his book, *Why Firms Succeed* (1995).

In the early days of medicine, the prestige of a physician was largely determined by that of his patient, and not the efficacy of his or her treatments. Urgency prevented critical analysis and the adoption of anything like a scientific approach. Similarly, today the professional manager is faced with pressing problems that often give way to hurried solutions found in some book or a management consultant's presentation.

However, like the physician of old, the manager of today is not dishonest. The *artifacts* of management and organizational design are not sufficiently rich. There is no foundation to which a manager may refer that is scientific in every sense of the word. Instead, he or she relies on pictures and "laundry" lists, and a relatively vague understanding of their complex interrelationships.

Modern medicine has benefited from basic science, yet remains an art. Management and organizational design will also depend on the experience and judgment of people. We propose to enrich that judgment with a scientific framework. We propose *design by architecture*.

3.7 CORE CONCEPTS

Market arrangements	Employment relations
Informating	Knowledging
Culture of engagement	Network structures
Process integration	Lateral relations
Vertical information linkages	Horizontal information linkages
Uncertainty	Ambiguity
Equivocality	Information richness
Information amount	Core capability
Core competence	Vision framework
Design fit	Design by architecture
Generic structure components	Generic structure types
Organizational learning	Organizational knowledge
Virtual organization	Information carrying capacity
Information channel	Core technological capability

CHAPTER 4

A NEW APPROACH TO ORGANIZATION MODELING

4.1 THE MISALIGNMENT OF ORGANIZATIONAL EFFECTIVENESS AND ORGANIZATIONAL DESIGN

The definition of organizational effectiveness (OE) varies with culture and context. For example, Japanese firms may define OE in terms of market share or employee turnover rates. In contrast, American firms may define OE with financial measures, such as profitability or return-on-equity. Both views are right and honest. Their respective contexts are different, so their definitions of success are different. Though their perspectives differ, their quests for improvement do not. Each engages in behaviors intended to change the organizational parts and the way they work together so that the whole benefits. This is organizational design.

One major problem area with existing design practice concerns "architecting" the organization to maximize organizational effectiveness. Older methodologies of organizational design fail to systematically account for constantly changing business needs, new and emerging paradigms (e.g., knowledge), and organizational goals, as well as the extremely flexible, dynamic strategies needed to achieve this effectiveness.

A new approach is proposed to address the uneven aligment illustrated in Figure 4–1. The solution is an innovative architectural framework. In formulating this architectural framework, we ask questions such as:

1. What is the focus of traditional OT approaches to organization design?
2. What is the business value of traditional approaches (i.e., affect on OE)?
3. What are the dimensions of competitive advantage?
4. How can various isolated viewpoints be integrated into a larger organization model?
5. What is an organization model? How do we architect an organization?

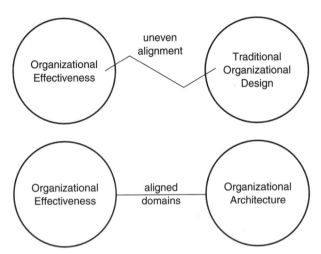

FIGURE 4–1   The Difference Between Conventional Organizational Design and Architecting the Organization

In establishing a new framework, several perspectives must be considered such as strategic, structural, competitive, business process, information technology, etc. New approaches employing object technology have begun to surface. Business-focused authors advocate "business engineering" (Taylor 1995), while IT professionals promote "object-oriented organizational modeling" (Czech, Fjermestad, and Jonsson 1995). Though they make a contribution to our understanding, they invariably offer little more than a repackaging of old ways in new wrappers. Typically, business or organization modeling is reduced to capturing "business rules" in "business classes" that characterize an IT application. This is analogous to building lasers without a knowledge of physics. Such "new approaches" do not adequately address the areas of organizational design and improved effectiveness. They are not built on a solid framework of organizational research—the subject matter that is the foundation of organizational design, for there is no underlying organization level architecture!

Our approach is different. We have broadened our perspective to include OT, recent organizational and business literature, as well as information modeling. We *build* an effective organizational architecture by using the *materials* of organization theory and literature, *framed* with information modeling concepts. We call this framework organization modeling—OM (see Figure 4–2).

Our analysis indicates that the main problem in the misalignment of OE and organizational design is a failure of context: structural, strategic, human, business process, and so on. The absence of an architecture has resulted in a misalignment of organizational design with the wider organization. *It is organizational architecture that promotes different perspectives, while integrating them into a whole.*

The lesson learned from organizational research is that there is no "root cause" to misalignment among organizational domains. Organizations are complex composites with an almost unlimited variety of behaviors. What is needed is an approach that codifies these behaviors. These behaviors and their interrelationships arise from an architectural framework, and embody the design of an organization.

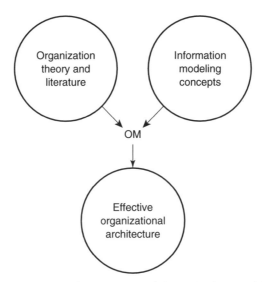

FIGURE 4–2   Architecture-Based Organization Modeling

4.2   BUILDING AN ARCHITECTURAL FRAMEWORK

We propose to make *organization materials* and their application in business *disciplined*. A disciplined approach to organizational architecture means a framework by which we may arrange an organization's pieces—how they communicate, how they change, and how they constitute the whole.

An organization model, framed with a certain discipline, gives organizational designers the architecture required for maximum business benefit. In the same manner that a disciplined approach to information systems provides an unambiguous specification of information, organizational design may also be structured, even if some organizational pieces are not explicit, such as tacit knowledge. Organizational design means the ability to capture and communicate the components of an organization—even if individual pieces are not fully defined!

Each domain of the organization—organizational constructs and derivative management philosophies—may be architected with behavior. By focusing analysis on behavior, we "hide" the problem of associating organizational constructs with dissimilar structural properties, such as organizational structure and business process. See Figure 4–3.

It is only during implementation that behavior is operationalized into structure. For example, an information specification becomes program code and data structures, a specification of organizational structure become functional reporting relationships, and so on.

The manager—in his or her head—knows what is desired, but does not know how to specify it. OM gives the manager a vehicle to describe and elaborate—in simple language—the architecture of the organization. The architecture of the organization is the framework through which it is designed and through

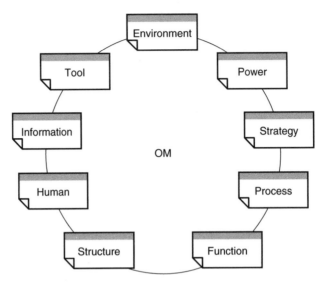

FIGURE 4–3   Integrating Organizational Constructs

which it emerges. Its components include core organizational constructs (e.g., strategy, structure), derivative management philosophies (e.g., culture, learning), and their interrelationships. The behavioral relationships manifest themselves in the behavior of these components. On the theoretical side, managers have the richness of OT; on the practical side, they have bits and pieces of organizational architectures: simulation tools, financial spreadsheets, information systems. Managers and organizational planners have everything except the thread—the model—of how to go from one to the other. For managers, it is a transition from chaos to successful decision making. For organizational planners, it is a transition from the expected organizational design to a successful organizational architecture that really satisfies his or her intent.

Finally, let us state the obvious: organizations are not buildings or bridges. They contain people, and therefore, unlike physical structures, the notions of architecture, engineering, and construction are all intertwined. Like strategy, architecture is formulated and formed. Architecture includes people too!

4.3 THREE VIEWS OF MODELING ORGANIZATIONS

Our approach to organizational design embodies three views of modeling. The first concerns the *richness of ideas*. This refers to the appropriateness and robustness of the concepts upon which you construct your architecture. In OM, the concepts derive from both OT and business literature. These concepts are used to describe organizational domains. These include strategy, people, culture, learning, information, quality, etc., as well as their interrelationships.

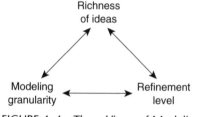

FIGURE 4–4   Three Views of Modeling

The second viewpoint of modeling pertains to the *level of modeling granularity*. This refers to successive levels of decomposition of a given object. In OM, the objects of granularity are organizational domains, each of which may be decomposed. For example, the domain known as process may be modeled starting with the "top" process type, *interorganization*, and its decomposition into successively lower levels: *organization, business process, work cycle, task,* and *activity.*

The third viewpoint of modeling concerns *scope and refinement.* As we will subsequently discuss, our level of understanding is a continuum between the current philosophy concerning organizations on the one hand, and the real world on the other. Finally, no level exists in total isolation; on the contrary, each level influences every other level. The three viewpoints are illustrated in Figure 4–4.

REFINEMENT LEVELS

The third perspective of refinement embodies the first and second perspectives—our richness of ideas and a specific level of granularity. The refinement levels are illustrated in Figure 4–5.

Philosophy of organizations. The first level of refinement concerns the relationships among organizations, people, and society. The place of organizations in the lives of people and their cultural and political institutions is critical to organizational

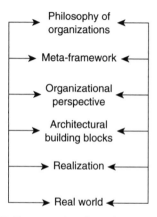

FIGURE 4–5   Refinement Levels in Organization Modeling

design. An organization's invariant derives from its cultural context, and forms its unvarying organizational rules that dictate design. This is discussed in the next section.

Meta-framework. The meta-framework concerns the structuring mechanism by which we choose to understand organizations. The meta-framework for OM is the object meta-model discussed in Section 4.5.

Organizational perspective. The principles that manifest themselves in the behavior of organizations. Organizational perspective is governed by two factors: (1) the organizational materials selected and (2) their positions in the organization. As we have been discussing, OM uses organizational constructs as its materials. Their manifest place in an organization exists as a series of layers, discussed in Chapter 5, *The Layered Organization.*

Architectural building blocks. The fundamental constructs that serve as the architectural underpinnings of an organization. The OM building blocks are revolutionary constructs—*organization molecules*—that are uniform across all organizations. Examples of organization molecules include process, information, structure, and culture. We introduce molecules in Chapter 6, and discuss several in detail in subsequent chapters. Chapter 7 discusses the alignment of these architectural building blocks.

Realization. This is the implementation of building block specifications. In OM, the operationalization of a molecule is within the OM refinement model discussed in Chapter 8. As we will discuss, the OM refinement model is bilateral in direction—it includes both top-down decomposition and bottom-up emergence.

Real World. The organization as it actually exists. The real-world organization participates in the formation of building block instances; that is to say, organizations have deliberate and emergent characteristics that manifest themselves in the development of organizational domains.

It should be observed that OM is a broad construct that embodies all dimensions of modeling. OM is not a technique of implementation. OM does not originate with analysis or even strategy, but with philosophy. By the time organizational design has started, there already exists a *pattern* or *direction* that constrains the manager's decisions. This direction was established at the philosophical level where managers, either consciously or unconsciously, have already defined their *organizational context.* This context establishes what is possible and what is not. In the same manner that IT decisions are effective only in an organizational context, organizational decisions are effective only in a philosophical context.

4.4 PHILOSOPHICAL CONTEXT

Organizations do not exist in isolation. Structure, culture, reward systems, methods of operation, and so on derive from their social, political, and cultural contexts. This larger *environmental context* determines the parameters of design.

Lester Thurow (1996) observes that "to ignore the social aspects of humankind is to design a world for a human species that does not exist."

These "social aspects of humankind" influence an organization's fundamental principles. An organization does not consciously act in accord with these principles; on the contrary, it interacts within an environmental context that constrains both its design and operations.

THE ETERNAL TRIANGLE

Environmental context is essentially composed of *people*, their *society*, and their *organizations*. People have historically expressed their values through cultural and political institutions (i.e., society) while turning to an economic entity (i.e., organization) for sustenance. These three environmental components interact in what we term the *eternal triangle*. The interactions produce unequal consequences. At different points in an organization's history, one component may exercise the greatest power or possess the highest value.

The relative value of individuals, organizations, and societies in different regions of the world rests upon a cultural distinction. For example, there has been a difference in the value accorded the three elements in the U.S., Continental Europe, and Asia. The apex of an eternal triangle represents the element that has cultural precedence. The other two elements at the base of the triangle are subservient to the apex. This is illustrated in Figure 4–6.

Each region represents a historical tradition that impacts organizational design. The importance of the cultural perspective is that each is characterized by a different invariant. Each culture is a direct consequence of the invariant associated with its respective eternal triangle. Therefore, it is not surprising to discover very different organizational types in these three great cultures.

Each society is in flux—no one part of the world adheres exclusively to any one classification. As shifts in power move the culture type from one category to another, societies change perspectives.

TYPE 1 Invariant: A *socio-cultural invariant* is associated with the semantics of the eternal triangle. This is a broad and commonly accepted view of culture. Generally, when we use the word "culture" we imply the social phenomena that are generic to the entire ethos, including belief systems, values, relationships, laws, and so on and so forth. Examples of a Type 1 socio-cultural invariant are individualism in the U.S. and community in Japan (Thurow 1992).

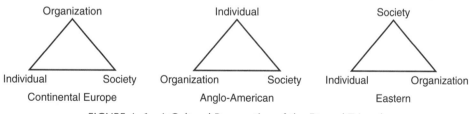

FIGURE 4–6   A Cultural Perspective of the Eternal Triangle

TYPE 2 Invariant: An *organization invariant* is a manifestation of a Type 1 invariant in a particular context. This context may be a family, an entire society, or, as we discuss in this book, an organization. A Type 2 invariant is more specific than Type 1. An example of a Type 2 organization invariant is the type of reward system an organization maintains—individual vs. group rewards. Type 1 invariants surround and largely constrain Type 2 invariants.

Organization invariants derive first
from the eternal triangle (TYPE 1),
and second from its manifestation in a
particular organization (TYPE 2).
Both are called culture.

Various Meanings of the Word "Organization"

A question that arises concerns the meaning of "organization." In Chapter 2, we presented the traditional view of an organization as a social entity existing to accomplish certain goals. In a socio-cultural context, the behaviors in which we are interested—those that implement the invariant of an organization—are derived within a context of *organizing* or creating an *organization* of ideas or people.

The meaning of the word "organization," then, is associated with its context. Below, we briefly describe its connotations, particularly as they pertain to the "organization" as a social entity designed to accomplish certain goals.

1. *Classification and categorization.* The arrangement of facts or things into a particular pattern. One such common pattern is a hierarchy. The hierarchy is commonly applied to the natural world.
2. *Discipline.* The activity of bringing discipline and order to an otherwise chaotic situation or (lack of) understanding.
3. *Structure.* Developing a meaning or morphology for a given situation.
4. *Relationships.* Developing alliances among constituents. These may be either formal or informal.
5. *System.* Organization is synonymous with the word "systematization," including regulation, feedback, etc. This may be applied to a knowledge area or an entire organization.

The relationship of an organization's invariant to each of the above descriptions needs to be made apparent. The theme of modeling is "organization." In OM, we specifically are making reference to all meanings. For example, *organizing* is the activity of creating patterns or associations. It includes dimensions of each of the above descriptions, all of which lead to the development of a socio-cultural invariant, which, in turn, governs subsequent *organizing* activities in creating and maintaining economic organizations.

INDIVIDUALS, ORGANIZATIONS, AND SOCIETY

The interactions between individuals, organizations, and society form patterns of behavior. Each set of patterns characterizes a particular social culture and its invariant (TYPE 1). It is important to note that these patterns constrain the behavior of organizations, but that each organization may counter the norm. In the U.S., for example, many organizations are characterized by self-interest and low *esprit de corps*. This appears to be consistent with the individualism that characterizes American culture. Nevertheless, John Kay (1995) points out that Hewlett-Packard and Procter & Gamble are two organizations that are characterized by community and high employee loyalty. They run contrary to the larger American culture. Therefore, each organization may be both master and slave to its environment.

Below, we present a broad historical perspective that describes the three previously cited regions of the world within which organizations must exist.

CONTINENTAL EUROPE

The central "organizational" theme of European culture is that of *organizing actions*. It is organizing actions that have led to the creation of its institutions and social culture.

Bismarck collected fiefdoms and created Germany in an act of organization. The efforts of Napoleon to bring Europe into one sovereign rule was also an exercise in organization. A more successful exercise was exhibited by the Roman conquest of much of Europe. Roads established a *coordinating* mechanism that became an organizing principle that Europeans were able to leverage throughout their history. The British colonial legacies of the railroad and telegraph are two such examples.

Organizing actions, then, drive the change in political organizations and coordinating mechanisms that are so characteristic of Europe. The prominence of formal institutions—the Catholic Church, and the multitude of fragmented kingdoms and fiefdoms that characterize the medieval history of Europe—all resulted from organizing actions. Hence, Continental Europe is characterized by *organization* at the apex of the eternal triangle.

The French Revolution endeavored to transfer power from the monarchies to the common people. This again was an exercise in organizing activity. Another example appears in the theories developed by sociologists, such as Durkheim and Max Weber. These culminated in the development of the functional bureaucracies so common throughout the world today.

Continental Europe is characterized by "social discipline"—itself an organizing activity. This is seen in the highly planned and organized cities and social behavior common in Europe. Everything from town planning to dress codes and etiquette is essentially European in origin. In contrast, Asian cities have never been planned, but have evolved as needs arise. (Aside: This is characteristic of organizational change in Asian societies. This addresses the age-old question as to whether organizations evolve or are planned. We argue that it depends on the socio-political context which we term the eternal triangle.)

ANGLO-AMERICAN

The American Revolution succeeded in transferring power from the few to the many. The foundation of Anglo-American society is the freedom afforded the *individual*. Through their democracy, individuals are at the apex of the Anglo-American triangle.

The theme of individualism leads to individual development and inquiry. This, too, leads to scientific achievement. In this case, the achievements are personal. There is a reason, after all, for the large number of Nobel prize-winners from the U.S. (However, it does not necessarily follow that high personal achievement leads somehow to collective achievements. In fact, it does not!)

In contrast, in organizations, the individuals at the apex of the Anglo-American triangle are the principal *stakeholders* of the organization—the owners and senior management. This is evident in the prominence given the "CEO" in U.S. organizations. This is also reflected in the pay strategy of American firms—to *accumulate* as much wealth as possible by the few at the top of the hierarchy (Block 1996).

As important, it follows from this logic that there exists an economic rationale to British and American organizations, but no social one. The primary measure of value or success in individual-centric societies is economic. Politically, this form is characterized by a high degree of freedom; consequently, a great deal of latitude is given to both individuals and organizations.

EASTERN

Eastern cultures are characterized by a history of small communities and spiritualism. Communities of people survive by *sharing resources* among their members. The structure of society in the East has always been cohesive, based mainly on family values. Even Eastern kingdoms had less impact on the daily lives of individuals than their counterparts in Europe.

The tendency of the Eastern ethos has been to consider issues that concern the world or humanity at large. It involves ideals that are lofty. This is irrespective of the fact that it is often difficult to put them into practice. The consideration of whether such ideals are practical is hardly the issue. (Pragmatism has been largely a legacy of the West and not of the East.)

The East is rich in philosophy and religiosity. Concepts such as giving and sharing have always been an important part of the Eastern ethos. An outstanding example of this is the principle of "Sangha," which is one of the three most important tenets of Buddhism. Theoretically, a Sangha is a huge collection of monks who are in complete consonance with each other. It consists of what may be described as "many bodies but a single heart." It follows that *society* is at the apex of the eternal triangle in the East.

It is no surprise that Japan, perhaps the most extensively developed "Eastern" society, has been able to create an essentially socialist ethic without the drawbacks that arise in an "organizing" society (i.e., Europe) whenever socialism is attempted. The success of organizations where competition and a "single heart" coexist is apparent.

4.5 A META-FRAMEWORK

The meta-framework is the paradigm by which we choose to formalize our understanding of organizations. The core modeling principles by which OM represents an organization concern (1) behavior as a structuring mechanism, and (2) the notion of managed collections as a construct that may be applied to organizations.

AN OBJECT META-MODEL

Illustrated in Figure 4–7 is a meta-model of the object paradigm that may be used to model any domain of the organization—e.g., environment, strategy, process, information systems, and organizational structure.

An *object* in traditional information modeling is known as an *entity*. It is a physical thing, a concept, or an event. An object is constrained by its unvarying business rules—semantics specified as an *invariant*. An invariant is a reality-based *assertion* specifying the context of the business. An object, then, has a *real world equivalent*, and like the real world, may be represented by different views, or levels of abstraction.

As illustrated in Figure 4–7, an object or a collection of objects may be understood in terms of either its *structural* properties or its *behavioral* properties.

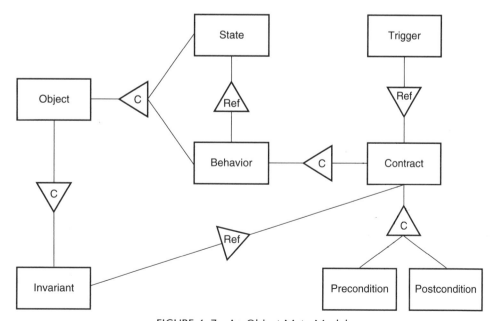

FIGURE 4–7   An Object Meta-Model

Behavioral properties (behavior) are defined by the set of operations available to an object, while structural property values (state) are determined by the application of the operations. Behavioral properties which are articulated in the behavior of an object are defined by the set of all possible operations available to the object. These operations are a set of rules that are followed when an object interacts with other objects or deals with its environment. Unlike an information system, it is not possible to specify, or even identify, all possible behaviors of an organizational domain. A few may be predefined, but many emerge from interactions with other domains.

At any given time, an object exhibits a certain behavior. This choice of the pattern of its behavior partly depends on its interaction with the environment and other objects, and partly on its own basic or "intrinsic" nature. However, whatever this essence may be, all that the outside or external observer perceives is the behavior pattern of the object. Looking at this pattern of behavior, the observer says that the object is in a particular state at such and such time. The state is not an intrinsic property of an object, rather, we as observers assign a state through our perception of its behavior pattern. Thus, it so difficult to perceive an organization's domains—strategy or culture, for instance. As behavior patterns constantly shift to adapt to a particular context, our perception of an organization's state also changes.

Each instance of a behavior is specified in a *contract*. A contract is implicit in the behavior it specifies. Contracts consist of assertions—a precondition (which is the situation before the contract can be executed), a postcondition (which is the situation after the contract is executed), and the constraints imposed by a corresponding invariant (which are rules followed during the transition from pre- to postcondition). Furthermore, a contract (i.e., a specific behavior instance) does not simply materialize, but must be triggered by a specific event. As shown in Figure 4–7, an object's state is not directly specified in a contract. It is specified by means of behavior. *The contract, therefore, is a mechanism for understanding an object.* (Framework 1992, Kilov and Ross 1994, Kilov and Simmonds 1996).

A pictorial representation of the relationship between an organization invariant, trigger, and pre- and postconditions is illustrated in Figure 4–8.

Observe that an invariant is in the "background," but it controls the behavior of objects in its domain. The same invariant can be instantiated in different ways. For example, the same statement of law may be interpreted differently by different lawyers. In an organizational context, this happens very often. People in different departments may interpret the "norms" of behavior and procedures in different ways. It may be that both parties are right, and their interpretations are honest, and yet they have a conflict between them. This is an example of how different cultural perspectives dominate our perceptions of the same real situation. Similarly, a trigger may initiate any number of behaviors. It is possible that a trigger may correspond to an object's precondition, as in a simple workflow process, or be a business event, such as an end-of-month time trigger that initiates a mailing of monthly statements. Unlike an invariant, a trigger need not be a rule that constrains an object—e.g., an end-of-month calendar event is independent of the behaviors it triggers.

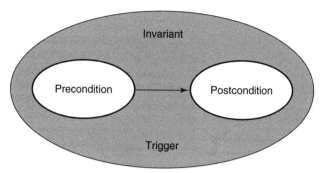

FIGURE 4–8   Relationship Between Invariant, Trigger, and Pre- and Postconditions

Pre- and postconditions are "states." An invariant is not a state (state is a function of time). An invariant is the background of procedures, operational rules, and relationships between objects which never change. The arrow in Figure 4–8 indicates a transition from one state to another. Contracts thus provide a dynamic aspect to modeling. From an IT perspective, a contract is a static set of rules which may materialize in the form of program code. But in an organization, contracts represent *dynamic interactions* between organizational domains—people, processes, tools, information, and so on.

A useful analogy in understanding the notion of an object is the concept of light. Light is said to have co-equally the properties of a wave and the properties of a particle. They are distinguished only by the context in which light is studied. Similarly, although an object has both structural and behavioral properties, it is distinguished by the context in which it is understood. The singularity of state and behavior is at the heart of the object paradigm. From an external observer's point of view, the question, "What does light really consist of?" is irrelevant. Let us leave such matters to the physicists.

MANAGED COLLECTIONS

Objects are almost always associated with other objects. Though behavior may be applied to an entity in isolation, this is rarely the case. As a rule, behavior associated with an object is governed by the semantics of its association with some other object. Another way of saying this is that behavior is "jointly owned." For instance, the generic associations discussed in the Appendix identify such well-understood, and commonly occurring, associations (e.g., dependency).

For example, a *parent* is a parent only because of a *dependency association* with a corresponding *dependent*. In this dependency example, there are three possible combinations of semantic arrangements. This is illustrated in Figure 4–9.

Behaviors associated with object A, object B, or {object A and object B}, are constrained by the *dependency invariant* (i.e., business and organizational rules). For instance, behavior may be associated with *parent* A, that is, object A and its dependency association. Similarly, object B does not exist in isolation, but is an

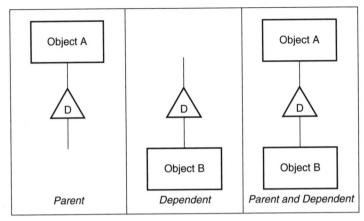

FIGURE 4–9   Behavioral Categories of a Dependency Association

object participating in a dependency association as *dependent* B. Finally, behavior may be associated with *parent* A and *dependent* B together. Each of these behavioral categories participates in behaviors constrained by their business rules specified in the corresponding invariant. In summary, we may say the following:

- Objects do not exist in isolation.
- An object's behavior is constrained by its associations with other objects.
- These are association rules (i.e., an invariant) which may never be violated.
- Object collections may be defined by the specification of their jointly owned behavior (Kilov and Ross 1994).

A collection of objects and their associations, constrained as a group, may be referred to as a *managed collection*. Managed collections are behavioral categories which are constrained by specific business rules specified in the objects' corresponding invariant. Furthermore, the behaviors associated with a managed collection are specific to the collection; a given collection will be constrained by a specific invariant and will have unique behaviors specified in corresponding contracts.

For example, Kilov and Ross (1994) have discussed the managed collection known as a *notification*. A notification represents the interaction of objects in the following way. A *notification* is emitted when a *monitored object* meets *notification criteria*. For example, a bank customer is issued a surcharge (notification) when his or her balance (monitored object) falls below a designated minimum (criteria).

A New Type of Association for Organizational Constructs: Composite-Subtyping

In OT, there are innumerable managed collections of organizational domains. Organizations consist of large numbers of very complex, interconnected managed collections of *different* organizational domains. Understanding and elaborating on these managed collections of domains is at the heart of organization modeling.

We now come to a problem in applying "traditional" information modeling concepts to organizations. In information modeling, when we model "business objects" we are really modeling their information content (i.e., a business class) which is destined for implementation in an information system. For example, the entity *employee* is an information class containing structural and behavioral properties of the class. However, it is very different from a *particular* instance of a human being. Managers must deal with both—the information class called *employee* and issues related to real people (e.g., motivation).

Let's illustrate the problem with a simple example. A work cycle in an automobile plant that paints an automobile a particular color is a portion of a business process. If this work cycle is fully automated, do we say that the robots and the information systems used to implement the process are components of the process (i.e., composition)? Or, are they *the* process itself (i.e., subtype)? *In fact, they are both.*

We postulate, therefore, that between organizational constructs of different types (i.e., environment, power, strategy, structure, process, function, people, information, tools) and their derivative management philosophies (e.g., learning, quality, change, culture, etc.), there exists a very complex association. This yet-to-be-identified association type (or types) forms managed collections among these organizational materials. By its very nature, an association between dissimilar constructs (e.g., people and process) is not clearly defined, and makes organizational design many orders of magnitude more complex than designing an information system.

What are the semantics of this yet-to-be-defined association? Using the example above, we postulate that it consists of properties of composition and of subtyping. The "composite" has properties associated with a *composite* in the traditional *composition* association (e.g., emergent and deliberate properties), while its "components" constitute "is-a" implementation constructs. Hence, we name this cross-domain generic association the *composite-subtyping association*. It approximates this very complex association among constructs.

Therefore, in OM, when we associate different organizational materials, we are using *this* type of association. We use the symbol "CS" in a triangle to identify the composite-subtyping. This is illustrated in Figure 4–10.

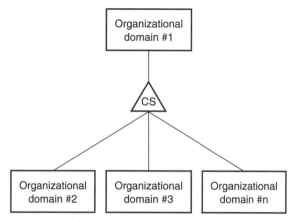

FIGURE 4–10   Generic Organizational Association Among Domains

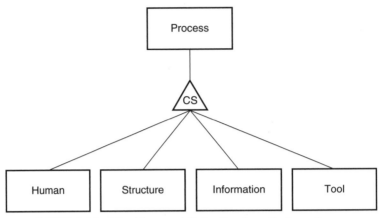

FIGURE 4–11   The Managed Collection for a Business Process

For example, the managed collection representing a business *process* really is a composite-subtype associating the organizational domains of *structure, people, information,* and *tools* that collectively *are* the business process, as well as its constituents and implementation constructs. This is illustrated in Figure 4–11.

4.5   ORGANIZATIONAL CONSTRUCTS AND BUSINESS OBJECTS

The IT professional states "We can model the organization with business classes." But what is it that the IT professional is really modeling? Is he modeling information objects and their relationships, or the situations in which the relationships occur? And what is the purpose of the model? When an IT professional models the organization, presumably it is intended to create an information system. This may be of little value, however, in designing an organization's processes, simply because the IT expert's view is "colored" by his intentions.

In contrast, when designing an organization's process, the manager or organizational planner, depending upon his or her experience and exposure to organizational literature, uses anecdotal or more formal descriptions of organizational constructs in order to arrive at a design. Often, this organizational design fails to achieve its purpose. This results in the organization's going through another cycle of reengineering. Such a situation invariably leads to tension, fear, loss of jobs, and so on.

Listed in Table 4–1 is a summary of the operational differences between organizational constructs and business classes.

The use of object technology, or object concepts, to represent "business classes" marks a significant improvement in aligning information technology with the organization. Object-oriented techniques may be used to specify the information component of business objects, that is, entities and managed collections of entities, during information systems analysis. However, claims that man-

TABLE 4–1 ORGANIZATIONAL CONSTRUCTS VS. BUSINESS CLASSES

Characteristic	Organizational Construct	Business Class
Who uses the construct	General managers	Information technology analysts
Level of analysis	Macro, sometimes micro	Micro
Focus of analysis	Organizational planning & design	Information systems development
Source of knowledge	Organization theory and business literature	Information technology theory and literature
Specification	No rigorous or formal schema Policies and anecdote substitute for architecture	Assorted, including contract, use-case, and structured constructs

agers will somehow be better equipped to make business decisions (e.g., business strategy) are erroneous at best, and deceptive at worse. As Bertrand Meyer has indicated, the IT-specification of "business classes" represents a view of the organization from the viewpoint of an information system. More accurately, it is only a view for a particular application. It is not a holistic view of that object—its interaction with respect to people, processes, structure, and many other organizational dimensions of an object.

From the viewpoint of the organization, the IT-view of business classes is of little value beyond the corresponding information system in which it appears. When a business object (e.g., John Smith) is viewed through an IT manager's eyes, it becomes a business class (e.g., *employee class*) with information properties. When a business object is viewed through a general manager's eyes, it becomes an organizational construct (e.g., a human being). The motivation of each viewpoint could not be more different.

THE ORGANIZATIONAL PERSPECTIVE

The IT perspective of the organization is immaterial because managers require a model of the organization—each of its components and their interrelationships—from the viewpoint of the organization. From the organizational perspective, IT is but one construct that must be interconnected with many others.

To illustrate the difference between an organizational construct and a business class, consider the following. Recall, from our discussion in Chapter 2, that *complexity* is a dimension of the organizational construct known as *structure*. Two kinds of people are usually interested in taking a close look at organizations: One is the OT researchers (using statistics); the other is IT systems developers (using business class models). OT researchers use variables, such as number of organizational levels, to better analyze this construct. However, the analysis of the data collected by statisticians tells us what these levels are in the current state, but does not offer a clue towards *what they should be*. Statisticians may carry out surveys, analyze the data, and correlate the number of levels with a measure of organizational effectiveness. An inference drawn from these correlations is theory building. In theory building, OT researchers propose hypotheses, which can be statistically tested.

Similarly, IT professionals look at the organization to create an information system. Systems analysts use techniques with varying levels of rigor—everything from textual descriptions to formal methods (e.g., "Z" specification language). The degree of precision used in specification does not affect the IT *perspective* of the analyst. Furthermore, the specification techniques used are not consistent (e.g., use-case vs. data flow diagrams—see Jacobson, Christerson, Jonsson, and Overgaard 1992).

Figure 4–12 illustrates the different perspectives, how they are currently unrelated, and how OM integrates them.

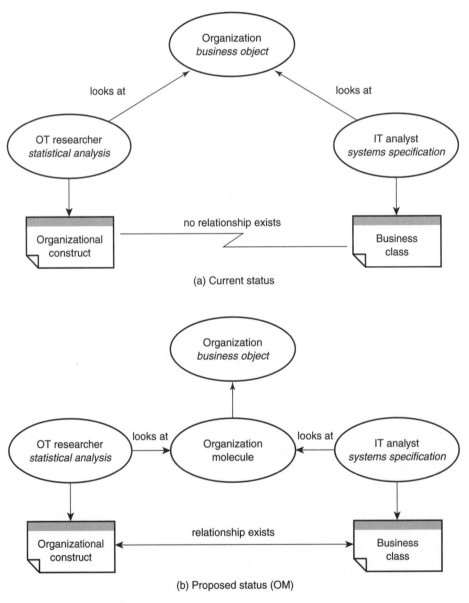

(a) Current status

(b) Proposed status (OM)

FIGURE 4–12   Organizational Vs. Information Perspectives of the Organization

BUILDING A UNIFIED FRAMEWORK

The OM framework creates a *unified organization model* that serves both organizational and IT analyses. *To the IT professional,* this means information systems that are aligned with the organization and its domains. For example, an information system designed to serve a business activity should have properties that "fit" with the requirements of a specific process task, as well as the people who participate in that task. This may mean information systems that elicit knowledge from an expert in a nonroutine task.

To the OT researcher, OM provides a framework for theory building, that is, a framework which supports his or her inferences as well as derived prescriptive guidelines for organizational design. OT researchers use statistics to analyze the relationships among organizational constructs, but offer no mechanism by which the manager may operationalize—make real—the design of an organization. OM enables organizational design with a framework that promotes specification, which may be operationalized.

To the manager, this brings the best of both these worlds: a simple, but useful model from which to design an organization—its structure, culture, information systems, business processes, and so on.

4.6 CORE CONCEPTS

Three views of modeling

Modeling granularity

Eternal triangle

Type 2 organization invariant

Composite-subtyping

Organizational effectiveness
and design

Disciplined organizational
architecture

Richness of concepts

Refinement levels

Type 1 socio-cultural invariant

Object meta-model

Managed collection

Deliberate and emergent properties

Unified organization model

Organization and information
perspectives

CHAPTER 5

THE LAYERED ORGANIZATION

5.1 A PARADIGM SHIFT FOR ORGANIZATION THEORY

This chapter advances the conceptual framework proposed in the OM approach. Three major directions of OM are presented in this section. The first direction provides some explanations and elaboration of the reasoning behind the development of this new approach. The second provides additional concepts which make the OM approach richer in many different dimensions. The third provides some ramifications of the basic ideas included in the OM approach. Together they represent a paradigm shift in our understanding of organizations—a language by which we may extend and change the notion of organization modeling and design.

EXPLANATIONS AND ELABORATION

From the outset, questions of the following nature arise:

"Why is it necessary to come up with new models when many conceptual models are already present in the field of OT? And why are these foreign words which are mostly unknown to the average practitioner in the field of management (such as an organization molecule) being introduced?"

The answers to these questions are manyfold. First, the need for the introduction of new models arises because the existent models are insufficient. This insufficiency becomes obvious when one raises critical questions on the present state of organizations in light of what is actually happening today.

Understanding dynamic organizations requires a rich language. As Fish (1996) expressed it, "What sociologists of science say is of course the world is real and independent of our observations but that accounts of the world are produced by observers and are therefore relative to their capacities, education, training, etc. It is not the world or its properties but the vocabularies in whose terms we know them that are socially constructed—fashioned by human beings—which is why our understanding of those properties is continually changing."

The current social climate in many organizations is radically changing. Corporations have downsized, following the new principle of becoming lean (and perhaps mean). Business transformation is the new fashion of the day. This is not necessarily because management is bad, but because the thrust of the environment is unbearable. The economic pressures are enormous and bring substantial changes in the way organizations are structured, and the way they operate, and so on and so forth.

The current state of management does not contain sufficient *artifacts* which can be used towards the development of theories for describing, modeling, and explaining the above changes. They do not enable the answer to the next question that arises, namely, how do we tackle these changes? The artifacts needed to take these changes into account must be both *descriptive* and *prescriptive*. They should be able to model both the *static* and *dynamic* nature of organizations. They should be able to adequately represent both *deliberate* and *emergent* properties of various organizational constructs.

The conceptual framework of OT, as it exists today, has primarily been the creation of either sociologists and psychologists, or practical administrators. The organizational perspectives discussed in Chapter 2, for example, were developed on a foundation of underlying social theories. These range approximately from the bureaucracy of Max Weber to the more recent quality movement based on teamwork. On the other hand, similar development also took place regarding the practical framework for OT, in addition to and in parallel with this development of a conceptual framework. This was led by managers and executives who actually practiced design and, in the process, developed their own practical philosophies. These range from Frederick Taylor in the early days of OT to Lee Iacocca in more recent times.

A New Perspective

The time is ripe for people with other backgrounds to jump in and contribute their energy to this endeavor. This does not mean, however, that the social and psychological perspectives or the conventional managerial field practices will be lost. In the first case, the contributions made by sociologists and psychologists remain valuable; in the second case, the habits of managers and executives cannot die suddenly. It is obviously wrong to pretend that there will be a revolutionary change in the near future.

At the same time, it is also wrong to assume that the status quo will remain forever. Change is definitely coming, both in philosophy and in practice. Therefore, there is a compelling need to take a fresh look at organizations in general. Such an observation must include both theoretical and practical aspects. Inevitably, the theoretical aspects will consist of new ideas and theoretical frameworks borrowed from other fields of inquiry. These other fields include the physical sciences, such as chemistry and computer science, and the theoretical sciences, such as logic and linguistics.

Such a combination is, in fact, very much in accordance with, and is a classic example of, a "paradigm shift" as discussed in *The Structure of Scientific Revolu-*

tions (1962, 1970) by Thomas Kuhn. Prior to Kuhn, scientific development was viewed as a kind of continuous progression, moving gradually closer and closer to the truth. This view is also known as *Logical Empiricism*. According to this view, all disciplines—physics, biology, chemistry, neuroscience, and even the social sciences—are progressively getting closer to the way things really are. However, according to Kuhn, scientific development is not a continuous progression. Rather, it occurs in a series of shifts from one view to another. Each view brings with it a new paradigm, a set of ideas, and a conceptual framework.

The idea of using the concepts of organization modeling in the development of a new design approach is thus such a *paradigm shift*. Inevitably, it will bring with it new models which are described by unfamiliar words that are either borrowed from other disciplines or are specially created for the purpose of description. People who find these words unfamiliar will have to learn this new language and will have to get used to the new models. However, this is not a large price to pay. Historically, each new paradigm has always brought new benefits. Paradigms which brought substantial benefits have survived. Those which did not, have died out. Whether a particular shift in paradigm will survive or not survive depends upon its success in solving current problems. A paradigm shift should be judged on the merit of the results it produces, irrespective of whether it is familiar or not!

AN EXAMPLE

Unfamiliar words, such as *organization molecule*, are being introduced because they carry an important connotation which is useful in the process of modeling. They make specification more *meaningful*, more *representative* of reality. The word molecule has obviously been borrowed from elementary chemistry and we assume that everyone, even the man on the street, has at least a vague notion of what a molecule is.

Let us recall that according to classical physical theory, physical reality consists of atoms and molecules. Atoms are the basic building blocks of all matter. These atoms combine with each other according to precise *rules* of chemistry. The result is the formation of *stable aggregates* which are called molecules. A molecule is the *basic constituent* of a chemical substance. It characterizes the substance in every respect. For example, a molecule of water is the *minuscule but authentic representation* of the "thing" that we call water, and so on and so forth.

Next, we note the following important fact: Although the molecule of water is constituted by the atoms of hydrogen and oxygen, it does not carry any of their attributes. The properties of water cannot be derived from, and understood on the basis of, the properties of isolated and individual atoms of hydrogen and oxygen. The properties are exhibited only when both hydrogen and oxygen occur in a combined form within the water molecule. Combining, thus, brings change in behavior. This explanation brings out the important fact that the properties of atoms are *deliberate*: They are given to us by nature. However, the properties of molecules are *emergent*: They emerge from the act of combining the atoms. Their properties depend on the nature of the bond. Moreover, they can be synthesized.

All these ideas applicable to chemistry and the natural world are valuable and can be usefully employed in the process of modeling organizations. They especially go hand-in-hand with the basic concepts of both information and organization modeling, such as specification, generalization, classification, inheritance, and reuse.

5.2 LAYERS OF ABSTRACTION

There are innumerable modes or techniques by which an organization may be represented. Each represents a view designed to characterize an organization premised on some set of core concepts. For example, the "Star Model" associates strategy, people, structure, rewards, and processes (in all possible combinations). Galbraith uses this "model" as a "framework" for designing organizations (Galbraith 1995). Another example is Benjamin's layered model of the organization to support change—by layering domains, such as vision, process, and data repositories (Benjamin and Levinson 1993).

The list of "organization models" for some purpose is seemingly endless. However, these models have a common thread. While they *do* reference the accumulated wealth of information concerning a particular organizational domain, they are little more than *pictures* in vague frameworks.

Current practice uses representation techniques that limit the advancement of organizational design. Existing techniques are not robust enough to capture all of the semantics of the constructs they represent. They are of little value in the formation of an organizational architecture, and thus, bring no formalism for specification, implementation, and integration. In effect, each continues the traditional method of design by executive summary, design by anecdote, design by case history, and so on.

The paradigm shift represented by OM embraces a new language for organizations that promotes thinking about and understanding organizations. This language brings forth elaboration of ideas, and ultimately, specification and integration of organizational domains.

A LANGUAGE FOR ORGANIZATIONS

The application of structure to the representation of organizations means that we must create a language for organizations. The core concept associated with specification in OM is that behavior may be used to understand, define, integrate, and operationalize organizational domains.

The assertion that organizational domains may be understood and specified in terms of their behavior is an application of information modeling concepts to organizational domains. Contracts specifying behavior may be used to understand and interrelate domains.

The problem of trying to integrate organizational domains with dissimilar structural properties (e.g., organizational structure, organizational learning, information systems, etc.) is solved through abstraction and the specification of behavior. That is, as we stated above, by choosing to understand and specify domains exclusively in terms of their behavior, we avoid the problems of association between structurally dissimilar objects.

For example, a stockbroker giving advice to a client may depend on a wide variety of information systems. The participants in this business task have very different structural properties, such as particular computing environments, data structures, and programs on one hand, and a particular stockbroker and client on the other. However, their integration is critical in business process design and in improving organizational effectiveness. This is relatively straightforward if we ignore or "hide" their respective structural properties and focus on their separate and integrated behaviors. This may involve the specification of an assortment of read operations on one hand, and knowledge-based interactions involving the stockbroker and client on the other. As we will see in Part 2, knowledge-based, nonroutine tasks are areas in which traditional business transformation techniques have difficulty, but are handled effectively with an integrated, architectural approach.

Structural properties are not avoided; rather, organizational domains, including IT, are more accurately specified and interconnected *first* through their behavior, and *subsequently* operationalized, where appropriate, through structural properties (e.g., reporting relationships, databases).

The OM layered model is the first of our structured representations. The difference between existing models and an OM layered model for the organization is that the former focus on broad organizational descriptions and loose associations, while the proposed OM model focuses on the behavior of corresponding organizational constructs, and incorporates a schema (i.e., contract) by which organizational specification and integration is possible. Furthermore, association between levels is through the new association type: composite-subtyping. As important, the layered model is the second of the OM architectural stages. It marks a continuation of an architecture-driven set of thought processes associated with organizational design.

Constructing a Layered Organization Model

The concepts we use to understand organizations are derived from OT. Organizational research identifies innumerable constructs, each of which portrays some aspect of the organization. Each construct describes a "fundamental" domain of the organization. These fundamental components of the organization represent its foundation—they change infrequently and are represented by the core organizational constructs with which we build a layered organization model. In other words, as illustrated in the following examples, a layered model of constructs used to describe an organization will remain relatively constant.

Classical Organization Theory. Illustrated in Figure 5–1 is an OM layered model of core organization constructs, based on "classical" organization theory.

In this model we make the following generalizations:

- The organization is a constituent of the environment.
- The organization communicates with the environment through its strategy.

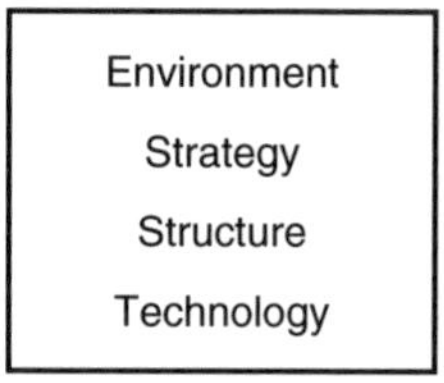

```
┌─────────────────────┐
│     Environment     │
│                     │
│      Strategy       │
│                     │
│      Structure      │
│                     │
│     Technology      │
└─────────────────────┘
```

FIGURE 5–1   Levels of Abstraction: Classical Organization Theory

- The organization's strategy is implemented through its structure and its technology.
- Technology is defined in economic terms—the transformation of inputs into outputs.
- Size is not directly shown—it is considered an emergent property of structure.

The Aston Group and Size.   Organizational research is not without controversy. The above illustration represents *our* interpretation of classical OT. No doubt, there are other views. For example, in our view of classical OT, we consider size to be an emergent property of structure. The Aston Group of Great Britain believes size determines structure. Accordingly, the Aston Group may layer organizational constructs as shown in Figure 5–2.

The Power-Control View.   A popular view of organizations is that they are political entities. The organization consists of contending groups, each seeking to exercise its power for its own benefit. In this view of power, a layered model would put *power* immediately below the environment, as illustrated in Figure 5–3.

Max Weber and Function.   As another example, recall that Max Weber elaborated on bureaucracy and the primacy of the division of labor in the organization of work. In this view, structure is designed to support a functional definition of work (i.e., technology). Thus, a bureaucratic view of the organization may appear as shown in Figure 5–4.

```
┌─────────────────────┐
│     Environment     │
│                     │
│      Strategy       │
│                     │
│        Size         │
│                     │
│      Structure      │
│                     │
│     Technology      │
└─────────────────────┘
```

FIGURE 5–2   Levels of Abstraction: Hypothetical Aston Group View
of Classical Organization Theory

```
┌─────────────────────┐
│     Environment      │
│                      │
│       Power          │
│                      │
│      Strategy        │
│                      │
│      Structure       │
│                      │
│     Technology       │
└─────────────────────┘
```

FIGURE 5–3   Levels of Abstraction: A Power-Control View of Organization Theory

The Systems View.   Current literature often makes reference to the notion of a horizontal organization—one based on a process view. In a given organization, suppose a process view supports the design of structure in terms of its business processes. Such a process-layered representation may appear as illustrated in Figure 5–5.

Refining the Systems View.   The core organizational constructs are not immutable. As organizational literature identifies fundamental shifts in our view of organizations, we adjust the core constructs accordingly. For example, only a short time ago a model of the organization would not have included information as a core construct; however, today excluding information from an organization model would be unthinkable!

As we apply current thinking to the OM layered model, we refine the classical set of models as follows:

- Decompose the concept of technology into constituent core organizational constructs.
- Include an information component.
- Emphasize the horizontal, process view (the systems view).
- Alter the concept of structure to support an organization of work rather than a division of labor. That is, in the refined model, structure is a constituent of the systems view. This says nothing about the type of structure, which may be functional, only that there is a structure which is involved in the process view of an organization.

We refer to these OM layers as a process view, illustrated in Figure 5–6.

```
┌─────────────────────┐
│     Environment      │
│                      │
│      Strategy        │
│                      │
│      Function        │
│                      │
│      Structure       │
│                      │
│     Technology       │
└─────────────────────┘
```

FIGURE 5–4   Levels of Abstraction: Hypothetical Max Weber View
of Classical Organization Theory

```
┌─────────────────┐
│   Environment   │
│                 │
│    Strategy     │
│                 │
│    Process      │
│                 │
│    Structure    │
│                 │
│   Technology    │
└─────────────────┘
```

FIGURE 5–5   Levels of Abstraction: A Systems View of Organization Theory

In this process view of our organization model, we have:

- Eliminated the functional layer of structure.
- Decomposed technology into the following:
  - a specification of its (i.e., technology) behavior—the process layer.
  - the organization of people supporting the process—the structure layer.
  - the people engaged in the process—the human layer.
  - the information required to support the process—the information layer.
  - the non-human artifacts required by the process—the tool layer.

Decomposing the technology layer resolves the problem of its definition. Technology has taken on different meanings in different organizations. By refining technology (as we understand it today) into its constituent core constructs, we are faithful to the original definition, while facilitating its elucidation across different types of organizations.

Observe that the process layer represents a behavioral abstraction of technology; that is, it is an abstract specification of the interrelationships between structure, people, information, and tools. This is an example of applying the object-oriented notion of "separating concerns." In this case, we are separating the specification of an activity {process} from its implementation {structure-human-information-tool}. This promotes understanding and analysis, and thereby facilitates optimization of each component in {structure-human-information-tool} as well as the composite specification itself {process}. Also, the managed collection

```
┌─────────────────┐
│   Environment   │
│                 │
│    Strategy     │
│                 │
│    Process      │
│                 │
│    Structure    │
│                 │
│     Human       │
│                 │
│   Information   │
│                 │
│      Tool       │
└─────────────────┘
```

FIGURE 5–6   Levels of Abstraction: A Process View of Organization Theory

of {process-structure-human-information-tool} is defined to represent a horizontal view of the organization, at some level of abstraction, such as business process or task (see Chapter 11).

For example, increasing the availability of information to a person performing a given activity decreases the need for hierarchical referral (i.e., behavior associated with structure). Or, as another example, information and the appropriate tools may decrease or even eliminate the need for a human component (as in an ATM replacing a human teller), though this may necessitate the creation or deletion of other activities (managing the ATM). These are examples of using our model to reengineer or optimize business processes.

Organizational Alignment.   The notion of *alignment* may be represented through different layered representations. For example, if an organization's culture and operations are along functional lines, it may be stressful to introduce lateral structures, such as teams. This is illustrated in Figure 5–7.

Though management may desire the benefits associated with teams, such a change in structure *first* requires a wider change in the organization of work—development of a systems view. To be effective, there must be *compatible* fit between the desired instance of structure (e.g., teams) and the layered representation of your organization.

GENERALIZATIONS CONCERNING THE LAYERED ORGANIZATION

> The layered organization is defined to be the levels of abstraction in the behavior of corresponding organizational constructs

A central concept of OM is that the organization can be sufficiently understood and integrated as a *nested set of behavioral specifications*. A specification at each layer is separate, yet constrained, by the specification of other layers. This results in a view of organizations as a complex composite of interrelated behaviors. The layers of abstraction form a pattern among core organizational constructs. The implications of this model are as follows:

- Each organizational construct (i.e., a layer) may be understood in terms of its behavior.

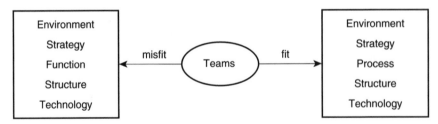

FIGURE 5–7   Misalignment and Alignment and the Notion of Teams

- Layers are defined and differentiated from each other by their corresponding behaviors.
- Behavior is an integrating mechanism in the organization.
- An organization's behavior has both deliberate and emergent properties.
- The behavior associated with each organizational construct is a level of abstraction of the behavior of "lower" organizational constructs.
- As emergent behavior, each layer contains properties corresponding to properties in lower levels.
- As deliberate behavior, each layer contains properties that distinguish it from its lower level components (otherwise, there would be no rational reason for its existence).
- Layers can be specified independently of each other. This is an example of how layering implements the notion of separation of concerns and assures correctness.
- The behavior associated with a layer represents a specification of the behaviors of lower layers, and an implementation of the behavior specifications of higher layers. It is not necessary to distinguish between specification and implementation.
- There is managerial choice at every level of abstraction—choice as to how to implement a higher level of abstraction, and choice as to what to specify for lower levels of abstraction.
- Each layer consists of "sub" abstractions within that organizational construct; that is, each construct may be modeled to any degree of granularity. For example, an organizational strategy may be decomposed into constituent strategies of function, product, marketing, etc.
- Reuse of the behavior specification of an element in any layer, implies reuse of all its component behaviors, that is, its lower level constructs.
- The layers of abstraction are not fixed. They represent the current state of understanding. For example, information is a construct that is relatively new—a layered model 20 years ago would not have included it. Furthermore, the managers of each organization must select the appropriate constructs for their organization.

BEHAVIOR VS. PROCESS IN THE LAYERED ORGANIZATION

The behavior we are modeling in the OM is both *generic* and *organization-specific*. OM behavior is generic to organizations of the same type. For example, functionally structured, and therefore functionally managed, organizations have behaviors in common that separate them as a group from, say, adhocratically structured organizations.

The behavior represented in OM is also organization-specific; that is, it describes persistent behavior associated with a corresponding OM layer (i.e., organizational construct) of a given organization. The behavior that characterizes an organizational construct is not the same as the process from which it was formulated. For example, strategic planning is a process, and is therefore an instance in the *process* layer.

OM behavior is that which is associated with an organizational construct: It has both planned and emergent characteristics. Recall from Chapter 2 that Mintzberg states that all strategy is both deliberate (i.e., planned in the strategic planning *process*) and emergent (i.e., formed from "lower" organizational components). Deliberate strategy is that which results from the strategic planning process, while emergent strategy is that which results from the behavior of each of the lower organizational components. The resulting composite behavior is the strategy of the organization: an instance in the *strategy* layer.

5.3 SAMPLE OM TYPES

The traditional view of an organization is that structure and work are organized functionally. In fact, there is no concept of "process." This may seem a bit odd; indeed, it runs counter to leveraging an organization's value-adding activities for competitive advantage. However, the popularity of information engineering approaches illustrates the difficulty organizations have in changing outdated models of themselves—even if it is to their advantage.

In contrast, a "modern" organization, one increasingly based on information (Drucker 1988), contains knowledge workers organized around the organization of work, as opposed to function, and is somewhat analogous to an *adhocracy*. Such organizations are better equipped to deal with an increasingly complex and turbulent environment (Peters 1988).

The difficulties of creating a "pure" adhocracy—including everything from vested interests in the status quo to structural inefficiency—have given rise to a third form, an adhocratic structure appended to a bureaucracy. Indeed, this is the most common method of operationalizing the adhocracy. Examples include formal methods of organizing such as the matrix organization, as well as less formal methods such as the use of task forces.

In terms of OM, we may model the organization as one of three general types, illustrated in Figure 5–8.

Naturally, there is correspondence between these three views and the generic structures described by Mintzberg (1983). However, generic structures and their many variations represent refinements that correspond to a particular set of organizational constructs. It is these constructs that must be identified for a given organization. The above represents a sampling of three arrangements of core constructs. Each manager must decide which constructs represent the core OM for his or her organization.

Characteristics of the functional perspective

- A traditional view of an organization.
- A machine bureaucracy.
- A functional organization and management of work (i.e., division of labor).

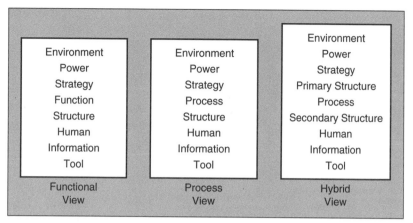

FIGURE 5–8   Layers of Abstraction of Organizational Constructs

- A fixed, unresponsive organization of work.
- Association with non-turbulent environments—a seller's market.

Characteristics of the process perspective
- A systems view of an organization.
- A "pure" adhocracy.
- A process, horizontal organization and management of work.
- A flexible, adaptive organization of work.
- Association with turbulent environments—a buyer's market.

Characteristics of the hybrid perspective
- Possession of elements of vertical and horizontal organizations.
- An adhocracy embedded in a bureaucracy.
- A functional view of reporting relationships (primary structure) and "centers of learning."
- A process, horizontal organization of work (secondary structure).
- A flexible, adaptive organization of work.
- Association with moderately turbulent environments.

One property of a hybrid organization is the existence of two distinct levels of structure. The primary structure represents the reporting relationships in an organization. This represents the traditional structure—the functional bureaucracy. One advantage of primary structures is that they are mediators for organizational learning among members of a particular profession. The secondary structure refers to the work relationships in an organization: the adhocratic addendum. This includes both the formal structures (e.g., project teams), as well as the informal organization (e.g., informal arrangements between individuals and the tasks they perform) (Nadler and Tushman 1984).

The OM-type selected is a reflection of how the manager wants to organize and manage his or her organization—the whole and each of its components. This must be qualified, however, by the philosophical context in which the organization finds itself, and the willingness of its management to override this context if it feels this will improve its effectiveness. For example, popular IT-planning approaches, such as information engineering, utilize the functional view. Naturally, these approaches are orthogonal to the organization of work—the process view. Accordingly, the literature demonstrates that information engineering is most suitable in non-turbulent environments, where the functional OM-type is dominant. In turbulent environments, where the process OM-type is appropriate, information engineering has produced misaligned information systems.

The central theme represented by the OM layers of abstraction is that a particular OM type determines the nature of subsequent organizational specification.

5.4 CONTRACTS AND LIBRARIES

As has been stated previously, a traditional contract is a precise and complete specification of behavior. It is a specification of some component of the organization to any level of detail. All relevant assertions—invariant, trigger, precondition, and postcondition—are specified within its context. Recall from the Appendix that contracts may be decomposed into constituent contracts. In an organizational context, for example, a corporate vision may be decomposed into strategic business unit (SBU) strategies, which in turn are decomposed into specific functional, product, and marketing strategies.

Contracts may be stored in libraries and made available for organizational tasks in the same manner that we use software libraries in the development of information systems. We introduce here a new concept: a library of organizational constructs. In the same manner that programmers create a library of code in which they make deposits and withdrawals, a manager may create and populate an organizational library. An organizational library contains a repository of knowledge accumulated from internal and external sources. The sources include organizational literature, analytical specifications, best practices, and so on. However, there exists a major difference between a library as is commonly understood and an organizational library. The former is an unstructured collection, while the latter is an architected structure of integrated contracts. The contract library facilitates the creation and the storage of the architecture of an organization. It may be used as the basis of organizational design, as well as a mechanism to facilitate organizational learning. The organizational library contains the specifications of current strategies, organizational structures, information systems, organizational culture, etc., as well as past experiences and decision results.

Furthermore, an organizational library may contain more generalized specifications from academic and business sources from which we may borrow. That is, we do not have to reinvent every organizational specification: We may reuse more generalized specifications to construct specific ones. Generally, the contract abstractions associated with each domain may be categorized as layers of abstraction, as shown in Figure 5–9.

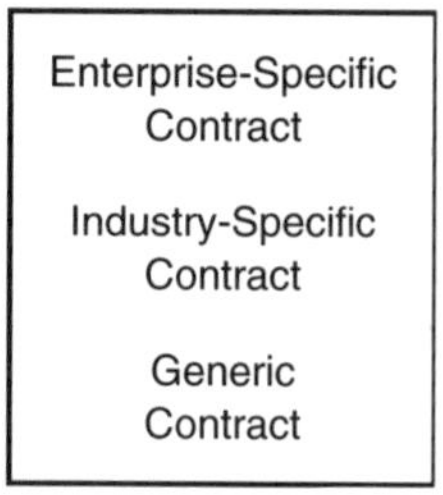

```
┌─────────────────────────┐
│   Enterprise-Specific   │
│        Contract         │
│                         │
│    Industry-Specific    │
│        Contract         │
│                         │
│        Generic          │
│        Contract         │
└─────────────────────────┘
```

FIGURE 5–9   Contract Abstractions

One may question whether or not contracts—business rules and corresponding behaviors—may be specified in a general way and applied to organizational domains. Actually, organizational rules—strategy, process, and so on—*have* been defined (in an imprecise and incomplete way) and used in everything from strategic planning to designing organizational structure, though most practicing managers may be unaware of this fact.

STRATEGY

For example, Porter has defined generic business strategies (i.e., differentiation, low cost, and focus), in effect, generic strategy formulations (Porter 1985). These formulations can be made formal by reassembling the rules into contract specifications. To any of these contracts may be conjoined assertions for a specific strategy. For instance, as a result of a *differentiation* generic strategy contract, a firm may specify a *product-specific contract* requiring certain "signaling criteria" in order to differentiate it from that of a competitor (see Porter 1985).

These contracts—generic and specific—may be stored in a "strategy library" and subsequently reused in the specification of new strategic contracts. Good strategic planners do this (unconsciously) all the time (without explicit contracts); by explicitly defining these strategies in the form of contracts and depositing them in libraries, they will be more formal and more likely to be reused.

BUSINESS PROCESSES

As another example, let us consider the process layer. In the process layer, we construct a process model for our organization through the specification of an organization's business processes. This is a high level of abstraction and is specific to our particular organization. However, we do not have to re-invent processes or process components. We may "reuse" industry-specific contracts.

Examples of industry contracts in the process layer include loan processing (banking), baggage handling (airline), course grading (education), and structural design (engineering). Naturally, we do not simply reuse any industry contract, but rather, scan the environment and choose the contract that is best in class—*best practices*.

Similarly, there are many generic level contracts for the process layer. Examples include order processing, billing, purchasing, and facilities management. Each of the enterprise or industry contracts may "reuse" generic contracts.

ORGANIZATIONAL STRUCTURE

As a final example, let us consider the structure layer. Recall from Chapter 3 that Mintzberg (1983) has proposed five generic structures: the simple structure, the machine bureaucracy, the professional bureaucracy, the division structure, and the adhocracy.

Other "generic" modifications may be formulated: The matrix structure is an example of an adhocratic addendum to a bureaucracy, commonly used in the aircraft manufacturing industry. Again, each generic and industry specific structure may be documented, specified, and stored in a library for future use in formulating enterprise-specific structures.

This rationale holds for behavior specification in any domain in the organization; existing generic, industry, and enterprise-specific rules may be specified as contracts and stored in libraries so that they may be reused. Furthermore, by specifying domains of the organization in the form of contract abstractions of each other, there is greater likelihood that information systems, business processes, organizational structure, and strategic plans will be integrated and optimized.

5.5 CRYSTALLIZATION IN ORGANIZATIONAL DESIGN

You may ask, what is so new about the layered approach to modeling? After all, haven't several writers used some form of layering, either explicitly or implicitly, to explain properties of organizations?

We respond that the OM layers present a dramatic departure in thinking about layers. In OM, the philosophy and layers associated with an organization mark only the beginning of modeling. As mentioned above, layered models are vague representations used by business executives, sociologists, and psychologists who, by their training, are not very scientifically disciplined. This is because of both the history of OT and the basic nature of its disciplines. The discipline of the business executive is management; the disciplines of the sociologist and psychologist are based on human behavior and interactions. Each of these disciplines does not lend itself to an exact description, which may be called scientific.

As we argue, to be meaningful an architecture must be implementable. This is what distinguishes OM layers from other layered models. In OM, the layered model is the second architectural stage of the thought processes associated with organizational design. (Recall that the first architectural stage is the development of an organization's socio-cultural context and invariant.)

Crystallization is a process of going from the undefined to the defined, from chaos to order. It concerns itself with the thinking processes that we perform while modeling. It provides the linkages between thoughts, ideas, and other notions. If we consider the ideas and notions as individual items of knowledge, these linkages provide the meanings. They provide both the semantics and the syntax of the modeling process. They provide the schema of connecting the individual bits and pieces of knowledge into a coherent whole.

For example, the notion of a business process consists of other notions or ideas. These represent our knowledge about people, how they are organized to do work, the information they use to do work, and the implements required for the process to be successfully executed. As we shall see in the following chapter, what we have just described in natural language can be made precise with the construct of a *process molecule*.

In subsequent chapters, we provide a series of molecules. The list is not exhaustive, but serves as a guide for several important domains of an organization that may be crystallized into a molecule. The designer must additionally "tune" the molecule to correspond to the philosophy and layered constructs that exist in his or her respective organization. For example, what does structure mean in *your* organization? Is it functional? Is it process-oriented? Is it decentralized? The molecule provides the designer with the rules of the game; the designer merely applies them.

The process of building a molecule for a given domain involves taking the knowledge areas referred to above as components, and connecting them together in a specific way. We suggest the domains of OT as a starting point. As you will see, this unique way of combining knowledge domains creates a composite specification of behavior in the form of a contract. This specification of behavior addresses many of the properties of organizations, such as the emergent properties of strategy that Mintzberg has identified. In this latter case, the result is a strategy molecule with a set of strategy contracts describing the behaviors associated with an organization's strategy.

5.6 CORE CONCEPTS

A paradigm shift for OT   Layers of abstraction

A language for organizations   Layered organization model

Three generic OM-types   Organizational contracts and libraries

Organizational alignment and fit   Crystallization

CHAPTER 6

ORGANIZATION MOLECULES

6.1 SCULPTING ORGANIZATIONAL ARCHITECTURE

Organizations are difficult to design. The manager is confronted with a milieu of entangled relationships, insufficient information (i.e., uncertainty), unclear sources for answers (i.e., equivocality), and conflict among contending interests. What should the manager do? Does he or she make a decision with a rational, analytical approach (i.e., deliberate), or an historical one that draws on experience (i.e., emergent)?

The concerned manager avoids anecdotal solutions, and usually turns to some form of authority for guidance—a framework within which he or she may make a specific decision. The search for a design framework is usually confined to two sources: the traditional training associated with business schools, or the pronouncements of the popular business literature. Unfortunately, each has strengths and weaknesses that are difficult to balance; the positions emanating from these two sources are essentially unconnected.

Traditional organizational texts present a static picture of an organization. They frame the organization with research using statistical analyses. As a result, there is seldom more than a casual reference to new business imperatives, such as business process transformation and total quality management (TQM).

In contrast, popular business texts grapple with the issues of the day—sometimes faddish, sometimes not—but usually with the intent of giving managers new tools to deal with a turbulent environment. They present a more dynamic view of organizations; however, they are rarely grounded in any form of organizational discipline.

We propose a framework that brings together the best of both approaches—one framed with the materials of OT, but sufficiently flexible to include new management and business imperatives. This building block of the OM architecture is known as the organization molecule. This is illustrated in Figure 6–1.

Galbraith (1995) describes the underlying principles of an organizational design framework to be "design policies." To be sure, a policy framework is necessary to establish a pattern for change; however, it is only a procedural guide. The ingredient that determines successful design is the framework to which design policies are applied. This framework is the model of an organization. Design

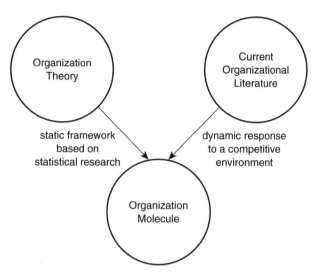

FIGURE 6–1   The Static and Dynamic Dimensions of OM

success is directly related to the contents of this organization framework—its breadth and depth, its adaptability to change, its sources of information.

One cannot design complex organizations through executive summary. The complexity of organizations requires a disciplined approach to their design. In the same manner that the architecture of a building must support its detailed engineering and construction, organizational design requires an architectural framework that supports its engineering and implementation. Organizational design requires a *framework that is constant* throughout the design process—from formulation through implementation—even as its contents emerge through execution.

6.2 ORGANIZATION MOLECULES

The OM layers of abstraction represent the core organizational constructs that a manager has decided are relevant to his or her organization. These core organizational constructs are objects themselves. Each participates in many associations, giving rise to overlap between layers. Elucidation of the associations of these constructs and their derivative management philosophies (i.e., organizational domains) give rise to the building blocks of organizational design: *organization molecules*. The organization molecule is the schema that we choose to frame organizational design decisions—the whole and each of the parts. *In OM, the organization molecule is the building block of organizational design.*

Organization molecules are *managed collections* of constructs that have unique properties as a *collection*. Molecules may be constructed within an OM layer, or between layers. For instance, a business process molecule includes elements from the human, information, structure, and tool layers.

An organization molecule is defined so that we may address a particular organizational problem or domain within a consistent architecture. The area of concern may involve a core organizational construct, such as strategy, or a derivative management philosophy, such as culture. Current management interests may be addressed with a molecule or a collection of molecules—business process change, for instance, references the process and information molecules.

The assembly of organizational constructs corresponding to a given OM is the same across organizations. *What differentiates organizations in their approaches to organizational domains is their manifest behaviors with respect to the assembly of constructs, not the existence or arrangement of the assembly.* Such behaviors represent the "outcome" of the interactions.

The observation that assemblies are constant across organizations suggests a framework that may be architected. That is, we may associate constructs with a uniform *meta-model*. We may think of an assembled meta-model as a molecule—an arrangement of atoms (i.e., organizational constructs) that together constitute a composite assembly. In the same manner that a molecule of *water* is the same everywhere on earth, an organization molecule designed for an organizational domain (e.g., business process), is the same in every organization. What distinguishes organizations in their approach to a problem domain is their specific behaviors—instances—of the molecule.

6.3 THE GENERIC ORGANIZATION MOLECULE

The architecture of a molecule may be generalized with the concept of a generic molecule. The generic molecule is a framework that is comprised of the following characteristics:

- Enables the analysis and design of some organizational task, such as business process reengineering.
- Uses the OM layers of abstraction of a given organization to identify relevant core organizational constructs.
- Is extensible so that current and future research in management will manifest itself in changes to an organization's assembly of molecules.
- Provides for the specification of an organizational domain in terms of the interaction among corresponding core organizational constructs.
- Provides for the elucidation of deliberate and emergent characteristics of organizational domains.
- Supports the notion of abstraction. This is necessary, for example, to support the specification of a business process, work cycle, and task. Each of these represents different levels of abstraction of the construct "process."
- The concept of a generic molecule is itself generic. That is, the generic molecule consists of many types (which we will provide subsequently), each of which is a generic molecule in itself. Examples of generic molecules include process, information, and culture molecules.

- Types of organization molecules may be aligned to permit the specification of an organizational construct in terms of local and organization-wide behaviors.
- Instantiation of a particular molecule is organization-specific.
- Refinement (planned or emergent) of a molecule represents the implementation of a corresponding organizational domain.

Using the OM framework, it is possible to define a generic architectural schema that conforms to the above requirements. This is illustrated in Figure 6–2.

This picture describes a molecule as a specification {organizational domain} consisting of any number of specific core organizational constructs. The core organizational constructs are represented as layers of abstraction in OM—e.g., environment, strategy, process, structure, human, information, and tool. The interactions of a specific arrangement of constituent organizational constructs represent the specification of the corresponding organizational domain.

Finally, using the notion of a contract, we may characterize a given {organizational domain} through its behavior. That is to say, {organizational domain} as a set of behaviors, each of which corresponds to a particular interaction of specific organizational constructs—its components. We may think of this interaction as corresponding to some level of fit. The interaction of components, then, both describes (emergent) and implements (deliberate) an {organizational domain}.

The linear specification of the generic molecule is as follows:

fit: CS (organization domain, {org construct$_1$, ..., org construct$_n$})

In this format, the name of the association appears first—*fit*. The name of the generic association appears next—composition-subtyping *(CS)*. This is followed by the name of the specification (*organizational domain*) and its components (*organizational constructs*). The same schemata is followed in the specification of all specific molecules (e.g., process, strategy).

INSTANTIATING AN ORGANIZATIONAL DOMAIN

Instantiating an {organizational domain} means that we specify a given domain in a corresponding contract. Recall from Chapter 4 that a contract is composed of four parts: the precondition that declares the required inputs and states that must

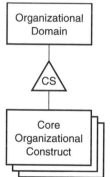

FIGURE 6–2   The Generic Organization Molecule

exist before that contract may be executed, the postcondition that describes the outputs, the trigger that initiates the behavior, and the invariant that describes what must remain unchanged. The assembled invariant, trigger, pre-, and post-conditions are known as contract assertions.

The instantiation of a contract for a given {organizational domain} requires that the designer understand the relevant organizational and domain-specific assertions: those that govern an organization's invariant, business rules, and the desired behaviors. See Figure 6–3.

Observe that the invariant and trigger for a contract both consist of two types of assertions: business rules and an organization's invariant. Business rules correspond in some way to an organization's economic activity. They derive from industry and company practice, government or professional regulations, and col-

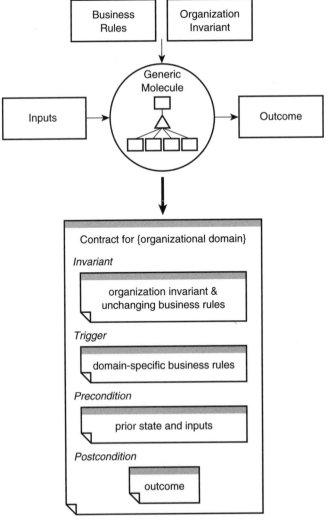

FIGURE 6-3   Generic Contract Specification for an Organizational Domain

lectivity govern the behavior of organizations in a given industry. We discuss business rules in more detail in Chapter 12.

An organization invariant derives from the nature of an organization, and its relationships to people and society. This refers to the effects of the eternal triangle on a given organization discussed in Chapter 4. In a specific organization, this manifests itself in the form of *culture.*

There is an additional caveat: A given organizational domain may be specified at varied levels of abstraction. Therefore, when identifying corresponding assertions, the designer must first ascertain the level of abstraction that is being specified. For example, if one is designing a {process}, is its specification for a particular business process, work cycle, or task? And which specific {process} abstraction is being specified—the auto assembly business process, the customer order-entry work cycle, and so on?

Generally, then, when designing a contract specification for a given {organizational domain}, such as {process}, we must identify the following parameters:

- Level of abstraction (e.g., business process, work cycle, task, etc.).
- Specific abstraction to be instantiated (e.g., field repair is an instance of a work cycle, etc.).
- Corresponding assertions for that specific abstraction.

Illustrated in Figure 6–4 is a contract for *hire an employee,* a specification in the domain {process}. This is a high-level abstraction corresponding to the {process} subtype known as a *workcycle.* The contract specification *hire an employee* decomposes into several constituent {process} types known as tasks, such as *advertise for a new employee, interview candidate, select candidate,* etc. Naturally, each constituent specification may be similarly specified in a contract.

INSTANTIATING FIT THROUGH FORMATION

Observe that the notion of fit is prominent in the generic molecule. The instantiation of an organizational domain reflects the fit of each of the constituent organizational constructs. That is to say, a given instantiation of fit for a corresponding molecule represents the appropriateness, rationale, and utility of the interaction.

Hire an Employee
Invariant
The organizational subunit has budgeted for an employee.
Trigger
A signed personnel requisition.
Precondition
There are no qualifying internal candidates.
Postcondition
The candidate is an employee.

FIGURE 6–4   Contract Specification for Hire an Employee

Fit is established through instantiating a molecule. There are two means by which molecules become instantiated: *deliberate formulation* and *emergent formation*. For example, in the case of a *routine business task* (e.g., auditing) behavior is entirely formulated by means of specification. In the case of a *nonroutine task* (e.g., financial management) or an *ill-defined* domain (e.g., culture), behavior is *formed*, as opposed to formulated.

Formation is a dimension of learning and adaptation and includes the following stages:

- *Conceptualization.* Understanding the essence of the {organizational domain}.
- *Learning.* Understanding both the conceptualization of the {organizational domain}, and the mix of constituents and their interactions that together implement the composite {organizational domain}.
- *Operationalizing the learned behavior.* Specifying and implementing the corresponding behaviors of constituent organizational constructs.
- *Adaptation.* The subsequent refinement of the conceptualization of the {organizational domain}, its mix of constituents, and their interactions.

Organizational formation is an extension of Mintzberg's notion that strategy is formed, as well as formulated. For example, the strategy molecule has a fit that we label strategy formation. Strategy formation includes all the static and dynamic aspects of strategy, consisting of the strategy concept itself, its specification, and its execution. A specification is as much a result of conceptualization of the desired effect, as it is a result of its implementation and adaptation. This results in a combination of both deliberate and emergent characteristics of strategy.

> Organizational formation is the manifestation of deliberate and emergent properties through the specification and operationalization of a molecule—the conceptualization of a given domain, and the learning, operationalization, and adaptation of the corresponding constituent behaviors.

INSTANTIATING CONSTITUENT ORGANIZATIONAL CONSTRUCTS

The organizational constructs that are selected to be components in a specific molecule are derived from organizational literature, and depend, naturally, on the problem domain—what we are referring to as the composite {organizational domain}.

For example, if we are instantiating a process molecule as part of a business process design effort, the constituent organizational construct information may be refined into either rich information (implemented with people) or information amount (implemented with computer systems). The selection of the refinement path for information is governed by the nature of the {process} specification. Routine tasks require sufficient amounts of information, whereas nonroutine tasks require rich information.

Instantiating constituent organizational constructs requires a systematic process of operationalization. Recall from the previous chapter that a specification at any lower level of abstraction represents an implementation of some other, higher level of abstraction. Therefore, we may state that the implementation of a given specification, {organization domain}, is implemented through the specification and operationalization of constituent {organizational constructs}. The specification of a particular instance represents the operationalized refinement path. In the previous paragraph, the choice was between refining information into either *rich* information, information *amount*, or some combination of the two.

The selection of a refinement path is the job of the organizational designer— we refer to the selection process during implementation as *managerial choice*. Managerial choice is never easy. We give structure to the decision making process with the OM refinement model discussed in Chapter 8.

6.4 EXAMPLES OF ORGANIZATION MOLECULES

For illustrative purposes, below is a brief discussion of two representative molecules: the process and information molecules.

PROCESS MOLECULE

Let us first look at the nature of a business process. A process is not a tangible thing. Rather, it is an abstraction of interrelationships between people, work structures, information, and tools. The process abstraction may be represented in a contract specification. The process molecule, then refers to the specification of the activity {process}, and the actual combination of elements {human-structure-information-tool} used to implement the activity. Naturally, because of the existence of organizational formation, these same constituents {human-structure-information-tool} determine the emergent characteristics of {process}. See Figure 6–5.

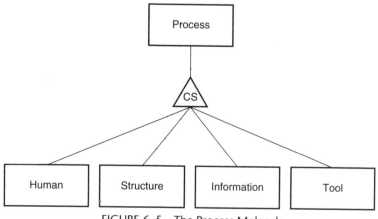

FIGURE 6–5   The Process Molecule

Reference to a process molecule, {process}, is a reference to the entire process molecule illustrated above—{process-human-structure-information-tool}. Observe that the inputs and outputs to the process are not directly shown in a picture—they are part of the contract for the process itself. That is, process inputs are specified as {process} contract preconditions, process outputs are specified as postconditions, while business rules and the invariant are each specified as triggers and invariant, respectively.

The linear specification for the process molecule is as follows:

work: CS (process, {human, structure, information, tool})

Observe that the concept of *work* manifests itself in the form of an *interrelationship* between people, their work structure, necessary information, and any required tools (such as computers).

INFORMATION MOLECULE

As illustrated in Figure 6–6, the specification of {information} may be operationalized with a variety of components. Information technology is the name commonly given to {information} implemented through the {tool} subtype known as "computer." The other primary {tool} subtype is "document." Increasingly, however, it is becoming clear that much of the information required in a learning organization is supplied through lateral relations, that is, through the human and structure constituents in the information molecule.

The linear specification of the {information} molecule is as follows:

information formation: CS (information, {human, structure, tool})

The source of information affects its character. Computer tools (i.e., information technologies) are a good source of large *amounts* of information, while lateral relations are better sources of *rich* information (Daft and Macintosh 1981, Goodhue, Wybo, and Kirsch 1992).

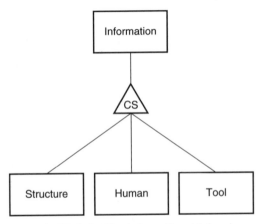

FIGURE 6–6 The Information Molecule

6.5 ELABORATING ORGANIZATION MOLECULES

During the process of instantiation, it is usually desirable to elaborate—i.e., refine—the core organizational constructs that comprise the component subtypes of a molecule. By "elaborate" we mean that a given core organizational construct that is a component in a molecule may be subtyped or decomposed into *its* constituents. Elaboration makes a design more understandable, explicit, and specific to a given domain instantiation. This is illustrated in Figure 6–7.

Recall from Chapter 5 that the core organizational constructs represent stable constructs that change infrequently. The core organizational constructs are used to create a layered model of a particular organization as well as the structural arrangement of molecules. As we stated above, molecules are constant across organizations. However, it is sometimes possible to refine a molecule into a more dynamic representation, depending on the current organizational research that the designer may utilize.

For example, the process molecule is a specification representing the interaction of {human, structure, information, tool} constituents. This scheme for process specification is constant across all organizations. However, not too many

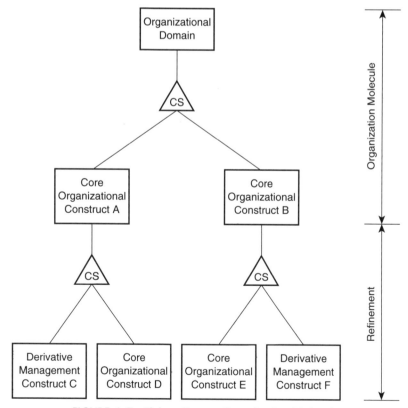

FIGURE 6–7 Elaborating an Organization Molecule

years ago, the component {structure} would have been understood to be a functional structure, while today it may be subtyped into both functional and a variety of lateral structures, such as teams. The type of structure depends on the particular organization and the process being specified.

As another example, the component {tool} in the information molecule once referred primarily to documents, while today it refers primarily to computer sources. The information molecule itself, including its constituents, is constant. What has changed are the possible refinement paths. Once this path is chosen, instantiation becomes easier, and of course, is specific to an organization.

For example, illustrated in Figure 6–8 is the culture molecule, its refinement, and the resulting elaborated culture molecule. It is the fully elaborated molecule that is instantiated with specific values, and becomes the actual design.

SINGLE- AND MULTI-DIMENSIONAL PROPERTIES

Observe that the culture molecule, its refinement, and its elaboration convey *several* dimensions of people and information. This is because people and information may be multi-dimensional, and they play several roles in the culture domain. *People* have roles in a process context, as well as possess a broad, more psychological view of their experiences in the organization (i.e., *memory*) and the environment (i.e., *world-view*). In a like manner, *information* is a component in a task and

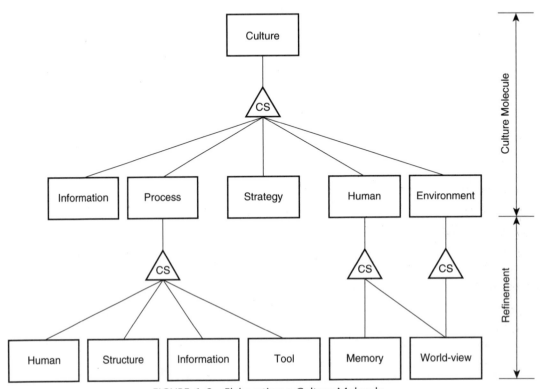

FIGURE 6–8   Elaborating a Culture Molecule

may be as simple as an update operation to a database. Or, *information* may be organizational and may represent organization-wide access to business strategies, tactics, policies, and so on.

Thus, each domain of the organization has single and multiple dimensions. A single dimension represents a specific, local context—it would typically be seen as a leaf in an elaborated molecule. When this domain is itself specified, as a composite composed of *its* constituents, it assumes the properties of a multi-dimensional construct.

GUIDELINES ON ELABORATION

- We elaborate where composite-subtyping, subtyping, or decomposition displays constructs that are not apparent from a particular molecule of the domain under consideration. In the above *culture* molecule, decomposition of *human* and *environment* constituents reveals the constructs *memory* and *world-view*.

- We elaborate where composite-subtyping, subtyping, or decomposition displays constructs that are known to have prominent effects on the domain in question. For example, in elaborating *culture*, we decompose *process* because each of *its* constituents has an isolated effect on the specification of *culture*, if only through its participation in *process*.

- We elaborate to identify current thinking on *dynamic* and *static* properties corresponding to components of a given molecule.

- We elaborate to identify the single dimension of an otherwise complex construct with multi-dimensional characteristics.

- We elaborate to identify a particular *perspective* the designer intends to implement.

6.6 PEOPLE, ORGANIZATIONS, AND IMPRECISE CONTRACTS

The primary purpose of OM is to propose an organizational architecture, and thereby, make organizational design disciplined. In traditional information management, this has meant concepts and techniques that manifest the *explicitness* of the information domain. A common assumption among IT professionals is that explicitness is both required and beneficial in the development of information systems.

In the much more complex world of organizations, this is not the case. Wherever people are involved, *implicit* assumptions are the general rule. From a purely conceptual viewpoint, the IT professional may state that he is not interested in the internal motivations of people, only in their explicit behaviors. Such an argument is at the foundation of object-oriented information systems.

To extend this argument to human beings, however, is to go back to the 19th century and consider people as machines. Hopefully, we have moved beyond such primitive thinking. In fact, internal motivation does matter! Moreover, these "things of the mind and heart"—trust, motivation, mutual respect, etc.— distinguish those organizations with a competitive advantage from those with a disadvantage. A meaningful organizational architecture, therefore, must account for both the explicit and implicit character of organizations.

THE RATIONALE FOR PRECISE CONTRACTS

We have argued that several organizational domains *may* be precisely specified with contracts. If organizations were machines, and if they were fully understood, this would be possible. However, neither assertion is close to being true.

The notion of a precise specification has a certain appeal to IT professionals. This is because computers are machines that require precise statements of code in a predefined format. If the implementation (i.e., the code) must be precise, it makes sense to have explicit and precise specifications of that code to remove any ambiguity or doubt concerning the intention of the program. That's the way machines work.

The IT professional is not alone in his or her desire to make things explicit. The success of Taylor's Scientific Management may be attributed to the desire (and value system) of managers who liken an organization and its employees to a machine. It is desirable for managers to apply the frameworks appropriate for machines to that of people and the entire workings of the organization. This makes decision making easy since, after all, it is straightforward to think about job skills, titles, and the design of functional activities. In contrast, it is much more difficult to architect organizational memory, culture, a network structure, or the design of empowered work teams.

The "organization-as-machine" is neither sustainable nor desirable. The demands of the competitive market, the knowledge required and possessed by people, the natural tendency of educated people to resist non-democratic, hierarchical institutions, the availability of information, and so on—all contribute to the perception that the old ways are no longer acceptable.

THE COMPETITIVE ADVANTAGE AFFORDED BY IMPRECISE CONTRACTS

This leads us to the real world. People and organizations are not machines. Each may be architected, but the architecture must be sufficiently flexible to capture all of the semantics in the real world. This includes the way people interact, the way strategy is formed (as opposed to formulated), the structuring of organizations, the informal alliances people make with each other, how culture evolves and manifests itself, how people and organizations learn, how people are motivated, and so on and so forth. Little can, nor should, be "precisely" described.

One strength of the organization molecule is that it provides a schema in which precision is possible, but not mandatory. A molecule provides a framework for understanding by identifying how the interconnectivity of specific domains (i.e., components) establishes the specification of another domain (i.e., composite). The application of a contract specification to that composite domain gives us a specification of its behavior. It may or may not be fully explicit.

Hard Architecture. Tools and data, together with what we will subsequently call routine knowledge, may be precisely specified; otherwise, we may not know how to implement them. Routine processes may be specified precisely so that we may optimize our workflows. We may even explicitly identify job skills, roles, and behaviors of people and structure in a particular process. Certain dimensions of people and their structure, then, may be specified in a "precise" manner. We call the collection of such precise contract specifications the *hard architecture* of an organization.

Soft Architecture. In contrast, the knowledge-based organization of the 21st century is competitive only in terms of its explicit complexity, tacit knowledge, and its hidden behavior. Competitive advantage is accorded those organizations whose semantic associations cannot be precisely stated or identified, and therefore, can not be easily imitated (Kay 1995). Such relationships comprise informal structures, people, learning, culture, and external relationships with suppliers and customers.

> Competitive distinctiveness derives from those behaviors that cannot be copied or understood by competitors. Implicit assumptions and complex associations characterize such behaviors.

This soft architecture of an organization is a primary source of competitive advantage. A soft architecture "specifies" the imprecise behavior associated with multi-dimensional, high-level constructs. This includes people, culture, and organization learning, but may also include (at high levels of abstraction) information and business processes. Furthermore, a soft architecture is characterized by multiple and complex alignment among domains.

RELATIONAL CONTRACTS

John Kay (1995) has proposed an architecture based on "patterns of relationships" that confers a distinctive capability to an organization. These relationships address those behaviors of an organization that are best described implicitly. Behaviors that are described with both explicit assertions and implicit assumptions are known as *relational contracts*.

The employment contract between an organization and a professional employee is an example of a relational contract: certain properties are precisely defined, such as salary, while other properties are only vaguely described, such as job responsibilities.

Relational contracts between the firm and its employees, and among employees, constitute an internal architecture. External architecture refers to relational contracts between a firm and its suppliers and customers. Network architecture refers to relational contracts among collaborating firms. All three cases are examples of a "soft" architecture based on relational contracting.

The success of a relational architecture rests on its association with organizational knowledge and cooperative (as opposed to individualistic) behavior. The organization invariant (i.e., context) necessary for implementation is *reciprocity*. The *reciprocity* invariant has three dimensions:

- An expectation of long-term relationships.
- A sharing of rewards for collective achievement.
- A structured informality.

6.7 INTERRELATING HARD AND SOFT CONTRACTS

An entirely hard architecture—one with precisely defined contracts—is not feasible in anything but the most simple, generally automated organization. A fully and precisely specified architecture is not desirable—the advantage it confers on the organization is short-lived.

The relational contract is one dominant form of "specification" in effective organizations. A soft architecture—one with a large share of relational contracts—does not necessarily lend itself to economies of scale or scope. Its assumptions are implicit, complex, and not easily understood.

In fact, a successful, knowledge-based organization has an architecture composed of hard and soft contracts. Generally, each type of domain may, and should, be specified with contracts of varying degrees of precision. For instance, with unskilled people performing routine activities, it may be possible to precisely specify the roles they play in an organization with a labor contract (the labor contract is an example of a precise specification).

6.8 ARCHITECTURE AS STRATEGY-IN-THE-LARGE AND STRATEGY-IN-THE-SMALL

Architecture and culture are not the same. Culture is a *pattern of behaviors* that may be *unaligned* and not necessarily desirable. Some organizations have a weak culture, while others have a strong one. Culture is "the pattern of learned basic assumptions that has worked well enough to be considered valid, and therefore, to be taught to new members as the correct way to perceive, think, and feel in relation to the problems of survival and integration" (Schein 1994). This pattern of behaviors is composed of an inner "mind-set" of members of an organization and their overt behaviors.

What we have stated above concerning culture—that it is a pattern of behaviors—may similarly be said of each organizational domain. That is, an organization's business processes form an identifiable pattern of behavior, as does its information systems, its structure, and so on. Each domain, then, is specified in a corresponding molecule, and when operationalized, manifests itself in a very specific form known as a pattern. Each individual pattern, then, is represented by a molecule and may be considered an organization's *strategy-in-the-small*.

In contrast, architecture is a *pattern of patterns,* and serves as an organization's *strategy-in-the-large.* The explicit behavior associated with a molecule is specific to an organization and is represented by instantiating a molecule. When we connect molecules, we are aligning the organization along very specific "threads" and thereby establishing a pattern of patterns. For example, establishing correspondence between process and information molecules serves to align the business processes of an organization with its information systems.

Recall from Chapter 4 that the behaviors associated with an organization's philosophy and culture identify an organization's invariant. Thus, instantiating the culture molecule creates a particular pattern that serves as an invariant during instantiation of subsequent molecules, such as learning or strategy. The culture molecule is on top, other molecules are constrained by culture, and together the complex composite of hard and soft instantiations represents an organization's architecture. Philosophy and culture, then, are central components of architecture.

6.9 CORE CONCEPTS

Organization molecules	Building blocks of organizational design
Fit and composite subtyping	Instantiation
Organizational formation	Elaborating an organization molecule
Precise specifications	Imprecise specifications
Relational contracts	Hard and soft architectures
Strategy-in-the-large	Strategy-in-the-small

Stages of organizational formation: conceptualizing, learning, operationalizing, adapting

Single- and multi-dimensional properties of organizational domains

Architecture as a pattern of patterns

CHAPTER 7

ALIGNING ORGANIZATION MOLECULES

The great challenge of management is to shape the organization so that all of its pieces work together in consonance. Ideally, these aligned components resonate with each other in a unique manner and become a source of advantage. These pieces are said to be in *alignment* when their respective behaviors correspond with one another.

The contingency model of organizational behavior developed by Nadler emphasizes the transformation process and the "fit" between organizational components (Nadler, Gerstein, and Shaw 1992). The optimum interaction of organizational components leads to organizations with a good "fit." Nadler has identified four major components: work, people, the formal organization, and the informal organization. The work component, defined by Nadler as the "basic activity in which the organization is engaged, particularly in light of its strategy," is said to have a "fit" with the other three components. And it is fit that determines success, more so than the individual components: "Effectiveness is driven by the relationship among components rather than by the inherent characteristics of individual components" (Nadler, Gerstein, and Shaw 1992).

Labovitz and Rosansky have written specifically on "the power of alignment." In their view, alignment should exist along vertical and horizontal dimensions. Vertical alignment exists between strategy at the top and people at the bottom. Horizontal alignment exists between internal processes and external customers. Each alignment linkage represents a two-way communication, and when aligned, vertically and horizontally, all four organizational pieces become aligned with each other. (See Labovitz and Rosansky 1997 for details.)

As a third example of alignment, Henderson and Venkatraman (1993) have advanced the strategic alignment model (SAM) for IT and the organization. The SAM identifies two areas of *strategic fit*: business strategy and organizational infrastructure, and IT strategy and IT infrastructure. Similarly, SAM identifies two areas of *functional integration*: business and IT strategy, and organizational and IT infrastructure. In this way, business and IT strategies, and organizational and IT processes are each subject to alignment.

Clearly, both academics and managers recognize the importance of alignment. In this book, we generalize the notion of alignment to all domains in a consistent and formal framework.

Distinctiveness comes from organizational pieces and how they fit together. The process of designing a single domain creates an organizational *architecture-in-the-small*. Through alignment, we construct an organizational *architecture-in-the-large*. Each type of architecture is a source of competitive advantage.

7.2 INSTANTIATING DOMAINS

We have argued throughout this book that design includes the specification of each domain of the organization. Some of these domains, such as structure, exist in all organizations; others, such as learning or TQM, may *appear* more discretionary. However, this is not the case! In any organization, domains exist and are instantiated, consciously or through deferral. A molecule is either instantiated by a designer, resulting in a domain with deliberate and emergent properties, or is neglected by management, and is therefore instantiated entirely with emergent properties.

For example, an organization may choose *not* to adopt TQM as a philosophy; nevertheless, a quality molecule exists and *will be* instantiated through correspondence of each of its component constructs. Subsequently, management may become aware of the *realized* quality molecule through surveys that indicate customer dissatisfaction, declining market share, and so on. For example, in the late 1970s, American auto manufacturers became painfully aware of their quality domain and its specification. In response, they decided (with mixed results) to instantiate their quality domains rather than leave things to chance. Knowledge of a quality molecule would have hastened management's awareness of the quality issue and the benefits of deliberate design.

Each domain in an organization will be instantiated, and will effect other instantiations. To maximize organizational effectiveness, it is preferable for management to proactively design and integrate domains through molecules.

7.3 CORRESPONDENCE AMONG DOMAINS

Each organization has a "mix" of domains that are consciously or unconsciously instantiated. If domains are instantiated through management deferral, misalignment may likely exist between what the organization designs (e.g., structure) and what it neglects (e.g., quality). The result is performance that does not meet expectations. However, even if domains are deliberately instantiated, the designer must still establish correspondence to avoid the effects of neglect. No domain exists in total isolation. Each should be consciously instantiated and correspondence established among related domains.

The specification of a domain is through its corresponding molecule. The specification of a molecule must support and be supported by the specifications of other molecules. However, alignment is a difficult task. Interconnecting domains is neither trivial nor obvious. *Domains are perceived from different viewpoints, depending on who is looking and the context in which they are looking.*

For example, *information* to an information specialist is perceived primarily through its operational components; if the information specialist is IT-focused, it is understood through *computer* components in the information molecule. In contrast, a business designer perceives information as one component in a complex interaction of information, people, and organizational structure, and therefore, he understands information in terms of its *participation* in the business activities specified in the process molecule. Figure 7–1 illustrates the alignment between two perspectives: the process and information molecules. If different views are to be successfully designed and implemented, each must make sense in terms of the other.

For example, a business process such as *financial investment* involves non-routine tasks. Nonroutine tasks require rich information. The specification of the components of the process molecule and the entire information molecule must each support access to rich sources of information. Immediate access to both *de-*

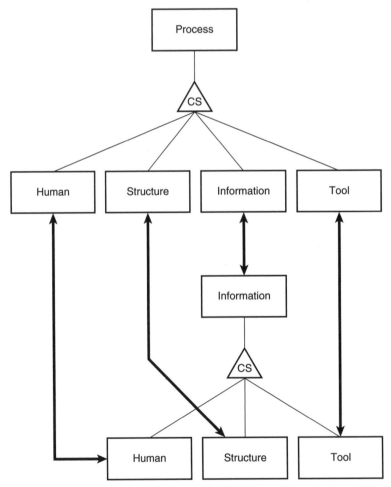

FIGURE 7–1   Correspondence Between the Process and Information Molecules

tailed and *summarized* information that supports multi-dimensional analysis is required.

Illustrated in Figure 7–2 is a sample design solution for *financial investment*. Naturally, there are a variety of solutions, and Figure 7–2 is for illustrative purposes only. Observe that alignment may exist between different subtypes of the same construct. In this example, the *structure* component in the process molecule is a *team* of investment specialists. This corresponds to a *hierarchical* subtype of structure in the information molecule. Structure is instantiated in the information molecule with a series of *functional departments*, each representing specialized knowledge in an investment area, such as equities or bonds. That is to say, the *functional* equity and bond departments may be aligned with the *lateral*

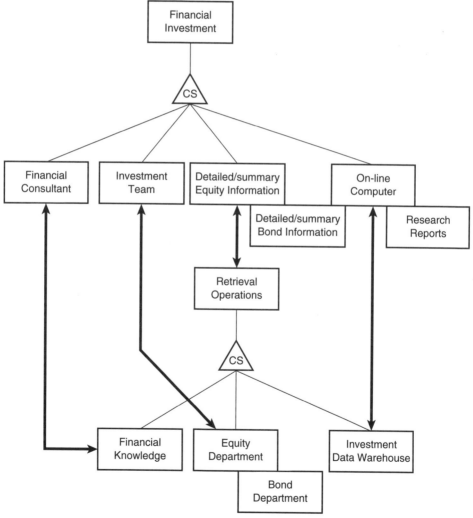

FIGURE 7–2   Correspondence in the Process and Information Molecules
for Financial Investment

investment team. This is a typical mix of structures found in organizations. Lateral structures, such as teams, are usually associated with the organization of work, and hence are found in the process molecule. Similarly, functional structures represent knowledge areas, and are typically found in the information molecule.

There is a caveat here: Alignment exists only if operationalized, that is, if the members of the investment team are indeed populated by drawing people from the equity and bond departments. Alignment, then, must be realized, not merely specified (see Chapter 8).

Note that this is an example of how correspondence between molecules is achieved through *alignment* (i.e., property correspondence) as opposed to *integration* (i.e., property equality).

7.4 ALIGNMENT AS A DRIVER OF CHANGE

Organizational change is a function of alignment. Certain instantiations and molecules support change more than others. Information is perhaps the most significant domain in this regard. But even with information, its transformation capability is achieved primarily through alignment—i.e., its degree of interconnectivity with other domains. This is evidenced by the impact which information has had on both structure and business processes.

Establishing alignment between molecules can dramatically change the character of an organization in a way that specification of individual molecules in isolation cannot. Organizational designers can initiate alignment between molecules, and thus direct the transformation of the organizations they manage. Below are three examples of organizational transformation related to alignment.

- *Structure.* Structure may be used to establish alignment between information and process molecules. This may transform the structure of organizations from hierarchical to process-specific lateral structures.
- *Information.* Using the organizational construct of process and the management philosophy of organizational learning as drivers, we may change the character and distribution of information in an organization. Information may be designed to fit the requirements of the process, and may include knowledge creation and knowledge workers.
- *Culture.* Using organizational learning again as a driver, we may align people with the culture molecule and enable the establishment of an organizational culture that is innovative. Organizations with innovative cultures are adaptive—their culture is based on learning.

The first example is one with which we are all familiar. The downsizing of organizations is primarily driven by the widespread access to both *task-specific* and *organizational* information. Alignment between information and structure molecules illustrates how correspondence may produce *immediate* change in an organization. In this case, information is the *driver*, people and tools are the *mediators*, while structure is the *target* of change.

The second example requires significant management commitment. Though the benefits of a learning organization are intellectually acknowledged, organizational learning is yet to be implemented on a large scale in most large firms. However, in an environment that demands knowledge-based organizations, *rich* information will become increasingly valuable. Moreover, once we identify and use people as sources of rich information, we will be positioned to move to the next level of learning: the development of specific knowledge creating processes.

Finally, the last example of alignment is relatively new and may have dramatic, long-term benefits to the organization. Information can transform the culture of an organization from one shackled by its history to one that is adaptable to the environment. An adaptable culture is one that is characterized by an ability to change "the rules of the game" as the competition dictates. In an increasingly turbulent environment, organizations with innovative cultures have a distinctive competence. Building learning-culture alignment requires substantial management vision and commitment.

7.5 BUILDING ALIGNMENT THREADS

Establishing correspondence between domains is a never-ending management task. For example, consider aligning the process molecule during a particular management initiative, such as business process reengineering (BPR). Correspondence is established among process components and each of its specifications. Additionally, correspondence must be established among the related molecules if the original molecule, the process molecule, is to be successfully implemented. This is illustrated Figure 7–3.

There are three dimensions associated with the notion of alignment. The first concerns internal *consistency* within a given domain. Does a specification make sense in terms of the proposed implementation? Do components contradict each other or do they reinforce the specification? The second dimension follows from the first: *compatible* alignment with associated domains in different molecules. Is a given specification supported by other existing or proposed specifications? Does it make sense to proceed with implementation, or will other domain specifications simply undermine the intent of the design? Finally, alignment must be viewed as a *dynamic* activity. Is there a new management initiative or philosophy that the organization has or should adopt that will reinforce existing domain specifications? Or will a new initiative undermine the existing complex of domains? Each is a serious management concern and is discussed below.

CONSISTENT ALIGNMENT

The first stage of alignment concerns the development of a *consistent* molecule specification itself. We refer to this as consisting of *self-contained alignment threads*. The specification of a domain has a certain intent; to be fully successful, each of its components must be mutually supportive. In the example illustrated in Figure 7–2, each of the process molecule components is brought into alignment with each other and

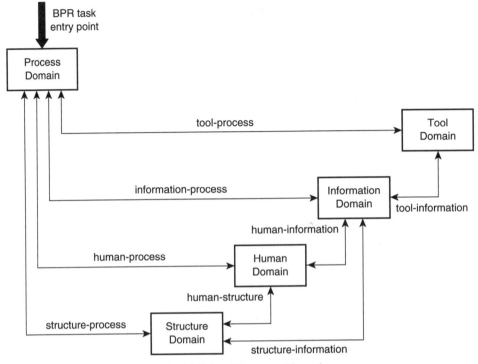

FIGURE 7–3   Alignment Threads

with the composite process specification. As another example, consider designing a process for *collaborative* systems development. This is more likely to make sense if structure is specified as lateral as opposed to hierarchical. Lateral structures, in turn, are more easily supported with information covering the entire life-cycle instead of information for phase-specific tasks. Each component, then, should support every other component. This is illustrated in Figure 7–4.

Self-contained alignment threads have two dimensions. The first concerns selecting the appropriate components to satisfy the intent of the designer (i.e., composite specification). This is embodied in the molecule itself. The second addresses the correspondence among the components of the molecule. Successful implementation will be more likely if molecule composite and component specifications are consistent.

Compatible Alignment

The next stage of alignment involves *multiple alignment threads*. Multiple alignment involves the establishment of *compatible specifications across molecules*. For example, a given business process may be designed with the expectation of local, process-specific information. But if the organization level information molecule does not support decentralized information (e.g., client/server, distributed), the finest process molecule specification from the viewpoint of a business process designer will not be supported by the organization's information infrastructure.

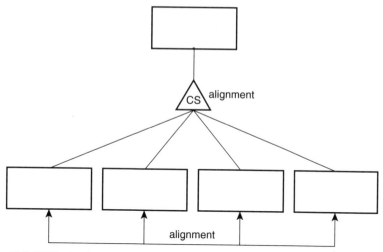

FIGURE 7–4   Consistent Alignment: Self-Contained Alignment Threads

Similarly, if your process molecule requires cooperative behavior among the participants in the process, but if your culture molecule does not support shared rewards, you have yet another misfit. Multiple alignment, then, ensures that a local specification is compatible with the specifications of the entire organization. This is illustrated in Figure 7–5.

DYNAMIC ALIGNMENT

Since each domain is connected to some other domain, alignment will engulf the entire organization. And this is exactly the case—changing one domain of an organization may impact, and be impacted by, every other domain. Effective managers recognize that implementing multiple alignment threads is the meaning and challenge of organizational design. Alignment is a never-ending journey.

Alignment is implicated with any new management philosophy. This, too, is a dynamic activity since some "new" management practice is published every day. Furthermore, there is an aspect of alignment that has much broader implications. This concerns a drastic and radical change in the social and political context which we discussed in Chapter 4. For example, the "New Deal" introduced by Franklin D. Roosevelt changed the position and relative importance accorded people in American society. This changed the management philosophy with regard to managing employees. There was, for example, an immediate rise in the strength of unions and management's willingness to work with them.

As another example, consider the effects of learning on an organization. Learning, as we will see in Part 2, brings forth emergent characteristics. Alignment threads (consistent and compatible) will be adjusted in real time, as people execute, learn, and adapt their alignment threads to their process tasks.

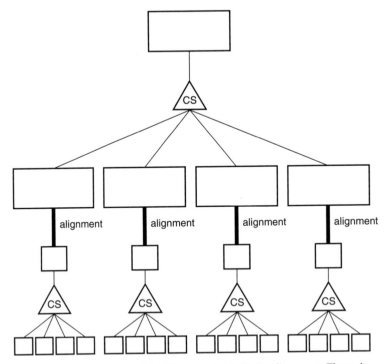

FIGURE 7–5   Compatible Alignment: Multiple Alignment Threads

7.6 ALIGNING HARD AND SOFT ARCHITECTURES

Rigorous specification, even the formal methods of mathematics, is the glue of a hard architecture. In contrast, the soft architecture of relational contracts *cannot* be engineered. They represent relationships—*imprecise* statements of mutual obligations and benefits. *Reciprocality*—an exercise in understanding and respect—is its glue.

Each type of contract is as relevant as any other. The hard and soft architectures represented by precise and relational contracts, as all behaviors, are interdependent. Moreover, each type of contract facilitates the alignment of the other. Precise contracts tend to *enable* the implementation of relational contracts, while relational contracts facilitate the *effective application* of precise contracts. This is illustrated in Figure 7–6.

For example, Edgar Schein claims that information technology enables the development of a type of culture that is self-learning. This type of culture is known as *innovative culture*. In OM terminology, the instantiation of information and culture molecules elicits behaviors that characterize innovative cultures, such as *adaptability* and *learning*. These are examples of relational contracts—there is no precise specification of adaptability, only an "understanding" between the organization and its employees that each employee is expected to adapt to a changing work environment.

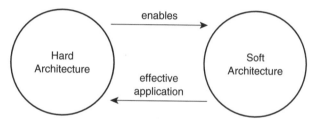

FIGURE 7–6 Aligning Hard and Soft Contracts

Similarly, the existence of an innovative culture permits the effective application of *new and changing* business processes and information systems. That is to say, specific culture molecule instantiations (e.g., adaptability) facilitate the acceptance of different and changing process and information instantiations. This may manifest itself in the form of new products in new business processes.

7.7 AN EXAMPLE: CULTURAL ALIGNMENT

Organizational literature describes frameworks for a variety of management problems that are, in effect, alignment models. Certain relationships are prominent because of their perceived value to effectiveness. For example, organizations constantly strive for "strategic alignment." The premise is quite simple: Organizational components should be synchronized with the firm's strategy. Similarly, an organization may desire to change its underlying culture and thereby induce a permanent change in the organization of work, performance, and management. We term these activities *cultural alignment*. It is through culture that alignment becomes an enabler of change itself!

For example, as described in Chapter 6, John Kay maintains that competitive distinctiveness is a function of an organization's architecture—or more precisely, its relational contracts governing the responsibilities and behavior of organizations and people. The success of implementing relational contracts is directly tied to the notion of reciprocality.

When we dissect the Kay architecture using the language of OM, we discover that the "sources of architecture"—informality, the expectation of shared rewards for collective achievements, and the expectation of long-term relationships—represent an *invariant* and the implementation of structure and culture contracts. That is to say, we can take the valuable Kay approach, and make it *disciplined* using the OM architecture. In so doing, we identify incomplete and inconsistent areas. Thus, using OM, we can *extend* the Kay framework so that we may prescriptively analyze both the soft and hard architectures of an organization.

Illustrated in Figure 7–7 is an *extension* of the Kay model within the OM architecture. We consider this to be one example of cultural alignment (no doubt, there are others). We consider this an example of cultural alignment because its implementation affects an organization's invariant and culture first, and

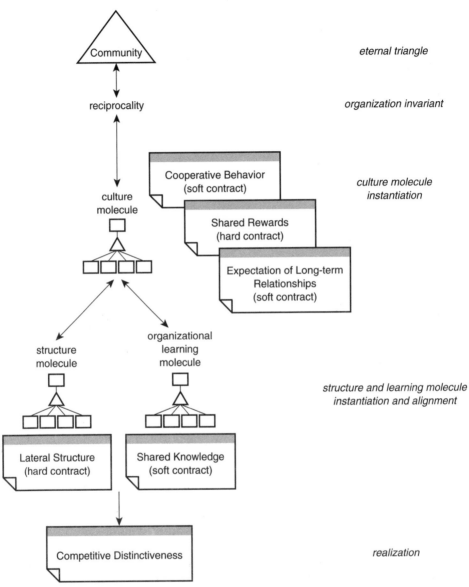

FIGURE 7–7 Extension of the Kay Architecture in OM

subsequently every other organizational domain. Recall that in OM, culture molecule instantiations form part of an organization's invariant (along with the invariant derived from the eternal triangle).

We believe that the social context required for relational contracting and the development of competitive distinctiveness is a commitment to *community*. In an environment where only individuals accumulate wealth, it is difficult to establish the notion of community.

The success of a relational architecture rests with its association with organizational knowledge and cooperative (as opposed to individualistic) behavior. The organization invariant (i.e., context) necessary for the implementation of community is reciprocality. This invariant serves to instantiate three culture contracts: the expectation of long-term relationships (a soft, relational contract), the sharing of rewards for collective achievement (a hard, formal specification), and a commitment to cooperative behavior (a soft contract).

The Kay architecture describes highly effective organizations; in the OM framework we can more clearly see its specifications and interconnectivity. OM permits the organizational designer to use the Kay architecture as a *seed*, and *additionally* align other domains of an organization—information, for example. Accordingly, the Kay approach of describing relational contracts (i.e., a soft architecture) is enriched in OM by the establishment of a full repertoire of domain contracts (hard and soft) and their subsequent alignment threads. This is illustrated in Figure 7–7 by the alignment of the eternal triangle and the organization invariant, culture molecule instantiations, and corresponding structure and learning molecule instantiations. As alignment progresses among molecules, the organization soon achieves a greater degree of competitive distinctiveness and increased effectiveness.

7.8 ALIGNMENT AND ORGANIZATIONAL EFFECTIVENESS

Alignment and OE are based on three criteria: consistency, compatibility, and dynamicity. As discussed above, consistency is meaningful correspondence *within* a domain (e.g., a process molecule). Is the intent of a process specification workable within the specifications of the process components? Compatible alignment is correspondence *among* domains—across molecules. Is a given process specification supported by the *organization's* information, structure, tool, and cultural specifications? Consistency, then, describes what should be specified; compatibility describes whether or not it is achievable. Both must be satisfied if the organization is to derive benefit. Consistency and compatibility represent a traditional view of OE.

Dynamic alignment is an extension beyond the conventional meaning of OE. Consistency and compatibility represent static states of an organization. The implication is that organizations are effective at a given point in time based on some degree of consistency and compatibility. In contrast, dynamic alignment represents a dynamic view—one that implies that organizations must constantly change, improvise, and modify themselves to be effective at all points in time.

A coordinated and successful organization is possible only in the context of alignment. For example, U.S. firms have learned that creating a lateral structure in the form of *teams*, in and of itself, produces little effect on the organization. Moreover, maintaining individual rewards while expecting "team" achievement only *magnifies* the misalignment in an organization. Lateral structures are of little value in sequentially designed business process, or in an organization whose culture emphasizes individualism, outsourcing, or large differences in pay scales.

The cultural alignment example above is an example of compatible alignment. There is meaningful correspondence with a belief system grounded in *community,* the organization invariant *reciprocality,* the manifest cultural behaviors of *cooperative behavior, shared rewards,* and the *expectation of long-term relationships,* and corresponding instantiations of structure and learning molecules. When each of these *behaviors* is implemented, that is, given structure, competitive distinctiveness is *realized.* As we shall see in Chapter 8, realization is the stage of implementation where behaviors, structures, and their interconnections are operationalized.

EMERGENT PROPERTIES OF ALIGNMENT

In addition to enriching architectures such as the Kay framework, OM illustrates an important class of properties that manifest themselves as a *consequence* of alignment. Properties such as competitive distinctiveness or distinctive competence are *emergent* properties of a set of domains that correspond to component specifications *and* their associated multiple alignment threads.

The notion of competitive distinctiveness exists only after the successful *realization* of several molecule specifications and corresponding alignment threads. We have seen this illustrated in the OM-extension of the Kay architecture—distinctiveness is possible only after the implementation of compatible molecules such as learning and structure, and after the appropriate invariant is in place. This is a consequence of realizing culture specifications and its alignment threads!

For example, one distinctive competence of Toyota is its *assembly* quality. This may appear to be an emergent property of process, but it depends on the existence of compatible specifications and alignment threads among several molecules, such as process, culture, quality, structure and learning.

DIRECTIONALITY AND CHANGE STRATEGY

In the illustrations used in this and other chapters, we have shown each alignment thread between associated constructs as a line with an arrowhead at each end of the line. A question that arises concerns the symmetry (or asymmetry) of the alignment thread. The answer concerns the nature of alignment, and its dependency on *context* and *change strategy.* Domains have *no* intrinsic characteristics that dictate the direction in which correspondence is established. Direction is established as a consequence of a particular change strategy.

For example, in the design of a business process, we may specify certain on-line retrieval operations. Part of the infrastructure that makes this happen is a relational database. Which drives the correspondence—a business requirement for an on-line operation or a relational database? It is likely that during the introduction of relational technology, IT drove correspondence: the information and tool components, as well as the business process itself, were brought into correspondence with the demands of relational databases. Today, the reverse is true, and relational databases simply implement on-line retrieval operations defined in a business process. Note that this speaks to the observed role of information technology in the design of business processes: IT may serve as an *enabler* or a *di-*

rection setter. More recently, the same may be said of the Internet and e-business. New IT often acts as a driver of radical change, but in time, assumes the role as a enabler of incremental change.

We see documented examples of this two-way correspondence every day. For example, the strategic alignment model defines four strategy perspectives among selected constructs (Luftman, Lewis, and Oldach 1993) as follows:

- *Competitive potential perspective.* The associated directionality is *IT-strategy* leads to *business strategy* leads to *organizational infrastructure.*
- *Technology potential perspective.* The directionality is *business strategy* leads to *IT-strategy* leads to *IT infrastructure.*
- *Service level perspective.* The directionality is *IT-strategy* leads to *IT infrastructure* leads to *organizational infrastructure.*
- *Strategy execution perspective.* The directionality is *business strategy* leads to *organizational infrastructure* leads to *IT infrastructure.*

In each perspective, the source domain, known as an *anchor domain*, drives the change. The second domain, known as a *pivot domain,* represents the problem area that is being enhanced, while the last domain, known as an *impacted domain,* is the area that is changed as a consequence of the change to the pivot domain.

Observe directionality is asymmetrical, and is a function of the strategy adopted for change. Once the change has been executed and correspondence established, the direction no longer matters. When the next organizational change effort is planned, a change strategy will be selected (i.e., a perspective), the relevant domains selected, and direction established as a consequence of both the context and its change strategy. Thus, correspondence and directionality among organizational constructs is a function of the change strategy, and rarely of any intrinsic properties of the constructs themselves.

7.9 DEGREE OF ALIGNMENT AND MANEUVERABILITY

The degree of alignment is the *level* of correspondence established among molecules. No correspondence can ever be complete. This is the "gray" area between fit and misfit. Gray areas are a reality of life—all organizations are characterized by partial alignment.

Information engineering, for instance, defines information planning in terms of *complete* data integration. In contrast, Goodhue, Wybo, and Kirsch (1992) have suggested that partial data integration is more successful and effective in organizations. That is to say, an information strategy requiring partial data integration around, say, selected "critical" entities, may be more aligned with an organization's processes than a strategy requiring total data integration.

Consequently, we say that *partial data integration* has a greater degree of alignment than *complete data integration.* Accordingly, firms with partially integrated data have more effective information systems and business processes— precisely because there is a higher degree of alignment between them than otherwise. This enables the organization to leverage the alignment threads themselves—to operate more effectively and to adapt to a changing environment.

CONTINUOUS MANEUVERABILITY

This property of organizational architecture, quantified in terms of the degree of alignment, is *maneuverability*. Ultimately, the degree of alignment, and hence maneuverability, is a function of an organization's culture. It is through culture that an organization's invariant (i.e., context) is established. Context determines the nature of a specification and its potential for alignment. A culture that is closed is one with *unchanging* manifest behaviors. This leads to a stagnant organization—one which has difficulty adapting to a competitive environment.

Cultures that are open are cultures that are *self-learning:* They have the necessary invariant, such as reciprocality, to establish aligned cultural and learning contracts. Culture and learning molecules establish a baseline by which adaptability becomes a characteristic of other molecules. That is to say, the scope and extent of organizational design is a function of its culture. This property of culture is yet another representation of maneuverability.

One may ask, "Is not maneuverability an emergent property of culture?" This is somewhat like asking, "Which came first, the chicken or the egg?" *Culture is a special type of molecule.* Culture contracts serve as an organization invariant for the specification of other molecules. The alignment of culture and learning molecules facilitates additional instantiation of culture contracts, which in turn leads to the greater alignment among many more molecules than otherwise. The resulting behaviors and alignments are characteristic of an innovative culture (Schein 1994). Innovative cultures are associated with inventive organizations. Innovative cultures, inventive organizations, and maneuverability are mutually dependent, and together form the basis of effective organizations in highly turbulent environments.

7.10 CORE CONCEPTS

Alignment	Competitive advantage and architecture
Organizational fit	Correspondence among domains
Alignment threads	Consistent alignment
Compatible alignment	Dynamic alignment
Strategic alignment	Cultural alignment
Alignment and effectiveness	Maneuverability

CHAPTER 8

THE OM DESIGN PROCESS

8.1 REFINEMENT AND MANAGERIAL CHOICE

It is well-known that an architecture, no matter how elegant, may not be implementable. The utility of an architecture is determined by its implementation. It determines how an organization is structured, how information systems are developed, how control mechanisms are instituted, how business processes are formulated, how people are compensated, how managers manage, and so on.

Design can not be separated from implementation. There is no such thing as a good design that is not well implemented. As John Kay (1995) states: "Was Napoleon's defeat in Russia a failure of strategy or implementation? It hardly makes sense to ask the question, because in the hands of a skilled strategist, formulation and implementation are inextricable."

Designing an organization requires managerial choice at every stage of development: choice associated with the constructs chosen by management to represent the organization, choice with respect to the organizational domains which management is interested in proactively designing, choice of alignment among organizational domains, and choice of operationalization.

Throughout the design process—establishing an organizational baseline, identifying domains that are in need of design, specifying an organization's invariant at all levels of abstraction, instantiating appropriate molecules, and refining molecules into an implementation of one's own design—refinement may follow any number of paths.

The core organizational constructs which a decision maker includes in the layers of abstraction represent the first necessary choice. Concomitant with this is the identification of an organization's invariant. One important purpose is to establish a baseline that reveals where the organization is and where it would like to be.

The next series of choices concern the business and organizational problems and issues which management needs to address. This may include everything from process transformation and cultural change to new information systems, and so on. This is accomplished by selecting the appropriate molecule.

Refinement of specifications leads to implementation. Decision points during implementation indicate the refinement path chosen. Recall that in Chapter 7, we gave a brief example of refining information into either rich or quantitative information. The choice depended on whether the process specification represented a routine or nonroutine task; routine information requirements are refined into quantitative information (i.e., amount), whereas the information requirements of nonroutine tasks are refined into both quantitative and rich information.

The process of refinement is a critical element in organizational design. Below is an example of the process of refinement in the IT arena and the role of choice in the "final product" of design. This is followed by a general OM refinement model and associated design guidelines.

REFINEMENT: AN EXAMPLE FROM IT

The decomposition of a contract specification into its constituent specifications (i.e., subcontracts) is known as contract refinement (Woodcock and Loomes 1988). Recall that a contract is an implementation of some "higher" level contract, and a specification of what is to be implemented at some lower level. That is to say, as we "refine," we decompose the corresponding contract specification of behavior into component contracts in the next "lower level."

However, things do not decompose so nicely: There is choice at every layer. For example, let us examine the refinement of the information contract introduced in the Appendix, *Create an accountant instance*, illustrated in Figure 8–1.

Create an accountant instance, in the information layer, is independent of any tool implementation. If we choose a relational implementation, this information contract refines into *Insert an accountant tuple*, in the tool layer. We can refine even further, into a particular relational tool (e.g., DB2) contract, *Insert into accountant_table Values (...)*. This DB2 contract is at a lower level of abstraction in the tool layer. If we choose a hierarchical implementation (e.g., IMS), we will decompose along a different path and therefore develop different contract specifications.

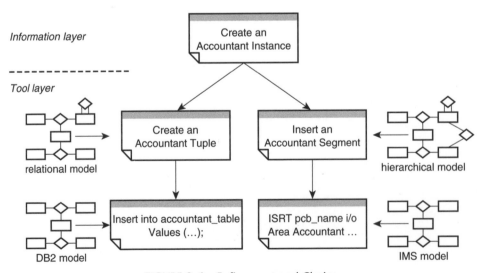

Information layer

Tool layer

Create an Accountant Instance

Create an Accountant Tuple

Insert an Accountant Segment

relational model

hierarchical model

Insert into accountant_table Values (...);

ISRT pcb_name i/o Area Accountant ...

DB2 model

IMS model

FIGURE 8–1   Refinement and Choice

At every level of refinement, there is individual choice and a concomitant model that supplies information to our "decomposed" contract specification. That is, *there is always information from external sources*—models representing the corresponding level of abstraction in the OM, and the selection of the "path" during decomposition, or, correspondingly, aggregation.

The selection of the path is dependent on the desired context. Does the manager want a relational, hierarchical, or object-oriented environment, or some combination? *The answer often depends on the specification of some other molecule.* In this scenario, that specification is the instantiation of a tool molecule.

8.2 THE OM REFINEMENT MODEL

We may generalize the previous discussion into a framework that integrates and extends the concept of refinement with the OM approach to organizational design. For the same reason that it is not desirable to skip design and go directly from analysis to coding during the development of an information system, it is also unwise to formulate, say, a strategic plan, and immediately attempt implementation. As with information systems development, organizational design is characterized by stages of development.

The OM refinement model is a meta-schema that may be used to support the life-cycle phases of organizational design and is part of the OM framework. Successful implementation of an organizational specification requires successive refinement. This is illustrated in Figure 8–2, and elaborated in the next section.

The OM refinement model consists of six layers. Each layer represents a "refinement"—an implementation—of the next higher layer. Since the constructs associated with each layer are *formed* as well as *formulated,* and contain *emergent* as well as *deliberate* properties, there is two-way interaction between layers. This is illustrated in Figure 8–2 by the label "Feedback and Engagement."

FEEDBACK AND ENGAGEMENT

In a top-down prescriptive approach, the design process is deliberate, and its contents are formulated. To ensure adaptation, there exists a formal *feedback* process. In a bottom-up descriptive approach, design is emergent, and its contents are said to be formed. In this case, there is no need for a formal feedback process, since *engagement* along the refinement path ensures emergence. Engagement is the active involvement of people in a task—learning is concurrent with the task, and therefore its emergent characteristics obviate the need for feedback. Moreover, since alignment between analogous constructs in associated molecules is two-way (prescriptive and descriptive), it may require mutual adjustment between them. Both feedback and engagement often coexist are mechanisms that support dynamic alignment.

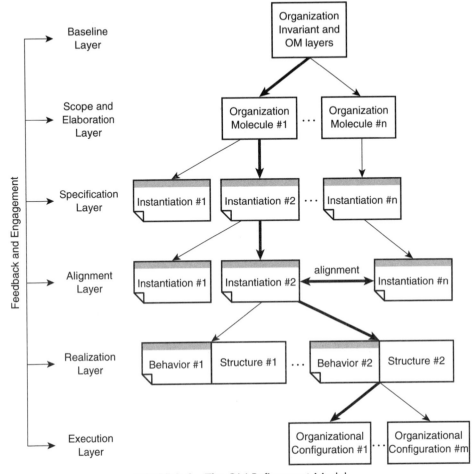

FIGURE 8–2   The OM Refinement Model

8.3 THE OM DESIGN PROCESS: REFINEMENT LAYERS AND GUIDELINES

The following is a discussion of the OM refinement model and its associated design guidelines. For each layer, we discuss its purpose and identify corresponding deliverables—i.e., what is required from associated activities before refinement may continue at the next lower layer. Similarly, if the process is bottom-up, the associated deliverables are required before emergence to the next higher layer is possible.

BASELINE LAYER

Purpose: Establish an organizational baseline
Key deliverables: Identify relevant socio-cultural invariant (eternal triangle)

> Organization invariant (current and desired)
> OM-layers (current and desired)

The primary purpose of establishing an organizational baseline is to promote analysis of the current and future type of organization you intend to design. The manager's first task is to identify the socio-cultural invariant (Type 1) that is relevant to the design issues. This may be the identification of an invariant that impacts the culture of an organization—for example, the existence of *community*. The second task is to identify specific organization invariants (Type 2)—for instance, reciprocality.

There are two sources of organization invariant: the eternal triangle and an organization's existing culture. What are the practices of your organization? Does it mirror the larger society's invariant? What is your organization's culture? Are its behaviors different from that of the eternal triangle? Is your organization rational? If you claim that it is, what are you doing that everyone else isn't? Another example of an organization invariant is the level of respect accorded employees. Each organization invariant corresponds in some way to those of the eternal triangle and the organization's culture.

The manager's next task during this phase is the identification of core organizational constructs that represent current and desired views of your organization. The set and arrangement of core organizational constructs constitute the OM-layers. Decomposition of organizational constructs within a layer is recommended only if it serves to identify your organization. For example, if your organization is largely focused on strategy, you may decompose strategy into corresponding constituent strategies, such as market, product, and function. The benefits of establishing an organizational baseline is that it focuses senior management on the type of organization it leads and defines its options.

These types of high-level invariants may sound vague or irrelevant. But the opposite is the case! OM-layers and a corresponding invariant establish your organizational baseline: where you are as an organization, what you desire your organization to become, and what you as an organizational designer are capable of changing.

Of course, invariants are not the exclusive claim of the Chief Executive Officer (CEO). Invariants, as with all organizational concepts, have deliberate and emergent characteristics. An invariant is formed, as well as formulated. The CEO may intend to have a rational, knowledge-based organization that respects its employees, but emergent forces may overwhelm deliberate intentions. For example, Peter Drucker points out that all organizations routinely claim that they value their employees, when in fact most neither believe (perhaps not consciously) nor exercise that claim (Drucker 1992).

SCOPING AND ELABORATION LAYER

Purpose:	Designate molecules
Key deliverables:	Molecules are identified
	Refinement of identified molecules
	Local invariant overrides

The scoping and elaboration layer supports the designation of corresponding molecules that support the resolution of a design issue. The process of designating a specific molecule includes:

- Molecule identification
- Molecule refinement
- Development of an associated domain (molecule) invariant

For example, if the design issue is business process reengineering, the process and information molecules will be identified as the design constructs with which to specify and implement, at both high and detailed levels of analysis, the business process under consideration.

The second step in designating a molecule is to elaborate on the molecule's constituent organizational constructs. This includes elaboration and decomposition. This was illustrated in Chapter 6 with the culture molecule, and is repeated in Figure 8–3.

The final step in molecule designation is development of an appropriate domain-specific invariant. This includes industry, professional, and departmental *business rules*. Note that these are invariants that are specific to your designated

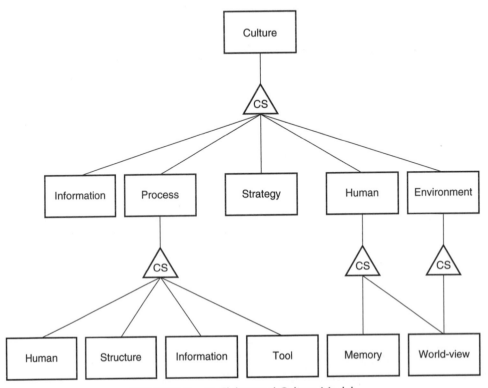

FIGURE 8–3   An Elaborated Culture Model

molecule, though they may correspond in some way to the organization invariant. Business rules are discussed in subsequent chapters.

Suppose that you desire an invariant that is contrary to your organization invariant. One solution may be to attempt a local override, perhaps at a departmental level. An example of an override is illustrated in Figure 8–4.

We make an important observation here. Organizations can not expect certain types of behaviors (e.g., knowledge sharing) without a corresponding invariant (e.g., community) and supporting instantiations of culture (e.g., shared rewards). If certain behaviors are desired, organizations must consciously adopt an appropriate invariant through corresponding instantiations of culture.

A larger issue here is that organizations have architectures, whether or not managers choose to understand that this is the case. Behaviors are interconnected and depend on contracts and their invariants—explicit by design, or implicit by neglect or otherwise.

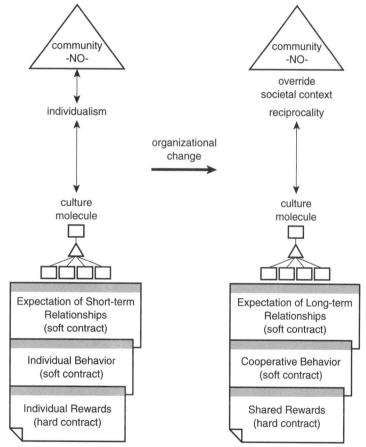

FIGURE 8–4 Overriding Organization Invariant with a Change in Culture

SPECIFICATION LAYER

Purpose:	Specification of organizational domains
Key deliverables:	Domain contract specifications
	Component instantiations (molecule constituent descriptions)

This layer is characterized by the specification of the desired behaviors of corresponding organizational domains. For a given organizational domain, this includes the specification of high-level (e.g., a given business process), and corresponding low-level abstractions (e.g., associated work cycles and tasks). Instantiating a molecule means specifying its domain in a contract, and identifying and describing its components.

In Figure 8–5, we highlight our example of a process molecule from Chapter 6 to illustrate instantiation of a molecule.

As we have often pointed out, a contract includes an organization invariant, and a specific invariant for the domain being specified. We have discussed examples of the former (e.g., reciprocality). The latter are business- and industry-specific invariants (commonly known as "business rules"). Examples of business rules are drug-testing regulations for the pharmaceutical industry, financial reporting regulations for publicly owned companies, etc. Another type of business rule is the existence dependency or cardinality. Cardinality is popular among IT professionals because it is easy to implement in databases. An example of this type of business rule is the requirement that a person have an account before being considered a customer.

A key element during this phase is the discovery of corresponding contract assertions. Up to this point, the designer has identified the organization invariant. This phase requires the discovery of all molecule-specific invariants and as-

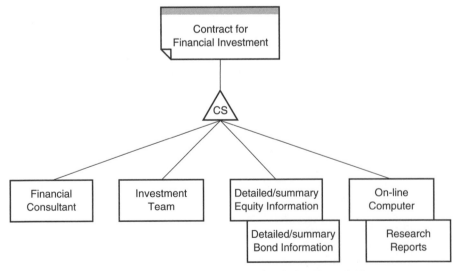

FIGURE 8–5   Instantiating the Process Molecule for Financial Investment

sertions. We say discovery, because here, too, assertions are formed as well as formulated.

Naturally, the designer will specify contract postconditions—the desired outcomes from execution of the molecule contract. These, too, may be formed. In fact, the postcondition will have to be compatible with the contract's other assertions and the constituent's assertions. For example, during a BPR effort, there is an expectation that cycle time will be significantly reduced—cycle time is a postcondition of a process contract. Additionally, cycle time is an emergent property that corresponds to constituent assertions, particularly those of the information component.

ALIGNMENT LAYER

Purpose:	Establishment of context between organizational domains (that is, align behaviors across associated domains)
Key deliverables:	Re-instantiations of domain contracts (if necessary) Establishment of consistency and compatibility

The alignment layer addresses the need to establish the context of each molecule. Since organizational domains are interconnected, establishing context means aligning molecules. The implementation of an instantiation is constrained by instantiations in related molecules.

For instance, in the IT-refinement example illustrated in Figure 8–1, the implementation of the information contract is determined by the instantiation of a corresponding tool component—either an IMS or DB2 instantiation. We are able to choose DB2, in turn, because of its correspondence to an instantiation of an IT-strategy molecule that specifies relational technology. Two separate refinement paths are made to converge in order to establish compatibility. This is illustrated in Figure 8–6.

In the example shown in Figure 8–6, the tool contract controls the context. Ideally, this is accomplished through coordinated refinement paths that are logically sequenced. In this case, refinement of the IT-strategy molecule should precede refinement of the information molecule. However, since there are few ideal situations, establishing context through compatibility may require re-instantiation of constituent specifications.

Instantiating a molecule means specifying its domain in a contract, and identifying components. These component descriptions will eventually have contract specifications in corresponding molecules. For example, a business planner may instantiate a process molecule to design a given business process, while an IT-analyst instantiates a corresponding information molecule to support that design. In Chapter 7, we illustrated a process molecule and its corresponding information molecule (Figure 7–2). This is detailed in Figure 8–7 to highlight the alignment of the process and information molecules. Each must be compatible with the other. Note that this example illustrates that specifications are compatible to the extent that they reinforce each other; they need not be identical.

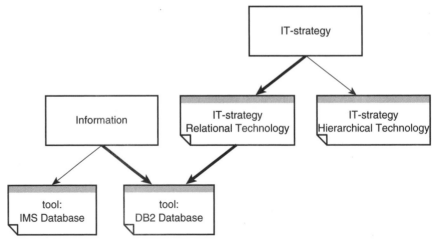

FIGURE 8–6   Compatibility: Refinement Path Convergence

REALIZATION LAYER

Purpose: Operationalize aligned behavior
Key deliverables: Identification of structural properties of molecules
                    Identification of timing and sequencing characteristics of molecules

Realization is part of the process of operationalizing aligned behaviors specified in molecules. Operationizing aligned behaviors means identifying corresponding configurations that consist of structural properties and any special timing, sequencing, and delays imposed by those properties.

For example, realizing a business process means establishing work- and physical-document flows. The popular "IS-maps" and "should-maps" used during BPR are pictorial representations used to structure the business process during realization. The combination of process molecule instantiations during the specification phase, and a variety of "maps" during realization, provide the necessary details to reengineer and improve business processes.

Generally, then, realization takes a contract specification of behavior and operationalizes it into a variety of structural diagrams. The most commonly employed are the process, queuing-process, and causal diagrams. The first is quite popular in BPR; the "IS" and "should-maps" are, in fact, process diagrams. These are linear mappings of activity flows representing the structural characteristics of a system. They are based purely on the flow of time. To further refine a business process "map," it is advisable to use, in addition to a process-diagram, both queuing-process and causal diagrams. Queuing-process diagrams are characterized by stochastic considerations; hence, Peter Senge (1994) uses the term "stocks and flows diagram" to capture the waiting period and the piling up of activities. Furthermore, by using casual diagrams, the designer is able to identify the cause-and-effect relationships. These enable the designer to address all eventualities, unforeseen circumstances, and catastrophes.

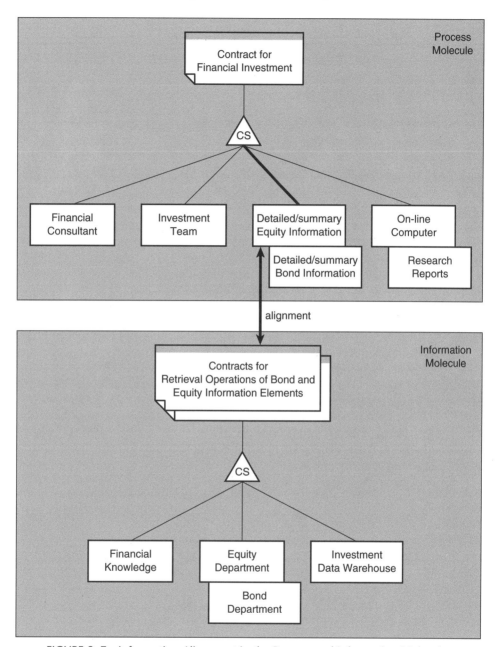

FIGURE 8–7   Information Alignment in the Process and Information Molecules
for Financial Investment

A summary of the *structural* diagrams used during realization is illustrated in Table 8–1.

As another example, consider operationalizing an information molecule contract. Realization includes writing the actual code—the transformation of information contract specifications into code and data structures. An information

TABLE 8–1   COMPARISON OF PROCESS, QUEUING-PROCESS, AND CAUSALITY DIAGRAMS

Property	Process diagram	Queuing-Process diagram	Causality diagram
independent variable	time	time	causality
dependent variable	activity	activity	activity and events
node	activity	occurrence of events	cause and effect activities (variables)
link	flow of materials, information, and time	flows and accumulations	causality
characteristic	illustrates the flow of work based strictly on time	flow is based on stochastic principles and the build-up of "stocks" or queues, depending on the probability of occurrence of events	flow is based on cause-and-effect relationships

contract alone is insufficient for programming; hence, the existence of "application architectures" during realization that address the same issues as queuing and causality. For example, realization constructs from IT include event, scenario, and creation charts (Walden and Nerson 1995). Of course, there are many more such constructs depending on the IT paradigm chosen; however, each is some form of a process, queuing-process, or causality diagram—that is, each describes flows, the effects of time, events, and causality. Also, at yet a lower level of refinement, realization includes the identification of tool subtype instances necessary for coding. For example, in the above section we identified a specific type of relational database technology (i.e., DB2).

Realization, then, serves to modulate both execution and alignment. It is during realization that specifications meet reality, and of course, alignment among the related specifications is fine-tuned in terms of their structural characteristics.

For example, consider the alignment between the process and information molecules illustrated in Figure 8–7. In this example, a lateral structure called *investment team* (in the process molecule) is specified and aligned with functional structure *equity* and *bond departments* (in the information molecule). Alignment is effectively realized if members of the *investment team* are derived from the *equity* and *bond departments*. That is to say, alignment involves two separate tasks: aligning behaviors (the above alignment stage) and configuring their realized structures (this stage—the realization stage).

Configuration is perhaps the most difficult form of realization—realizing alignment threads. This is where conflict among different perspectives must be resolved, or implementation will probably fail. It does not make sense to specify, no matter how desirable, a lateral structure (such as a team) if the appropriate members cannot be assembled from their respective departments.

EXECUTION LAYER

Purpose: Render, monitor, and adjust the results of implementation

Measure of organizational effectiveness

Key deliverables: Manifest contract postcondition

The execution layer is characterized by the performance of molecules—the delivery of corresponding postconditions. From an architectural viewpoint, OE is defined as the level of agreement between contract specifications for molecules (i.e., the postconditions) and the actual performance of the molecules.

For a process molecule, this may be a product or service. The performance of the molecule is usually characterized by adherence to the contract specification (delivery of a service or product meeting stated specifications), as well as meeting desired emergent properties of the molecule (e.g., reduced cycle time for a process molecule).

For example, consider executing the information contract discussed in the refinement example above. It requires refinement in the tool layer through transformation into structure: writing and executing a series of computer commands. That is to say, operationalizing an information contract requires the transformation of data and behavior specifications into structures (i.e., code and database structures) that represent the corresponding implementation. The processing of the code and data structures represents the execution of the corresponding information contract.

A key to the success of any architecture is the monitoring and assessment of the execution results. For example, execution of the more amorphous molecules, such as culture or learning, results in changed behavior patterns—e.g., a new world view among employees in the culture molecule. This may, in turn, require further adjustments in, say, the realization phase (e.g., implementation plan) before the desired behaviors (i.e., the performance of the contract) are fulfilled.

This may be said for any molecule contract—execution identifies the relative success of implementation, which in turn, may necessitate adjustments to molecule refinement, specification, alignment with other molecules, or realization.

8.4 DESIGN AND ARCHITECTURE INTERDEPENDENCE

Managers and planners design individual domains according to some design process appropriate for the domain in question—e.g., a particular BPR approach for process improvement. The processes are interrelated with the architectural framework of the organization.

In the OM framework, there is correspondence between the OM refinement model and the separate design approaches to structure, culture, business processes, and so on. The OM architectural framework is *methodology-independent*. This permits it to support a variety of design approaches for each domain. For example, Davenport (1993) has proposed a framework for business process reengineering that centers on five stages. A layer in the OM refinement model supports each of these stages. This is shown in Table 8–2.

The Davenport BPR stages are not sequential, and this is reflected in the sequence of corresponding OM layers in the above table. Also, the BPR stages, as

TABLE 8–2   OM REFINEMENT SUPPORT FOR THE DAVENPORT BPR PROCESS

Davenport BPR Stage	OM Refinement Model Layer
Identifying processes for innovation	Specification and alignment
Identifying change levers	Scoping/elaboration and alignment
Developing process visions	Baseline and alignment
Understanding existing processes	Specification and realization
Designing and prototyping the new process	Specification, alignment, realization, and execution

with process improvement generally, are iterations of each other, and similarly, recall from above that each layer in the OM refinement model is both deliberate and emergent.

As another example, consider how the OM refinement model supports the design of organizational structure and several other domains. As with BPR, there are innumerable approaches. For instance, let us examine the approach Galbraith uses to design organizations (Galbraith 1995). This is illustrated in Table 8–3.

Note that to fully implement the Galbraith approach, we are not confined to "structure" but must include elements of strategy, process, people, and information. This is really a form of "organization design." In effect, we must apply the OM refinement model to various molecules at different stages of refinement.

8.5 A SUMMARY OF THE OM DESIGN PROCESS

Table 8–4 is a summary of the OM design process.

TABLE 8–3   OM REFINEMENT SUPPORT FOR THE GALBRAITH DESIGN PROCESS

Galbraith Design Stage	OM Refinement Model Layer
Identify strategy	Baseline, scoping/elaboration, and specification
Identify structure	Specification and alignment
Identify key business processes	Specification and alignment
Identify key people	Realization
Identify roles and responsibilities of key people	Specification, alignment, and realization
Identify and design information systems	Specification and alignment
Identify and design performance measures and rewards	Specification, alignment, and realization
Training and development of people	Alignment, realization, and execution
Identify and design career paths	Realization and execution

TABLE 8–4   THE OM DESIGN PROCESS

Stage/layer	Purpose	Deliverables
Baseline	Identify organizational context	Identify socio-cultural invariants. Establish organization invariants. Create a layered architecture of relevant constructs
Scope and elaboration	Designate and refine domains Identify invariant overrides	Identify and refine molecules. Invariant overrides.
Specification	Specify current and desired behaviors	Molecule domain and component contract instantiations
Alignment	Establish context between domains (i.e., alignment between behaviors)	Re-instantiation of molecules to establish consistency, and compatibility among domain and component specifications
Realization	Operationalize aligned behaviors	Identify structural properties and operationalized characteristics—flow, timing, sequencing, queuing, cause-and-effect relationships. Structural configuration.
Execution	Monitor execution of molecules	Monitor contract postconditions (i.e., OE)
Feedback and Engagement	Dynamic alignment among domains	Adjustment of all above deliverables

8.6 CORE CONCEPTS

Refinement	Refinement path
Managerial choice	OM refinement model
Instantiation	Baseline layer
Scope and elaboration layer	Specification layer
Alignment layer	Realization layer
Execution layer	Organization invariant
Business rules	Invariant overrides
Realizing alignment threads	Architectural interdependence
Feedback	Engagement

Realization diagrams: process, queuing-process, and causality

CHAPTER 9

ORGANIZATIONAL PATTERNS

9.1 ORGANIZATIONAL PATTERNS AND CHANGE

Let us imagine we are driving an automobile. We come to a traffic light and notice that it is amber. What happens next? The light turns red. We expect it to turn red, and not green, because we have been conditioned to respond in a particular way to a specific pattern.

Organizations have patterns, too. These recurring behaviors are not as easy to recognize as traffic light patterns. Nevertheless, we know of such patterns by observing their emergent characteristics. When automobile executives, analysts, and customers say that Toyota manufactures high-quality automobiles, are they not, in fact, recognizing a characteristic associated with a pattern of organizational "fit"? When employees at Hewlett-Packard exhibit uncommon loyalty, are they not witnessing the consequences of a pattern of culture and internal fit? The same, of course, may be said of companies that manufacture poor quality automobiles, or who have disaffected employees. From well-defined patterns flow very clear and predictable behaviors and characteristics—desirable or not-so-desirable. In contrast, other organizations have no distinctive characteristics and operate in a quagmire. Their patterns are as blurred as their reputations.

As stated by Miles and Snow (1994): "How does a successful company go about putting together its particular package of essential organizational ingredients? What's involved in devising an effective strategy, organizing to pursue that strategy, and so on? There are no simple answers to these questions . . . Nevertheless, over the course of business history, many companies have achieved continued success—enough, in fact, to reveal a pattern in how success develops. To understand this pattern, we believe it is useful to think of success as achieving fit. Fit is both state and process. That is, if one were to take a snapshot of a successful company at a given point in time, the picture would show a strong external fit between the company and its environment . . . The same snapshot would also show a strong internal fit; that is, the organization's structure, processes, and managerial ideology would support the firm's strategy."

WHY STUDY ORGANIZATIONAL PATTERNS?

Patterns are useful. They help us organize and integrate knowledge at the organizational level. The characteristics evidenced by both successful and not-so-successful organizations are a consequence of their underlying patterns—

predictable behaviors that represent the level of fit within and among organizational domains. Simply stated, we study organizational patterns to avoid failure and achieve success.

Discovering patterns is an exercise in understanding architecture. In this book, we have defined a series of organizational patterns. Each is a representation of a domain called an organization molecule—a collection of constructs that can be formulated, implemented, and managed. Each molecule is a pattern corresponding to a domain, such as culture, process, strategy, or information. When we align molecules, we build more complex patterns representing collections of domains.

The organizational patterns associated with domains, or collections thereof, are responsible for the emergent properties that characterize success. These emergent characteristics are self-reinforcing—for instance, behavior patterns in organizations that create high employee loyalty attract people with a proclivity for allegiance. Therefore, the emergent properties associated with patterns are both a *consequence* and a *goal* of design.

For example, the characteristics mentioned above (i.e., product quality and employee loyalty) are emergent properties associated with complex arrangements of organizational components—that is, organizational patterns. The challenge of organizational design is that, while the emergent properties themselves are recognizable, the same can not be said of their underlying patterns. In fact, the patterns responsible for the emergent characteristics of an organization are often hidden from observer and participant alike. This is illustrated in Figure 9–1.

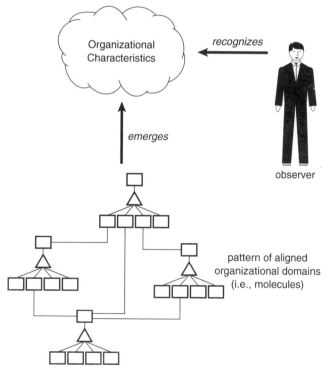

FIGURE 9–1   Emergent Characteristics of Organizational Patterns

Design practice too often focuses on the visible emergent properties of an organization, while ignoring the underlying pattern—somewhat analogous to a physician treating the symptoms and ignoring the disease. If an organizational domain is addressed, it typically is a fragmented piece of the whole. The entire pattern—each domain and its alignment threads—is almost never considered or even known to exist.

The *nature* of an emergent characteristic is determined by its pattern—a molecule, or a collection of molecules—while its *clarity* is defined by the level of alignment in that underlying pattern. For example, *cycle time* is an emergent property that is associated with the process molecule. During a BPR effort, the *level* of reduction in cycle time is a function of the specification of the process molecule, and its *degree of alignment* with corresponding constituents.

Emergent characteristics vary in complexity, as do their underlying patterns. Cycle time is an emergent property associated with a "simple" organizational pattern represented with a process molecule. In contrast, employee loyalty is more complex—it is an emergent property of the human and culture domains. Still other emergent characteristics are very complex—for example, competitiveness and inventiveness. These emergent properties are associated with complex patterns of several molecules. In this chapter, we will analyze and describe both simple and complex organizational patterns.

ORGANIZATIONAL ARCHITECTURE AND CHANGE

As we align the patterns of organizational molecules, an organizational architecture-in-the-large is formed. Organizational architecture, then, is a complex pattern—a pattern of patterns that will exhibit characteristics that are both a cause and consequence of organizational success.

> Organizational patterns exhibit clear characteristics. When we put these patterns together, we create organizational architecture-in-the-large, the properties of which determine organizational success.

Designing organizations includes instantiating, aligning, and operationalizing molecules. The result is an organization with emergent characteristics that, on the surface, identify a successful or unsuccessful organization. At a lower level of detail, these characteristics identify the level of pattern formation within the organization itself. To the knowledgeable designer, they point to the patterns themselves, identifying the internal levers that need to be pulled if the organization is to change direction and improve effectiveness. The process of architecture and strategy formation, then, involves identifying desired emergent characteristics and their underlying patterns, followed by the necessary instantiation and alignment activities. *Organizational change involves both strategy and architecture—moving from one instantiated pattern to another.*

9.2 PATTERN FORMATION

Patterns are associated with two separate but interrelated dimensions. The first concerns *process development*. An idea may initially be *unformed* or only vaguely understood. As we fill in the details, it becomes more definite. As we continue the design, our initial idea becomes more concrete. As we execute our design, it becomes still more defined. Each successive stage is part of operationalizing an idea into something more tangible. In previous chapters, we have referred to this process as *crystallization*.

To achieve organizational success, the emergent characteristics associated with patterns must be *seen*—by employees, by customers, by independent analysts. Along each stage of crystallization, then, the pattern must be made *evident*; otherwise, we will never know of its existence. We refer to the *visibility* of a pattern as its *manifest representation*. Figure 9–2 illustrates the association between crystallization and manifest representation, and its relationship to pattern formation.

Unformed ideas are neither visible (i.e., manifest), nor operationalized (i.e., crystallized). This characterizes the initial planning phase of a new idea or strategy (lower left quadrant in Figure 9–2).

Patterns are *partially formed* when either explicitly specified during the early stages of development (upper left quadrant in Figure 9–2), or, if not specified, through their execution (lower right quadrant). Organizations have plenty of both types of partially formed patterns. For example, in the case of information systems, "manifest/not developed" (i.e., upper left quadrant) systems abound. Any such system, sometimes called "shelfware," is typically a set of detailed requirements and specifications that are not implemented.

In contrast, many domains are not explicitly understood, yet they execute in the organization as partially formed patterns (i.e., lower right quadrant). This is quite common with an organization's culture. This pattern tends to be partially formed since its characteristics are rarely explicit (i.e., manifest), or well-understood.

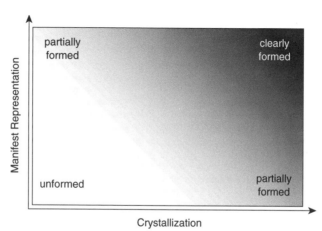

FIGURE 9–2   Pattern Formation

When properties are *operationalized* and made *explicit*, we refer to the pattern as *clearly formed*. Clearly formed patterns are executing behaviors with distinct and visible characteristics. These characteristics may be desirable (e.g., high product quality, high employee loyalty) or may not be desirable (e.g., low product quality, disaffected employees). A clearly formed pattern, then, is fully developed and operationalized, with visible characteristics.

ORGANIZATIONAL PATTERNS

Organizational patterns exist in OT. Many are fully formed patterns with definite characteristics. For example, recall from Chapter 3 that Henry Mintzberg has defined five generic structure types—in effect, patterns of structure with corresponding behaviors. These generic structure patterns have explicit characteristics—for example, the adhocracy is characterized by horizontal information linkages, complex and dynamic environments, low formalization, and many other specific characteristics that qualify this structural pattern as clearly formed. Observe that Mintzberg has actually defined a *complex organizational pattern*, though traditionally defined as "generic structure," that includes several domains—structure, environment, information, power, etc.

In contrast, many other organizational patterns are not very explicit, that is, not easily specified, operationalized, and measured. Michael Porter's generic strategies (i.e., low cost, differentiation, niche) are examples of partial patterns. Each strategy type is characterized by general properties that distinguish one strategy type from another—for example, "signaling criteria" for differentiation strategies (see Porter 1985). For the most part, however, the distinguishing characteristics of each generic strategy are only partially described in terms of an organization's architecture.

In Chapter 6, we introduced several organizational patterns—organization molecules. Each molecule is a generic pattern representative of its domain. When instantiated, a specific pattern is defined. If the molecule is aligned, the pattern becomes more manifest; that is, the organization's domains reinforce each other. If executed, we say the pattern is fully formed. However, if the molecule is misaligned, the pattern can never fully form since at least one, or perhaps several, domains contradict and work against each other. When domains are not aligned, their characteristics never become fully visible (i.e., manifest), and therefore, even if implemented, the pattern is only partially formed (lower right quadrant in Figure 9–2).

When alignment and execution extend to several domains (i.e., molecules), the entire arrangement of molecules, as a single collection, becomes manifest, and we say that a complex pattern forms. Such complex patterns that exhibit important and enduring organizational characteristics are generally acknowledged as being responsible for success. These characteristics (that emerge from complex patterns) include quality, loyalty, competitiveness, marketing-fit, structural-fit, and so on.

THE PROCESS OF PATTERN FORMATION

Patterns come into being through *planning*, *emergence*, or a combination of the two. That is to say, patterns are either deliberately designed (i.e., prescriptive), or arise through performance (i.e., descriptive). This is illustrated in Figure 9–3.

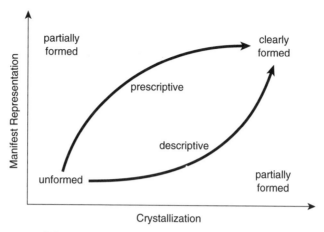

FIGURE 9–3   The Process of Pattern Formation

When patterns are planned (i.e., deliberate), their properties become apparent (i.e., manifest) *early* in their development. Organizational domains representative of the hard architecture lend themselves to planning through early specification of desired characteristics in corresponding molecule contracts.

Note that hard domains such as computer information systems lend themselves to specification; however, this in no way ensures that they will indeed be planned. We have all witnessed the development of an information system that seems to start with programming (i.e., realization). In effect, there is little analysis as the information system emerges through implementation.

The domains that form the soft architecture of an organization, such as culture and learning, tend to develop and become manifest through *emergence*. They are rarely planned. One of the contributions of OM is that we provide generic models (i.e., molecules) for each of these domains—soft as well as hard—so that pattern domains may be planned, rather than left to chance through emergence.

However, even if specified early in their development, characteristics associated with soft domains may only be implied in a relational contract. For example, the employment contract between a professional and an organization is vague in many respects—job responsibilities, for instance. However, during realization and certainly during execution, most ambiguity is removed, and the relational contract becomes more manifest. The manifest relational contract reinforces or undermines its underlying assumptions.

An important architectural consideration is the relationship between hard and soft patterns. Each does not exist in isolation from the other. In Chapter 7, we stated that the hard architecture of an organization may *enable* its soft architecture, while the soft architecture *facilitates (or retards)* the effective application of the hard. Organizational patterns, particularly those that are complex and not easily imitated, contain both hard and soft domains (i.e., molecules). This leads to three important design applications of the OM architecture:

1. The first is *effective alignment* among domains. As a quick glance at the molecules in Chapter 6 reveals, alignment involves elements of both hard and soft organizational pieces.

2. We may *raise* the manifest representation of the soft architectural domains by making each more explicit and the entire pattern more effective. For example, we may create specifications for soft domains such as culture and learning. This is effected through the instantiation of corresponding molecule contracts. These contracts contain assertions and therefore make the domain more manifest. Even in the case of a relational contract, assertions for assumptions and implications may be formalized in the form of invariants, pre-, and postconditions. This facilitates the planning of soft domains, and their integration into an entire organizational architecture.

3. Domain specification and alignment enables the design of *complex patterns* containing elements of both hard and soft architectures. The success of organizations such as Toyota and Hewlett-Packard is largely attributed to these complex patterns of organizational architecture.

9.3 THE STAGES OF PATTERN FORMATION

The process of *crystallization* takes place gradually in steps. At each step there is some amount of partial crystallization. Each step is a transition from a relatively more abstract state to a relatively more concrete state. It thus involves gradual concretization.

Evidently, here we are talking about different levels of abstraction. Recall that abstraction is the principle of "ignoring those aspects of a subject that are not relevant to the current purpose in order to concentrate more fully on those that are." Concretization involves filling in the details that have been left out. Also, these details get organized in an increasingly formalized manner. That is, though we separate the dimensions of crystallization and manifest representation for ease of understanding, both are, in fact, intertwined.

As a result, the amount of formalization in the representation as a whole goes on increasing as we proceed through the different levels of crystallization. Naturally, the relationships between the component details get fixed. They become static as if they are cast in stone. Once they have lost their dynamicity in the process, it is difficult to change them. Any change can be possible only by retracing the process of crystallization backwards, thereby going to a less concrete state, and re-crystallizing.

Early Vs. Late Manifestation

The OM design process described in Chapter 8 steps the designer through successive stages of crystallization. If the process emphasizes the planned (as opposed to emergent) approach to crystallization, the OM design is characterized by the *early* manifest representation of domains. If the process emphasizes emergence, manifest representation will be *late*.

A concern that naturally arises is the need for a formal approach to early crystallization: "Must every domain be planned? Isn't emergence sufficient?"

The short answer is that manifest representation, and therefore the intentions of the designer, will be more apparent if deliberately planned. Clarity builds on itself; the earlier and higher the level of manifest representation, the more unequivocal the final pattern. The exercise of specification raises the manifest representation level early in the design process, and therefore the final design will be more clearly formed than otherwise.

Anecdotal evidence suggests the importance of specification. Would a manufacturer rely on "goals" in place of rigorous specifications to build an automobile? The same may be said of developing information systems—experience has shown the IT professional that even detailed "goals" are not sufficient for developing complex software. In each case, some form of specification is required; furthermore, the richer the specification schema, the higher the level of manifest representation (i.e., the clearer the requirements), and the more likely the final outcome will be successful.

In contrast, late manifest representation postpones the application of knowledge in the crystallization process. This has the benefits of promoting wider application of knowledge downstream and greater organizational flexibility and learning. Late manifest representation is best when there is a requirement for user/expert knowledge, or when relational contracting is operational.

VISUALIZATION AND THE PROCESS OF CRYSTALLIZATION

During the early stages of crystallization—significant, even inspirational—change may be formulated. Opportunities for significant change are present during the fluid state that characterizes early crystallization. However, once crystallization has taken hold, real change becomes notably more difficult—involving both the undoing and re-implementation of design decisions.

> Change is a function of dynamicity, which in turn, is a function of early crsytallization.

Stepping through the OM design process is an exercise in *visualization*. Visualization is somewhat like composing a symphony or painting a picture. The artist starts with an image—the final rendering is visualized even if not fully formed. As the artist fills in the image, the composition begins to take form. The artist shapes according to the image, but the form molds the image, too. Planned and emergent, the molded image is a product of visualization.

Visualization applies to organizational design as well. Visualization is *not* a vision statement. Rather, it is a collection of decisions by which the strategic intent of management may be interwoven into the fabric of an organization's architecture. Typically, strategic intent is defined as the long-term ambition of the business. From an organizational design viewpoint, strategic intent means the *desired emergent characteristics* of the organization.

> Visualization is the process that interweaves strategic intent, architecture, and change

Starting with the cultural context of an organization, the interaction patterns among organizations, people, and society identify an organization's invariants. We have seen that the OM layers present a dramatic departure in thinking. In our approach, the philosophy and layers associated with an organization mark only the *beginning* of modeling—the initial stages of visualization.

Visualization, then, is crafted by accounting for desired emergent characteristics, culture, and the patterns of behavior representing domains—all the elements that together represent organizational architecture—and the strategy of change.

9.4 GRANULARITY

Patterns exist at every level of the organization. Levels have a certain granularity, which is preserved in their patterns.

Patterns are "things", not just ideas. They can be seen, felt, handled, and operated upon. In other words, they have a manifest form. They can be observed and recognized by anyone. They do not lie in the conceptual or subjective domain of human thought; rather, they lie in the objective domain of reality. They are part of the objective world.

This is not to say that a pattern is solely a set of executing behaviors. Rather, a pattern exists at every stage of crystallization (e.g., specification), and at every level of granularity in the organization. The more manifest is its representation, the more the pattern emerges and becomes recognizable—whether at a high or low level of granularity. For example, an information *specification* may be represented by (1) a natural language, (2) a series of pictures such as data flow diagrams, (3) a contract with structured language assertions, and (4) a contract with formal methods such as "Z." Each specification technique in the above series represents a more manifest, and therefore, clearer pattern.

Pattern Abstraction

Patterns exist in various forms. The highest level of granularity is the *organizational pattern*. This addresses the mix of socio-cultural context and organizational constructs we have been discussing in this book. When we move to a lower level of granularity, we discover *business patterns*—the mix of products and markets that flows from organizational patterns. At still lower levels of granularity there exist *service patterns*, and finally *information patterns*. Service and information patterns represent the "nitty-gritty" of business that an organization must deal with on a day-to-day basis. Naturally, there is no clear line that identifies where one type of pattern ends and another begins. *Each level is a set of behaviors that interconnects to behaviors of other levels.* This is illustrated in Figure 9–4.

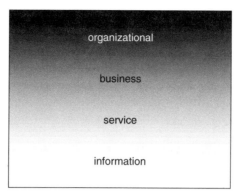

FIGURE 9–4   Levels of Abstraction in Patterns

ORGANIZATIONAL PATTERNS

Organizational patterns constitute the energy of an organization. This should be of great concern to management because these patterns govern lower level business patterns. However, most managers do not even recognize the existence of organization-level patterns. They think success rests solely on business patterns. While this may be true in the short term, sustained success can be accomplished only within an organizational context that creates *opportunities* for effective business patterns. Examples of organizational patterns include domains such as strategy, culture, process, and in fact, the layered organization models as well as each of the molecules we have been discussing in this book. Also, organizational patterns include *combinations* of domains (molecules) that combine to form complex patterns. Examples of complex organizational patterns include competitiveness, marketing-fit, continuous improvement, and inventiveness. Understanding, building, and integrating such patterns is known as organizational architecture.

> Organizational patterns are manifestations of organization invariants, layers of organizational constructs, organization molecules, and complex arrangements of molecules, the collection of which constitutes organizational architecture.

For example, Toyota is well-known for the assembly quality of its automobiles. This is an emergent characteristic associated with complex organizational patterns that have developed over several decades—in particular, those of the quality, continuous improvement, marketing, and process domains. The same may be said of Hewlett-Packard with respect to employee loyalty. Each organization is distinguished by characteristics that create opportunities for sustained success. These characteristics exist as a consequence of the patterns that constitute an organization's architecture.

BUSINESS PATTERNS

Business patterns comprise an organization's mix of products and markets. This is largely related to "external fit"—heuristics and associations corresponding to a complex mix of organizational domains, particularly the following:

- Business processes and products
- Market segments
- Market condition, penetration, and maturity
- Environmental complexity—competitors, geographic scope, cultural diversity, and, naturally, the alignment threads among the above

For example, BMW markets a distinctive type of automobile in a particular market niche. General Motors, in contrast, manufactures and markets a broader range of automobiles to a wide variety of customers. Each organization has created a very different business pattern. An organization's business patterns combine to form its business architecture.

SERVICE PATTERNS

Service patterns describe the organization of work in an organization. A casual glance at an organization's activities reveals an abundance of service patterns, such as, *hiring an employee, a field repair to an appliance, issuing an insurance policy, writing a computer program,* and so on. Each is a set of activities, often repeated innumerable times, that embodies the business of an organization. Though an organization's *business rules* exist in all patterns, they are typically "seen" in service and information patterns. Representing business rules and work describing the behavior and structure of a service pattern is known as a *service,* or a *business model.*

It is important to note that different service patterns often share the same activities and information. For example, a *change in the life-style* of an employee (e.g., new child, divorce, etc.) is a *business event* that triggers a set of business tasks and information operations pertinent to such concerns as number of dependents, and health insurance. When the employee was originally hired (a different service pattern—*hiring an employee),* several tasks most likely addressed these same issues of dependents and insurance, as well as several others. Thus, one service pattern *(hiring an employee)* shares tasks and information with other service patterns *(a change in life-style).* Each set of tasks and underlying information patterns, as a collection, may be seen as a separate service pattern responding to a given business event.

The elements associated with service patterns—processes, events, business rules, customers, outcomes—may be clearly defined, and interconnected to a business and information architecture. Service patterns, then, are fragments of business processes—tasks and work cycles—and associated alignment threads. Of course, service patterns may be directly modeled with the process molecule.

INFORMATION PATTERNS

Information patterns concern information systems that support, enable, or transform higher level patterns. Typically, information patterns include both logical (technology-independent) and physical (technology-specific) dimensions. The collection of specifications and designs for an information pattern is known as an *information model*. Information patterns and their supporting frameworks (e.g., hardware, software, communication networks, documents) constitute an information architecture.

Examples of information patterns exist in every information system. For instance, the notion of subtyping is a common generic pattern that exists in both logical and physical models, and whose properties (e.g., inheritance) are made manifest in code. As another example, consider a "trivial" physical level information pattern—date fields six characters long (as opposed to eight characters and associated code). This simple pattern has the potential to create havoc in the year 2000, and may cost organizations billions of dollars to rectify—to change a relatively simple, physical information pattern from six to eight characters.

9.5 THE PATTERN CONTINUUM

Observe that in both pattern formation and granularity (Figures 9–2 and 9–4), we have used a shaded background to represent the changing level of pattern gradation which we call the *pattern continuum*. This may be a continuum of development as patterns emerge in the organization, or a continuum of pattern types where the line between, say, a business and a service pattern, is blurred. This is invariably the case: Patterns rarely have well-defined boundaries, only a complex web of interconnected behaviors.

As a consequence of the gradation in granularity of the continuum, we sometimes have difficulty distinguishing one type from another. This is to be expected. Real organizations exhibit patterns of all types, and each type is intertwined with another. As designers, we focus on a particular type of pattern (i.e., level of abstraction) to address a specific concern or opportunity. However, the effectiveness of a pattern is determined by its interconnectivity to other patterns.

ORGANIZATIONAL EFFECTIVENESS AND THE PATTERN CONTINUUM

As part of the OM design process, we interconnect a given pattern type with other types. For example, at a high level of abstraction, the process molecule describes an organization level technology chain (i.e., an organization level business process) that may be aligned with other domains to form complex organizational patterns. At a lower level of granularity, the same process molecule specifies the products, customers, and processes that constitute an organization's business architecture. At yet a lower level, that process molecule specifies the detailed tasks and work cycles which we have called service patterns. At a still further level of decomposition, we may specify the information content of business tasks to form information patterns. In summary, each level of *abstraction* describes the same organizational domain (i.e., process) at different levels of pattern granularity.

AN EXAMPLE FROM IT

Let us consider the lowest level of abstraction—the information pattern. We have suggested designing an information pattern in the context of its corresponding service pattern—in essence, creating different levels of abstraction within the pattern continuum. This establishes interconnectivity between information systems and the business processes and architecture of an organization.

In contrast, let us consider traditional approaches to information systems development (e.g., information engineering). They typically align information systems with an organization's business functions. These popular "stove-pipe" models have *no logical mechanism* for alignment with the characteristics associated with service and information patterns: events, services, customers, information, or outcomes. Hence, alignment between functions and other levels of abstraction in the pattern continuum is vague and inexact at best.

An explanation for the waning utility of information engineering is that information systems are developed within a functional context, and consequently cannot connect to an organization's business processes, markets, customers, products, and other high-level business and organizational patterns. Traditional approaches *isolate* information patterns from other patterns in the organization. In effect, the pattern continuum cannot form, and thus, organizational effectiveness is diminished. The goal of good design, then, is to establish organizational context by designing interconnectivity through all levels of the pattern continuum.

9.6 ORGANIZATION MOLECULES AND PATTERN FORMATION

Generally, we may say that explicitness is a function of the organizational domain (i.e., the molecule). Certain areas of the organization seem more clearly defined than others. Learning, for example, has a slippery connotation that, say, an information system does not have. Furthermore, timing is important—are we in the initial stages of crystallization, or are we further along in development? We would naturally expect, that as we move closer to implementation, the outcome will become clearer.

For example, an information contract may be precisely specified during the specification stage; a business process contract usually becomes more explicit somewhat later during development, strategy contracts still later, and finally, culture contracts may never be fully explicit. Furthermore, clarity is a continuum; we cannot say when a particular contract for a given domain becomes explicit—only that it becomes more so during crystallization. This is illustrated in Figure 9–5.

Observe that there exists a *pattern gap*—a difference in manifest representation between molecules at *every* stage of crystallization. A wider gap exists at the beginning than at the end of crystallization. Furthermore, the patterns associated

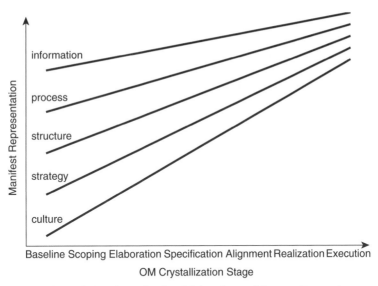

FIGURE 9–5   Organization Molecules and Pattern Formation

with "hard" molecules are more fully formed at every stage of crystallization than those that are "soft." Even when fully formed, the patterns associated with soft domains such as culture are less manifest that those of hard domains such as information. Each of these observations derives from the fact that hard domains may be specified with precise contracts, while soft domains are inherently imprecise (e.g., relational contracts).

Standard practice with hard domains—information, for example—is to attempt some form of specification during the early stages of crystallization. In contrast, soft domains such as culture are almost never specified during the early stages of development. At most, there is some vague idea of a cultural "goal." An actual specification is rarely attempted. Hence, there is a wide pattern gap during the early phases of crystallization.

During development, refinement activities are applied to domains of all types, and naturally, given the initial lack of rigor with the soft domains, the pattern gap closes. However, the inherent imprecision of the soft domains prevents them from ever being as manifest as the hard domains.

This imprecision carries through into execution. Here, too, the pattern gap narrows, but never closes completely. Even during execution, soft domains such as culture operate on assumptions and implicit understandings. Hence, fully manifest culture is never as explicit as fully manifest information.

How Techniques Affect Manifest Representation

Organizational domains are characterized by differing design techniques. Naturally, there are differences between domains—designing information systems, business processes, strategy, culture, and so on, require different design artifacts.

However, as we have argued throughout this book, the initial stages of crystallization in OM are common: determining baseline constructs and organization invariants, and developing contract specifications of domain behavior. It is only during realization that there is a divergence in the design artifacts.

A second difference exists *within* domains. Several domains such as information and process are represented with a variety of techniques. Each set of techniques leads the designer through the various stages of crystallization, but, depending on the set chosen, this is a substantial difference in clarity, that is, manifest representation.

AN EXAMPLE—INFORMATION PATTERNS

For example, during specification of an information domain, structured constructs such as data flow diagrams are more precise than descriptive text, but less so that those of contracts. Formal methods are still more precise. In each case, we are *increasing* the level of manifest representation by using increasingly formal techniques during the specification stage. This is illustrated in Figure 9–6.

Observe that differences in techniques create a pattern gap throughout the entire crystallization process. That is, the more rigorous the technique the more manifest the domain. Note: To simplify the discussion, we have used the four *specification* techniques illustrated in Figure 9–6 as a metaphor for the entire crystallization process. For example, data flow diagrams are used during the specification stage while an assortment of other structured techniques are used during realization. However, the metaphor holds: Approaches to software development that emphasize imprecise specifications carry that imprecision through later stages of development. That is, software development itself follows a pattern—each technique or diagram used embodies a philosophy, and that philosophy is

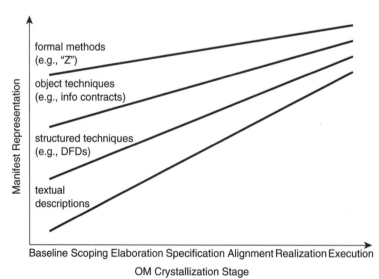

FIGURE 9–6   Information Techniques and Pattern Formation

followed during each stage of crystallization. Precise or imprecise specification techniques are typically followed by correspondingly similar implementation techniques.

Note also that the pattern gap continues to exist through execution. We have all seen this in the field: Information systems developed with precise techniques are more likely to behave as intended than those developed with textual descriptions of requirements.

AN EXAMPLE—BUSINESS PROCESS PATTERNS

The association between technique, manifest representation, and the resulting pattern formation is not confined to information, but extends to all domains. As another example, let us consider process design. Business process design may follow a series of crystallization stages, each with a different set of techniques. Popular techniques typically have no concept of formal specification; they use only a vague description of goals. Even during the realization stage, the popular approaches employ the process diagram—a simple workflow schema—to build IS and SHOULD maps. More sophisticated realization diagrams—*queuing-process* diagrams that record the effects of time, and *causality* diagrams that show cause-and-effect associations—are not widely used. Each of the popular approaches, therefore, neglects rigorous specification and alignment, and designs with incomplete process diagrams.

The results, of course, are unclear constraints on business processes (e.g., no specification of organization invariant and business rules), less interconnectivity with other domains (e.g., information, structure, people), resulting in less manifest representation than otherwise, and therefore, "reengineered" processes that are far less integrated and effective than envisioned.

Figure 9–7 illustrates the effect of different design techniques on manifest representation (i.e., the clarity of the intent), and the resulting pattern gap. The pattern gap may be seen as a measure of the relative effectiveness of different design approaches. Evidently, the richer the artifacts of design, the more manifest its representation, the clearer the intentions of the designer, and the more successful the process design effort.

The above illustrations for the information and process domains apply equally to all domains. The more rigorous the techniques employed, the clearer the formation of the corresponding pattern, and finally, the more manifest its emergent characteristics.

THE COSTS ASSOCIATED WITH PATTERN GAPS

The presence of a pattern gap, and its association with the artifacts of representation, highlight another issue that each of us has seen in the field. When a given domain, say, an information system, is developed with imprecise specifications, the customer usually has to accept either less than what is expected (i.e., less manifest representation of user intentions), or an additional cost that must be expended if the pattern gap is to be closed. That is to say, the richness of design arti-

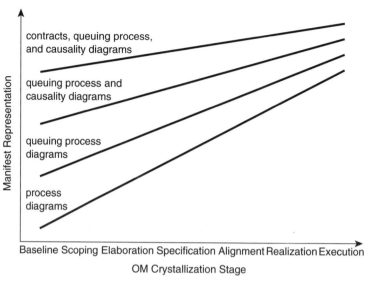

FIGURE 9–7   Process Techniques and Pattern Formation

facts is associated with the pattern gaps, the expectations of users, and the costs of adjusting those gaps.

The additional costs of closing a pattern gap takes various forms. For an information system, it may be the costs of subsequent releases of software. For a business process, however, the costs may be more substantial. To reengineer a recently reengineered process may not be feasible. The costs of using sloppy process design techniques are those associated with lost opportunities to fully leverage the BPR effort. With other domains such as culture, the costs are not so easily measured. They may come in the form of high employee turnover, or, more importantly, in lost competitiveness.

RAISING THE LEVEL OF MANIFEST REPRESENTATION

With OM, we may raise the level of explicitness during each stage of crystallization. Moreover, by creating molecules for each domain of the organization, and by using contracts to specify the behavior of each corresponding molecule, we introduce a formalism and thereby *raise* the level of manifest representation at the very start of crystallization.

Furthermore, the OM design process may be interconnected with existing approaches to designing any particular organizational domain, such as strategy, structure, process design, etc. The mix of different artifacts for each corresponding domain permits the designer to use "best in class" techniques, while applying the rigor of OM so that each domain may be aligned with another. The result is a substantially richer approach to organizational architecture and design than has previously been possible. In practice, this results in a greater level of manifest representation across the entire architecture of an organization.

There is an additional benefit to using OM. Many soft domains have never been given the rigor of a scientific approach that has customarily been applied to hard domains. What were heretofore amorphous constructs, such as learning and culture, may now be designed, often for the first time, and interconnected with other organizational domains. Furthermore, managers may do so with some sense of confidence—culture need no longer be left to the vagaries of the social sciences or to the experiences of executives. With the discipline of an integrated framework comes the *assurance* that goals may be defined, developed, interconnected, and measured.

9.7 LATTICES

Successful companies are characterized by complex patterns. These patterns exhibit clear properties—for example, competitive distinctiveness and good strategic fit. These organizational properties are long-duration characteristics that are largely responsible for sustained success. Not surprisingly, the underlying patterns responsible for such distinctive qualities are complex, not easily imitated, and depend largely on a mix of hard and soft contracts. We refer to these complex arrangements are termed *lattices*.

As with all patterns, the boundary between organizational patterns of differing complexities is blurred. Generally, simple patterns refer to instantiated molecules, while aligned molecules represent more complex patterns. Lattices are also complex patterns, but are distinguished from other organizational patterns in the following ways:

1. Lattices are sources of competitive advantage.
2. Lattices are complex patterns that are associated with specific, enduring emergent characteristics. These properties characterize successful organizations. Lattices are typically named for their distinguishing emergent property, such as *competitiveness*.

Organizational architecture includes simple patterns, lattices, and their constituent building blocks—molecules.

DESIGNING LATTICES

Building lattices is an exercise in building an enduring organizational architecture. This must be done systematically: We start with organizational philosophy and invariants, conceptualize our organization as a layered model, identify corresponding molecules, instantiate and align molecules, realize, execute, and iterate through all stages in the OM design process.

As we construct and implement molecules, alignment extends to increasingly more molecules, and eventually, complex patterns form. An instantiated molecule is a simple pattern; aligned molecules represent more complex patterns. As additional molecules are aligned, the resulting pattern becomes increasingly complex. Depending on the instantiations, the resultant emergent properties may or may not be desirable. Realizing correspondence through alignment is the technique underlying lattice development. This is illustrated in Figure 9–8.

We see evidence of the importance given to emergent properties with patterns every day. For example, business process transformation usually has as one of its goals the reduction of cycle time. Recall that cycle time is an emergent property associated with the process molecule. By using the process molecule and following the OM design process, cycle time will indeed be reduced.

The point is that the successful designer has a vision of changing a particular emergent property (e.g., cycle time), but understands that to make this happen in the real world requires a systematic approach to the specification, alignment, and execution of the constructs associated with the process molecule—process, and {human, structure, information, tool}. Only then will emergent properties such as cycle time be effected.

Accordingly, to be successful, the designer must start with the basics, and build to lattices. If you attempt the quick hit by directly designing complex patterns, you will fail as surely as a building contractor will fail if he or she builds a skyscraper without a firm foundation!

EXAMPLES OF LATTICES

Recall from Chapter 7 that we described *competitive distinctiveness* as an aligned set of specific instantiations of the eternal triangle, organization invariants, and the culture, learning, and structure molecules. This collection gives rise to an organizational characteristic known as competitive distinctiveness.

Generally, then, we argue that a collection of specific molecules manifests a specific emergent property type, such as competitiveness. When instantiated in a

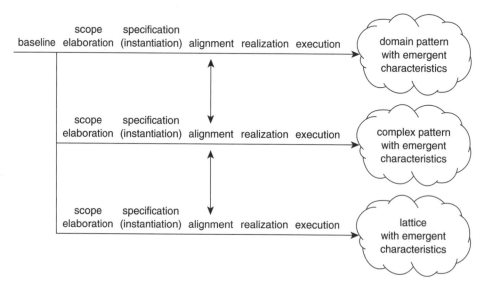

FIGURE 9–8   Constructing Organizational Patterns and Lattices
Through Incremental Alignment

particular way, the emergent property takes on a particular characteristic (i.e., an instantiation of the emergent property), such as competitive distinctiveness.

Lattices are usually named for their primary emergent property. As an example of a lattice we have discussed above, Figure 9–9 illustrates the lattice known as competitiveness.

Recall that John Kay attributed organizational success, in large part, to competitive distinctiveness. Architecturally, this is an instantiated (and aligned) competitiveness lattice. Furthermore, the instantiations are very specific, or the lattice (i.e., competitiveness) will be misaligned. When this lattice is *specifically instantiated and aligned, the pattern itself becomes instantiated*—that is, it will have the *emergent* property of *distinctiveness*. Competitive distinctiveness is illustrated in Figure 9–10.

PATTERN FIT AND MISFIT

The level of emergence of an organizational characteristic (e.g., distinctiveness) is proportional to the level of fit in its underlying lattice—the number of construct instantiations (i.e., specific design decisions) that reinforce each other. This level of visibility is a function of the level of fit among constructs in the corresponding lattice.

When patterns are aligned with specific instantiations, the special properties we have been discussing begin to emerge. A failure to understand the impact of alignment has led organizations to design constructs in isolation from one

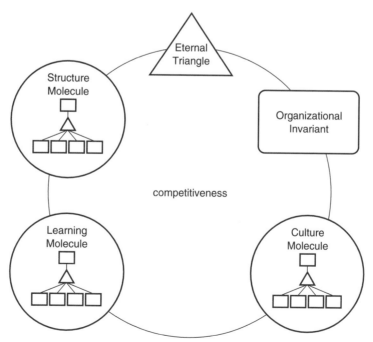

FIGURE 9–9   The Competitiveness Lattice

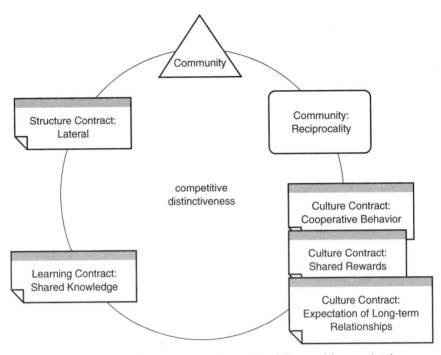

FIGURE 9–10   Distinctiveness: An Instantiated Competitiveness Lattice

another. Consequently, despite the best intentions, managers create (i.e., plan) patterns containing instantiations that contradict and work against each other. The result, of course, is the absence of desirable emergent properties. An example of "planned" fit and misfit for the competitiveness pattern appears in Table 9–1.

The illustration of competitive misfit is quite common in organizations. Managers *intend* to have cooperative behavior and knowledge sharing, *and* individual rewards, functional structures, and short-term employees. This typical plan is composed of design decisions (i.e., construct instantiations) that work against each other. Accordingly, distinctiveness rarely or only incompletely emerges.

TABLE 9–1   COMPETITIVE FIT AND MISFIT

Organizational Construct	Planned Contracts Resulting in Competitive Fit (distinctiveness)	Planned Contracts Resulting in Competitive Misfit (no emergent characteristic)
Eternal triangle	Community	Individualism
Org. Invariant	Reciprocity	Individual rewards
Culture	Cooperative behavior	Cooperative behavior
	Shared rewards	Individual rewards
	The expectation of long-term relationships	The expectation of short-term relationships
Structure	Lateral structures (e.g., teams)	Functional and lateral structures
Learning	Knowledge sharing	Knowledge sharing

This form of misfit is a classic example of management practice in many large organizations. The effectiveness of certain management or organizational practices becomes known, and subsequently is adopted as a patchwork overlay on existing arrangements. This is particularly true of such trendy areas as "team-work," "organizational learning," "knowledge management," and "culture change." The result is predictable—partial pattern formation and little distinctiveness.

EXAMPLES OF PATTERN-FIT FROM OT

John Kay has identified a generic type of competitiveness known as distinctiveness. We were able to formalize this concept by (1) identifying a generic competitiveness lattice (Figure 9–9), and (2) the corresponding instantiations that produce distinctiveness as one type of competitiveness (Figure 9–10). If any of the instantiations are not as defined, the distinctiveness characteristic would be less manifest (Table 9–1).

Similarly, Mintzberg (1983) has identified five types of structures that represent the manifest characteristic associated with a specific collection of properties. These properties may be taken as instantiations of the structure lattice. That is to say, each *collection* of lattice instantiations manifests itself in the form of a simple, machine bureaucracy, professional bureaucracy, divisionalized, or adhocratic structure. Moreover, each set of instantiations describes a pattern of fit for its corresponding structural form. In essence, Mintzberg has described five sets of aligned properties (i.e., pattern-fit), each of which represents a particular emergent characteristic of the structural-fit lattice. For example, the *machine bureaucracy* is characterized by the following properties, or instantiations of the structure-fit lattice:

- Eternal triangle: individualism
- Org. invariant: irrational, closed
- Structure: high formalization, vertical and horizontal specialization, functional form, bureaucratic
- Power: technocratic, some horizontal decentralization, significant flow of authority, top-down decision making
- Environment: simple, stable
- Information: simple systems, vertical flow of information
- Process: standardized, routine tasks
- Size: large

In describing the characteristics of each type of structure, Mintzberg has defined the appropriate fit for each set of instantiations. The above properties, for example, collectively describe the machine bureaucracy. If any of these properties were not as stated above (e.g., *low* instead of *high* formalization), the level of fit for the structural-fit pattern would be less than optimum. The resulting lattice instantiation (i.e., machine bureaucracy) would be less manifest, and therefore less effective than one with a higher level of fit.

9.8 ORGANIZATIONAL DYNAMICITY

The process of specifying, implementing, and actually moving from one pattern instantiation to another is, of course, organizational change. Knowing the direction of change and the desired effect is part of the process of strategy and organizational design. In an architectural sense, change may be thought of as the process of achieving fit—of continually changing organizational pieces and their linkages so that they work together more effectively and, consequently, create the emergent characteristics so closely associated with success.

However, we have observed that certain organizations seem better able to change than others. The ability to change is a function of the degree of alignment among organizational domains. Moreover, even with good fit, certain organizations seem better equipped to change than others. This is a function of the *specific instantiations* in an organization's architecture. The critical elements, then, in the *dynamicity* of an organization are three-fold:

1. The first is the level of alignment (i.e., fit) within and among molecules. Recall from Chapter 7 that we refer to this property—the level of correspondence between organizational constructs—as *maneuverability*. Recall, too, that maneuverability is the capability of an organization to *leverage* its components to withstand changes in its environment.

2. The second element is the set of *specific instantiations* in a given pattern or lattice. Not all organizational patterns are capable of changing underlying business patterns in the pattern continuum. Instances of one organizational pattern seem to create business architectures that are more flexible than those associated with different instances of the same organizational pattern type. Thus, *adaptive patterns* are those aligned, organizational pattern instances that have the ability to change underlying business, service, and information patterns.

3. As discussed in Section 9.3 above, dynamicity is more easily attained during the early stages of crystallization. This is a consequence of the fluid state characteristic of early design. Once implemented, the pattern is fixed; change requires *de-crystallization* back into a fluid state, new specifications and alignment (maneuverability and adaptiveness), and finally, operationalization back into a fixed state.

We, therefore, see that the organizational property of *dynamicity* contains two dimensions of pattern alignment: (1) the level of "horizontal" correspondence among domains that governs how well an organization executes in a changing environment (i.e., maneuverability), and (2) the character of the organizational domains themselves which governs how well an organization is able to change *other* patterns "vertically" in the pattern continuum—particularly its business architecture (i.e., adaptiveness). Finally, each of these dimensions is more easily established during early crystallization. This is illustrated in Figure 9–11.

For example, the competitiveness lattice described in Table 9–1 contains two sets of design instances—one producing highly recognizable distinctiveness, and

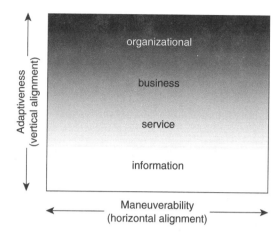

FIGURE 9–11   Organizational Dynamicity in the Pattern Continuum

the other producing much less, or no, distinctiveness. When AT&T was a utility with no competitors, its competitiveness instantiations promoted *rigidity*—deep functional structure, virtually no sharing of knowledge across functional subunits, and so on. The fit was good and *horizontal*—there was correspondence among the construct instances in the competitiveness lattice—but this was not distinctiveness. Rather, its emergent characteristic was *high-cost, effective service* that was suitable for a utility environment. Hence, AT&T was capable of withstanding changes in its technology and legal environments—it could leverage its alignment threads, and hence was maneuverable with respect to its environment.

However, AT&T's business architecture remained essentially unchanged over several decades—that is, its patterns were not adaptive, and hence, there was no *vertical* alignment. When AT&T faced competition, its competitiveness lattice, as well as other organizational patterns, *preserved* its business patterns in a *fixed state*. Its existing organizational patterns were not adaptable, and hence could not drive change to its underlying business patterns.

The lesson, here, is an important one—achieving horizontal fit is critical (i.e., maneuverability), but we must ask if the fit is adaptable. Does it promote change, or does it lock an organization into a rigid set of patterns? And do managers understand change? Do they have the wisdom to first de-crystallize before attempting new design contracts? Or do they unknowingly produce pathological change as one new rigid pattern encounters an existing one?

9.9 LEVERAGING THE LINKAGE BETWEEN ORGANIZATIONAL AND BUSINESS PATTERNS

A critical issue for an organization is the alignment of its organizational patterns and its business architecture—that is, its adaptive alignment. For example, during the 1970s and 1980s, Xerox was an organization that exhibited the desirable characteristic of *inventiveness*. Xerox Parc, the research arm of Xerox, is well known for its high-tech inventions. Yet Xerox's business architecture was entirely misaligned with this organizational pattern, and Xerox as an organization was under severe competitive pressure. Xerox could not benefit from its own inventiveness—its underlying organizational lattice was not aligned with its business architecture.

The lesson is simple, if difficult to implement. Certain desirable characteristics, and their underlying lattice patterns, can be leveraged only if aligned through all levels of the pattern continuum. Only then will their properties be capable of improving an organization's effectiveness.

The question that naturally arises concerns the technique for integration between organizational and business architectures. The key concept here is to recognize the existence of common organizational constructs across all pattern types. The primary difference is one of abstraction. At a high level of abstraction, organizational constructs are *multi-dimensional*—they cover several domains that exist at lower levels of granularity. At a low level of abstraction, they are *single-dimensional* and specific to a local context.

For example, the notion of a *product* or *service* is bound within the process molecule—product and services are postconditions of specific process contracts, and, of course, are also part of an organization's business architecture. The process molecule at one level of abstraction is an organizational pattern describing an organization's technology; at a lower level of decomposition, it is a business pattern describing its products; at still a lower level, it is a service pattern describing specific work cycles or tasks. Furthermore, the process molecule contains an information component which becomes an information pattern at the lowest level of abstraction. And so on and so forth—organizational, business, service, and information patterns are abstractions of one another.

9.10 PRAGMATIC MODELING

Architecture and the processes with which it operates are tightly coupled. The success of an architecture is largely determined by its ability to *mold* the processes of visualization and implementation. Visualization gives *direction* to an organization's patterns and their interconnectivity in the pattern continuum, while implementation provides the *assurance* that execution will fulfill intentions. The combination of architecture and processes, then, forms not only the foundation, but also the *character* of design, and ultimately, of the organization itself.

For example, the underlying methodology in information engineering is the so-called "waterfall" model. Such an approach embodies an enterprise-wide IT solution that is suitable to a highly stable and simple environment, one where local views are not substantially different from each other, or from that of the enterprise. The design constraints imposed by information engineering concerns the software development business process: Hierarchical structures are generally more suitable than cross-functional teams. In contrast, object-oriented architectures use "bottom-up" methodologies that are very good at delivering local solutions, work well in turbulent business environments, but do not appear to facilitate enterprise-wide IT synergies. In terms of the structure of the IT development process, object technologies lend themselves to the establishment of cross-functional teams, and as such, may not fit well with individual reward systems and functional reporting relationships.

Certain architectures, then, lend themselves to enterprise-wide solutions at the expense of local concerns, while others do the reverse. Furthermore, architectures and their associated processes (i.e., methodologies) *impose* design constraints on the organization's domains and how well they are aligned.

A questions that arises concerns the need to choose between different extremes, such as enterprise vs. local perspectives, teams vs. hierarchical structures, centralized vs. decentralized decision making, and so on. Is there a middle way, one that leverages the benefits of each pole?

Having it Both Ways

We illustrate the dilemma with an issue of growing concern—the configuration of the IT function in the 21st century organization. Traditionally, IT has been highly centralized, largely due to the newness and costs of the technology. This has been symbolized by the "mainframe culture" and the centralized power within the operations and data administration groups. With the introduction of PC and client/server technologies, power rapidly decentralized into the hands of the application groups. Moreover, this trend toward decentralization has extended into the business areas, where many IT-application groups now report to their corresponding business units. Outsourcing is a reasonable design option with the trend toward decentralization and the declining costs of coordinating technologies.

Several organizations have now questioned the decision to decentralize; in fact, some have begun to recentralize. Of course, they will never return to the mainframe culture again, but IT managers are searching for ways to leverage the benefits of both centralized and decentralized arrangements.

One solution has been described by Rockart, Earl, and Ross (1996). They have suggested the federated structure common in political organizations. In such a structure, the local units have *more* power than the centralized groups, but the latter are in control of those areas where there are economies of scale or scope—for example, standards, development tools, methodologies, common reuse libraries, etc. In effect, rather than choose one side of the coin or the other, the intent is to stand the coin on edge. But how can we do this? How can we have it both ways? Rockart *et al.* have suggested that the glue that pulls together the benefits of both centralized and decentralized IT is vision, strategy, and architecture.

Applying the Concept to Organizational Design

Organization theory as we know it is essentially Western in nature. A well-known characteristic of Western philosophy is its emphasis on an "either/or" belief system. One is, say, *either* Catholic *or* Jewish, but never both. In contrast, Eastern philosophy is characterized by a "both/and" framework. In Asia, it is perfectly acceptable to be *both* a Catholic *and* a Buddhist.

This same cultural division exists within organizations. For example, recall that Michael Porter's generic strategies (1985) of low cost and differentiation are seen by Western managers as opposite strategies. It is no accident, therefore, that Western firms adopt Porter's dualistic strategic concepts by choosing one or the other. It is equally no accident that Japanese managers choose both!

The configuration of an organizational architecture is also torn by this dilemma. Do we adopt a Western "either/or" view of organizations and develop an architecture that is either enterprise-wide or local, emphasizes one trendy domain (e.g., process) or another (e.g., culture), or develops a macro- or micro-view of the organizations? And so on and so forth. Or do we adopt an Eastern philosophy and build a "both/and" architecture? *Moreover, can we have it both ways—can we build an enterprise architecture, while designing local solutions, address hard and soft architectures, and even integrate each of the seemingly opposite possibilities?*

Design Radically, Implement Incrementally

The *design strategy* known as "design radically, implement incrementally" consists of those management decisions that create a vision of the organization, plan and design according to that vision, and yet, implement local solutions according to traditional business concerns, such as need, organizational impact, time, cost, and so on.

Visualization during early crystallization is the mechanism for "designing radically." It is during the early stages of crystallization that the designer exercises an organization-wide vision. Particular *domain* decisions are "implemented incrementally" in the form of specific molecules. Correspondence is established through alignment threads.

OM embodies the "middle way," the harmonization of seemingly conflicting dimensions of the organization. Characteristics of the "both/and" framework of OM are summarized in Figure 9–12.

1. *Invention and visualization.* Architecture must deal with reality, but to be useful it must support change and the development of new organizational forms. The need for *invention* is driven by *visualization*. This may be effected with the formulation of new lattices which address new models of organizational arrangements. For example, the definition of marketing and structural-fit lattices is motivated by the requirement to better align the marketing strategy of an organization with its structure.

2. *Abstraction and granularity.* Domains exist at varying levels of *granularity*. In fact, each level of granularity represents a pattern at some level of abstraction—organizational, business, service, or information patterns. Recall, for example, that the process molecule may exist in each of the four types of patterns.

3. *Dimensionalism.* Domains have *multi-dimensional* (organization-wide) and *single-dimensional* (local solution) characteristics. Domains have certain characteristics that are representative of the organization as a whole, while at a lower level of granularity their characteristics are localized. The two levels of granularity—one defining multi-dimensional properties and the other

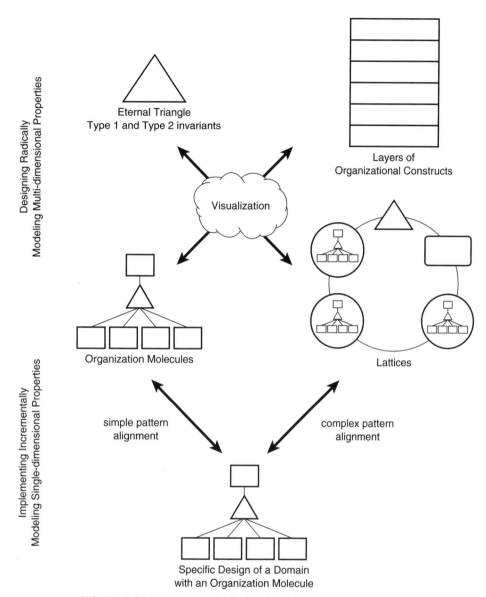

FIGURE 9–12   Designing Radically, Implementing Incrementally

specific, single-dimensional properties—are brought into correspondence through alignment threads.

4. *Degrees of contract formalism.* Organizations are characterized by *hard and soft contracts.* Not all behaviors in an organization lend themselves to complete specification, in fact, many are not even known. As a consequence of this gradation in the *specification of behavior*, we may specify certain domains precisely in formal contracts, others with relational contracts, and yet others may be identified by name only. It is this mix of precision in design that rep-

resents the real world, and it is the only way anything can be accomplished in an organization.

5. *Planned and emergent pattern formation.* Organizational patterns form as a consequence of either being planned (i.e., prescriptive), or through emergence (i.e., descriptive). Several domains are characterized by one course or the other. For example, information systems are usually planned, while culture typically emerges. How other domains, such as strategy, are formed is a subject of debate: They may have elements of both.

6. *Dynamicity and change.* Organizational change is a function of dynamicity—the fluid state that characterizes early crystallization. Moreover, dynamicity is facilitated by the pattern of alignment characteristics known as maneuverability and adaptiveness. It is this *mix* of pattern alignment and strategic intent that governs organizational change.

7. *Enterprise vision.* An enterprise vision is established through radical design. Recall that this includes (1) establishing an organizational baseline of sociocultural and organization invariants, (2) a layered model of constructs, and (3) identifying and elaborating molecules. If we now consider the complex arrangements among molecules—lattices with emergent characteristics—we have all the pieces to design radically. Harmonizing these *OM design constructs* to create an organizational vision is *visualization. Visualization* during early crystallization is the glue of "designing radically."

8. *Local design and implementation.* Specific *domain* decisions are "implemented incrementally" in the form of an operationalized molecule.

9. *Pattern alignment. Alignment* in the pattern continuum is the mechanism for reconciling the radical vision of the whole with the specific implementation of its pieces.

10. *The design process.* The OM refinement model embodies the "both/and" philosophy—the early stages support designing radically, while the latter stages support specific domain solutions and alignment with the broader organizational vision.

11. *OM constructs.* The organizational materials with which we design radically and implement incrementally are the OM constructs. This includes sociocultural and organization invariants (i.e., Type 1 and Type 2), layers of organizational constructs, organization molecules, and lattices. Collectively, they mold, and, in fact, are the patterns of an organization.

A Final Word on Pragmatic Modeling

What does a "both/and" architecture mean from the viewpoint of modeling as a discipline? Are we sacrificing understanding for muddle when we, say, name contracts rather than specify them rigorously?

As we mentioned in Chapter 1, we have accepted John Kay's contention that the real world of business is too complex to model completely. Each organization is unique, as is its situation. Recall, for example, that the assortment of schools in organization theory exist to address the variety of contingencies in which organizations find themselves.

Our purpose in OM is to account for organizational uniqueness by providing useful models, not mathematical completeness. OM is precise, but not 100% provable. There are situations in organizational life that do not lend themselves to formalism. This goes back to the reason an organizational construct can never become an IT "business object"—there will always be imprecision in organizations.

Each of the OM constructs—invariants, the layered model of constructs, organization molecules and lattices—is both general and specific. The difference between molecules and lattices, for instance, is somewhat vague. The same may be said of invariants and culture. We have deliberately created such a framework—so that managers may use OM to craft a vision for their particular organization notwithstanding its nebulous nature, yet design specific domains with some sense of assurance. Molding the mixture to create an organizational vision while providing specific solutions—that's what OM is all about!

9.11 CORE CONCEPTS

Organizational patterns

Emergent organizational characteristics

Crystallization

Pattern gap

Service patterns

Pattern continuum

Maneuverability

Organizational dynamicity

Pragmatic modeling

OM constructs

Linking organizational and business patterns

Architecture as a pattern of patterns

Pattern formation

Manifest representation

Business patterns

Information patterns

Lattices

Adaptiveness

Pattern fit and misfit

Visualization

Design radically, implement incrementally

PART 2

BUILDING A 21ST CENTURY ORGANIZATIONAL ARCHITECTURE

We continue our discussion of organization modeling by focusing on selected applications and issues. Each application addresses modeling issues which apply to a variety of domains (i.e., molecules) in the OM architecture. This includes relatively straightforward principles such as decomposition and inheritance, as well as the less clear areas of alignment. Accordingly, as we have done in every chapter, we introduce concepts that bring structure to an organization's architecture.

We discuss selected principles and techniques in the context of various well-known management paradigms. For example, we "characterize" processes by drawing correspondence between the process molecule and each of various frameworks, including Perrow's task model, Porter's value chain, and others. Our intent is to illustrate the utility and flexibility of OM by using it to create an architectural structure around popular management concepts, and, in so doing, incorporate these concepts into a larger organizational context.

Finally, we discuss areas that we believe are relevant for the 21st century organization. Each domain or management philosophy is an *organizational lever* to be pulled during the design process. While no domain may safely be ignored, it is clear that the 21st century dictates that some domains are more critical than others.

THE SEARCH FOR A 21ST CENTURY CORE ARCHITECTURE

Historically, organizational design has meant changing structure. As other constructs came to the fore, the central position of structure remained essentially unchanged. The issue had been refined from "structure" to "determinants of structure." Does technology or strategy determine structure? Is size more important? Or is it a combination of factors?

The game has changed. Discontinuous change, driven by globalization and information technology, has transformed the rules of change. Structure is too static and unresponsive. Even strategy presupposes planning and a certain stability. Strategic alignment has become a high risk venture—by the time a certain level of alignment is reached, the strategy may be outdated.

We believe that the sources of competitive advantage are shifting to those organizational constructs that characterize the *behavior* of an organization: *culture, people, process, information (data* and *knowledge),* and *learning (knowledge creation).* It is these constructs that represent the *core architecture* of a 21st century organization (see Figure P2–1). When aligned with one another, the domains of the core architecture provide an *infrastructure* for the other, more traditional and structural domains, such as strategy and structure. We envision domains and philosophies surrounding and intertwined with the constructs of the core architecture. Core architecture is the foundation of a 21st century organization, and from which structure, flexibility, quality and so on, flow. The remainder of this book is devoted to establishing a framework for designing a core architecture.

THE BUSINESS ANALYST OF OLD

The primary function of the business analyst of old had been to support the development of information systems for specific work tasks. The business analyst of old used textual descriptions to describe "business requirements" to an IT staff. During the 1980s, the requirements became more structured and included such artifacts as "data" and "process" models. These "process" models were partial business process models, typically data flows and functional decompositions—a collection of artifacts which IT professionals labeled "business" or "enterprise" models. Software development thus shifted from focused applications to "business area" analysis and development, the most popular form of which is known

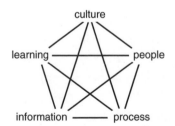

FIGURE P2–1   The Core Architecture of a 21st Century Organization

as information engineering. Through experience and research, we have come to recognize that such approaches produce little value for the organization as a whole—they represent the failed technology approaches described by Earl (1993).

Today, software development is a confused assortment of constructs—part information engineering, part collaboration, part object-orientation, and so on. Frameworks (e.g., fountain model—see Henderson-Sellers 1992) and techniques (e.g., information modeling—see Kilov and Ross 1994) are abundant. Methodologies are also abundant—just ask your favorite consultant!

THE BUSINESS ANALYST OF THE FUTURE

The role of the business analyst of the future, some would say today, will be more complicated. The emergence of communications technology, the complexity of knowledge, the human-machine interaction, the growing awareness of the importance of culture, and the emphasis on business process innovation has transformed the role of the traditional business analyst. He or she is no longer merely a communicator of requirements to an IT staff—but an *integrator of organizational constructs.*

The business analyst must address many complex interactions: data and knowledge, organizational learning paradigms, culture change, business process change, integration, and even invention. Knowledge creation and learning, collaborative problem solving and team structures, new hardware and communication technologies, and the prevalence of knowledge workers have made the business analyst key in the design of the organization as a whole. The business analyst must be an *organizational architect* responsible for defining and building the organization's new source of advantage—its core architecture.

CHAPTER 10

DIRECTIONALITY AND CULTURE

10.1 "NOTHING MATCHES!"

In his article, "Three Cultures of Management: The Key to Organizational Learning," Edgar Schein (1996) states that culture is "a set of basic tacit assumptions about how the world is and ought to be that a group of people share and that determines their perceptions, thoughts, feelings, and, to some degree, their overt behavior." Schein asserts that culture manifests itself at three levels, in effect, three levels of abstraction: deep tacit assumptions, espoused values that reflect what a group would like to become or the way it wants to be perceived, and its overt behavior that represents a compromise between the tacit assumptions, the espoused values, and the immediate situation. Because circumstances are so fluid, they frequently dictate behaviors that are inconsistent with each other, and with both the tacit assumptions and espoused values. Consequently, it is often difficult to ascertain the core value system of an organization by simply observing overt behaviors.

When we discuss the three-layered model proposed by Schein with professionals from a wide variety of industries, there is almost uniform agreement on the inconsistencies between tacit assumptions, espoused values, and explicit behavior. A frequently heard comment is, "nothing matches!" Perhaps more disturbing, inconsistencies are now expected and resented. The following quote from Schein (1996) well illustrates the mismatch between assumptions and overt behavior: "For example, many organizations espouse 'teamwork' and 'cooperation,' but the behavior that the incentive and control systems of the organization reward and encourage is based more on a shared tacit assumption that only individuals can be accountable and that the best results come from a system of individual competition and rewards. If the external situation demands teamwork, the group will develop some behavior that looks, on the surface, like teamwork by conducting meetings and seeking consensus, but members will continue to share the belief that they can get ahead by individual effort and will act accordingly when rewards are given out."

THE FORMATION OF ASSUMPTIONS AND BEHAVIORS

There is a danger in *consistently* behaving in a fashion that is not in accord with an inner value system—the value system either will be lost, or eventually change and bring itself into alignment with undesirable overt behaviors. The core value system of an organization will become buried if always compromised in the face of "situational contingencies." In such a case, the tacit assumptions that comprise the belief system of an organization will need to be rediscovered, and subsequently followed by a Herculean effort to bring the organization's overt behaviors into conformity with that "rediscovered" value system.

We believe that the notion of formation plays a role in organizational behavior, as it does in other domains (e.g., strategy). The above descriptions of the three manifestations of culture imply a linear relationship between levels. But there is no reason to believe that tacit assumptions are unaffected by overt behavior. Explicit behavior may transform a belief system, as well as the reverse. Figure 10–1, adapted from Schein (1985), illustrates the interaction of tacit assumptions and overt behavior.

Is each manifestation of culture equally important? The answer depends on the context. Certainly, if relationships are essentially transactional, the only cultural manifestation that is relevant to those involved, directly or indirectly, with an organization is its overt behavior. The hidden system of tacit assumptions and the espoused values are of no consequence. Perhaps this is one explanation for the observed inconsistencies—there is no inconsistency in light of transactional relationships, itself a culture contract that affects organizational behavior.

And in fact, organizations have increasingly viewed the relationships between themselves and their members—employees as well as customers, suppliers, and consultants—as transactional. We see this every day. For example, employees who have spent their entire work-lives with an organization are often forced to "reapply" as part of a reengineering process. Part-time and temporary employment are still other examples of transactional relationships.

The drive toward short-term relationships is so strong that organizations pursue this direction even if it is against their interests. Organizations overtly talk of the need for flexibility, redesign business processes accordingly, but then proceed to hire employees on the basis of short-term relationships. Perspective employees are hired on the basis of deep, narrowly scoped skills, and in effect, are positioned as contingency workers who are expendable as the organization changes. *By design,* loyalty, learning, and other characteristics of long-term relationships have been replaced with transactional ones.

Employees are almost never hired for their ability to learn new skills for yet undefined tasks—an importance faculty if an organization is serious about achieving flexibility in highly competitive environments. Organizational learning

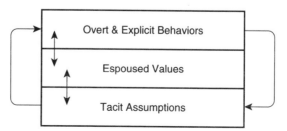

FIGURE 10–1   Levels of Abstraction in Culture and Their Formation—Adapted from Schein

critically depends on employees and their relationships to the organization and to each other. Such relationships arise only in the context of executing long-term commitments between people and organizations.

CULTURE-DRIVEN ALIGNMENT

We believe that the era of discontinuous change increases the importance of culture in organizational design. A strong culture controls behavior as much as, or more so than, any other organizational construct. Culture may facilitate or retard adaptation to turbulent environments. Ultimately, an organization's culture may be its primary source of competitive advantage. The level of alignment that derives from an organization's culture will largely determine its success in the 21st century.

As organizations run out of options to cut costs, they are increasingly being forced to increase their market, sell more, be more innovative, and so on. In the information era, organizations are turning to their primary source of innovation and "rich" knowledge—their people. The relational contracting to which John Kay refers is only the beginning of the realization that it is long-term relationships that confer sustainable advantage.

Organizations *must* consider their core belief system, if they are to bring overt behaviors into alignment and consequently make the organization more effective. Organization modeling can facilitate this process of building a strong, positive culture. Culture, in each of its manifestations, is an organizational piece, as is an information system, a business process, or any other construct. These pieces should be understood and brought into alignment and thereby made more effective. An organization can become more competitive by *designing* for desired behaviors and alignment threads that reinforce rather than undermine the design. A poor alternative is to "design by chance," and make decisions as if you were buying lottery tickets without knowing the odds of winning!

Look at it this way. Would you prefer to live in a neighborhood with its traditions and established relationships, or would you prefer a trailer park with its transitory relationships? Do you prefer to live in a society governed solely by market relationships, or are social relationships and democratic values as important—perhaps more so? Which metaphor characterizes your organization? In which type of organization do you want to work, manage, and lead?

10.2 DEGREES OF ALIGNMENT

We have seen that *fit* is an important dimension associated with organizational design. We have also seen that *alignment* is a more general principle that encompasses the traditional definition of fit, but also includes the level of consistency and compatibility within, and between, each domain of the organization, respectively.

The Need to Manage Reality

The "hard" architectural domains, such as information, are characterized by precise specifications—a consequence of the relatively "controlled" environment in which the domain operates. In a controlled environment, alignment could be assured, even rigidly enforced. In contrast, in the domains of the "soft" architecture (e.g., culture), behavior is governed more by assumptions than by explicit assertions. This leads to varying, but typically low, levels of alignment in the unarchitected organization.

An example from information technology (an essentially controlled environment) illustrates the concept of fit with *perfect alignment*. In an information model, a "dependency association" identifies a simple invariant: The existence of a child entity instance implies the existence of a corresponding parent entity instance. If the association invariant is not to be violated, certain behaviors (e.g., the creation of a dependent in the absence of a corresponding parent) are impossible. In this way, the integrity of the association is upheld. During implementation, this rigid control may and should be maintained. For example, in relational databases the concept of referential integrity enforces create and delete constraints between selected rows in corresponding tables.

As is commonly observed, the full alignment that characterizes the controlled environment of information systems is rarely the case. In fact, the reverse is almost always true. Organizations do not have the luxury of simply preventing behaviors that violate design intentions. In this book, we have given numerous examples of misalignment—e.g., the notion of teams in a culture of individualism. This is not to say that we do not adopt designs with *partial alignment*. On the contrary, managers do so all the time. What this does mean, however, is that managers recognize the varying levels of alignment that exist, understand their trade-offs, and consequently make informed, conscious decisions.

For example, what are the trade-offs involved with team structures and a reward system based on individual performance? Teams in a context of individualism will be less effective than teams in a context of community. On the other hand, rewards based on individual performance may lead to greater individual effort. The job of the organizational designer, then, is to reconcile the trade-offs: to identify those instantiations and alignment threads that *raise* the level of alignment for the organization as a whole—its degree of consistency and compatibility.

10.3 DIRECTIONALITY

When we further analyze the concept of alignment, we discover the notion of directionality. *Directionality* is the degree to which an organization's alignment threads derive from its invariants that characterize the core belief system which embraces the tacit assumptions of its culture.

The premise of directionality is simple yet profound: An organization may be responsive and successful in a turbulent environment, even though none of its constituents changes. The key to directionality is a clear *understanding* and subsequent *execution* of an organization's invariants and tacit cultural assumptions. Collins and Porras (see below), have described this composite of aligned values in terms of an organization's long-term goals and an attendant high level of alignment between organizational pieces.

That is to say, long-term success depends more on a well-defined architecture than a particular strategy or structure. Such an architecture derives from and is aligned with an organization's history and culture—invariants *driving* alignment, both vertical (i.e., adaptiveness) and horizontal (i.e., maneuverability). Directionality does not depend on what those invariants, tacit assumptions, values, and long-term goals are, only on the organization's alignment with them.

THE IRON BAR METAPHOR

Look at it this way. An iron bar contains iron molecules randomly arranged. When magnetized, the bar becomes a magnet—none of its constituent molecules has changed, only their direction. The larger the number of molecules thus arranged, the greater the resulting magnetic field—an emergent property that is a consequence of directionality among molecules.

An organization has more in common with a magnet than with an information system. It contains varying levels of alignment. When organizational pieces (i.e., molecules) have the same direction (i.e., alignment), they have well-coordinated behaviors and the organization as a whole exhibits purpose and desirable emergent characteristics. When constituents work against each other, the organization is characterized by frustration and confusion—i.e., a lack of direction. Consistent direction among the domains of an organization is far more important than the properties of the domains themselves! The force that gives consistent direction is, of course, an organization's invariants.

The notion of directionality addresses the importance of visualization and architecture. Writing in the *Harvard Business Review*, Collins and Porras (1996) have described how long-term success depends on an organization's vision framework: its *core ideology* (i.e., core values and purpose) and its *envisioned future*. Success in a rapidly changing environment does not mean a change in an organization's components; rather, both a consistent value system and engaging long-term business goals are responsible for sustained success.

From a modeling perspective, the notion of a core ideology corresponds to an organization's invariants, while an envisioned future corresponds to the emergent characteristics associated with its organizational and business patterns. Success is directly attributable to the level of adaptiveness (vertical alignment) that the organizational and business patterns have on the service (operational) and information patterns of the organization.

Organizations need to discover their core values and articulate a long-term vision which embraces their organization invariants, tacit assumptions, and organizational and business patterns. In each case, architecture will serve to facilitate the identification and specification of the organization's invariants and alignment threads, even as specific strategies, processes, structures, and other constructs change. Architecture is the *universal glue* that holds everything together—specific domain behaviors organized around stable invariants and long-term goals. That is to say, organizations may be successful as a direct consequence of the directionality maintained in their architectures.

10.4 RAISING THE LEVEL OF ALIGNMENT

Given both the existence of, and desire for, certain behaviors, questions naturally arise concerning the design of behaviors that are not supported, or are even undermined, by an organization's invariants. Is it possible for an organization to exhibit a variety of behaviors which are seemingly contradictory? Is it possible to override existing organizational invariants to account for local conditions? How can an organization maintain its directionality in the face of demands for a set of behaviors that are otherwise at variance with its invariants?

COMPENSATING FOR SOURCES OF MISALIGNMENT

Realization (i.e., implementation) is a common source of misalignment or low levels of alignment. An organization model, like an information model, is intended to specify a desired end-state. During implementation, however, there is always a certain amount of compromise. In each case, the model specifies the desired level of directionality, but circumstances impose partial alignment. This is fine. The point is that OM, like information modeling, is a framework where desired behaviors may be precisely specified, and if compromised during implementation, the "gaps" can be understood, measured, and subsequently reduced by implementing *other cooperating* behaviors.

For example, in the controlled environment of a database system, referential constraints are often permitted to be violated—for instance, foreign keys with "null" defaults. The database designer compensates for partial alignment with *subsequent, correcting behaviors* that establishes the desired level of alignment—a subsequent update operation to a null foreign key that produces correspondence with a primary key value.

As with an information system, realization is a common source of misalignment in an organization, one that may be corrected for with compensating behaviors that serve to reestablish directionality. But a more serious source of misalignment is the desire for behaviors that are often at odds with one another, or with the organization's invariants and culture. Misalignment in organizations takes the form of contradictory behaviors and organizational pieces that seem to work against each other. This results in organizational frustration and disaffection that ultimately leads to undesirable emergent characteristics.

In an *architected* organization, the solution to misalignment is to adopt a strategy that evaluates a proposed change *and* its alignment threads before realization. Moreover, our alignment strategy addresses both invariants and those concerns that arise from the proposed change (e.g., directionality, emergent characteristics) summarized below:

1. Evaluate the trade-offs—i.e., the benefits of the set of desired behaviors and attendant alignment threads, and potential conflicts with existing behaviors and invariants.
2. Evaluate the effects of the desired behaviors and attendant alignment threads on directionality, and consequently on the organization's emergent characteristics.
3. Evaluate the level of directionality consistent with the organization's core ideology (i.e., invariants), long-term goals, and the set of desired behaviors and alignment threads for our design.
4. Design for *that* level of desired directionality—the optimum level of desired behaviors and alignment threads required to support a sufficient level of benefit while maintaining the desired level of directionality.

Observe that when we speak of *desired behaviors,* we always group them with *attendant alignment threads.* And of course, that is exactly the point of design through an organizational architecture. Virtually all desired behaviors depend on, or impact other, behaviors and invariants, and consequently an organization's directionality and emergent characteristics.

Success, failure, or, for that matter, unintended effects can be directly managed in OM. The competitive advantage afforded a firm with an organizational architecture is apparent—the ability to analyze and design for varying levels of alignment. That is to say, an organizational architecture enables managers to manage *varying* levels of directionality.

10.5 DESIGNING FOR DIRECTIONALITY: AN EXAMPLE

Let us illustrate designing for a given level of directionality with a common source of organizational misalignment—the desire for teamwork and cooperative behavior in a culture of individualism. Here the central conflict is between the invariants of individualism and community, and between their alignment threads.

The culture contract of individual rewards and responsibility corresponds to the organization invariant of individualism, and naturally, the aligned reward system is based on individual performance. This represents the *predominant* set of alignment threads in most U.S. organizations. However, growing awareness of the benefits associated with the culture of cooperative behavior and the invariant of community (the predominant alignment thread in Eastern organizations) presents a dilemma for U.S. management: How do we facilitate a culture of cooperative behavior (a tacit assumption) within a context (i.e., invariant) of individualism?

LOW DIRECTIONALITY

One popular solution to this dilemma is to simply premise individual rewards on both invariants—individualism (i.e., individual performance) and community (i.e., group performance). This strategy creates two alignment threads to a single reward system. The implication, of course, is that the organization has established a second culture contract of cooperative behavior (corresponding to an invariant of community), in addition to the predominant culture contract based on individual behavior (corresponding to an invariant of individualism). The presumption is that the organization will derive the benefits associated with both invariants.

This classic design option is an old-time favorite, and unfortunately, an example of low directionality. This is illustrated in Figure 10–2.

We may summarize the alignment threads that lead to low directionality as follows:

- Two invariant and culture behavior threads that separately are aligned, but collectively are misaligned.
- Two opposite invariants representing a conflict of values (individualism vs. community), each aligned with its corresponding culture contract that is also in conflict with each other (individual or cooperative). At the organization level, the two {invariant - culture} threads are pointed in opposite directions.

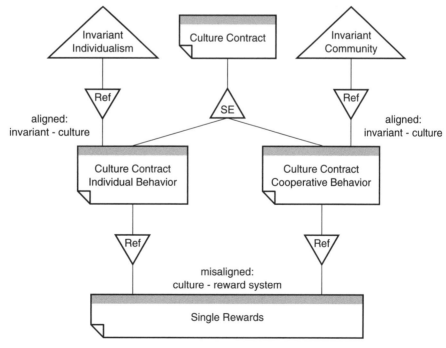

FIGURE 10–2   Low Directionality

- Two sets of culture contract threads {culture - rewards}, each of which works against the other, and each of which is misaligned—a single reward system that seeks to invoke two contradictory behaviors (individual and co-operative) has conflict designed into its threads.

The notion of having two conflicting invariants and corresponding cultural behaviors—each pointed in opposite directions—can only convey an unclear perception of the organization's tacit assumptions and desired behaviors. This is in spite of the fact that, *separately*, each {invariant - culture} thread is aligned; it is their *summation* at the organization level that produces a cultural conflict. Also, by creating alignment threads from two *different* culture contracts to the *same* reward system, management is attempting to produce a single behavior premised on two contradictory invariants—an effort sure to produce conflict and low alignment.

MODERATE DIRECTIONALITY

Another design option is to create a *second* reward system (i.e., shared rewards) that has a high level of alignment with the culture contract defining cooperative behavior. The conflict caused by two different {invariant - culture} threads remains, but there is greater alignment between each cultural contract and its corresponding reward system. This is illustrated in Figure 10–3.

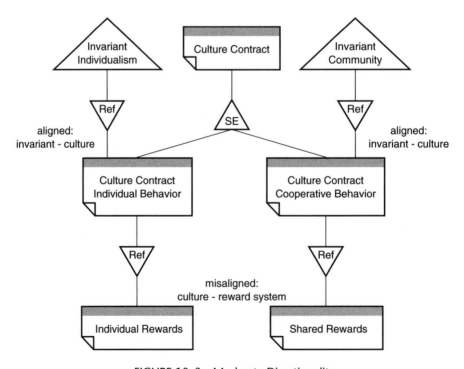

FIGURE 10–3   Moderate Directionality

To the extent that each culture behavior contract and its corresponding reward system is treated as distinct threads, this is not a bad solution. The {individual culture - individual reward} thread facilitates individual performance, while the {cooperative culture - shared reward} thread facilitates teamwork. Naturally, the group reward must be the same for each member of the group (or there is no group reward system), correspond to the value of the group's output, and be separate from individual bonuses. Unfortunately, in this case, the existence of two contradictory {invariant - culture} threads produces conflicting interpretations of an organization's tacit assumptions and invariants.

High Directionality

The highest form of directionality is found in those organizations where there is no conflict among invariants or culture contracts, and in which there is a high level of alignment among constructs. That is to say, directionality is maximized in an organization where there is a single alignment thread, rather than some mix that attempts to derive benefits from each type of thread. This is illustrated in Figure 10–4.

The theme here is simple: High directionality is a function of alignment without ambiguity, and not actual domain instantiations. Figure 10–4 illustrates two very different organizations (through the specification of very different behaviors), but each has high directionality.

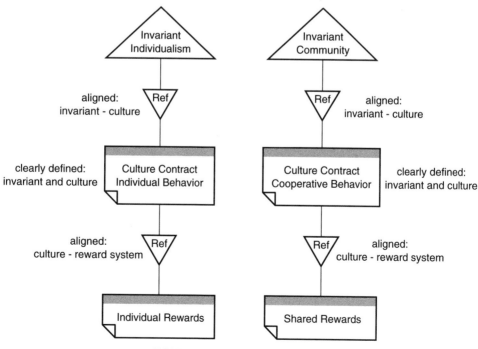

FIGURE 10–4   High Directionality

In this situation, management decides that the advantages associated with adopting a conflicting invariant in no way compensate for a loss of directionality. The drawback, of course, is that management is forced to choose a direction. It means that management can no longer deceive itself into believing that it can design individualism and community paradigms into the same organization (which management can do, since anyone can design anything), and expect to derive the benefits of both (which rarely occurs since the design itself is contradictory and cannot be successfully executed).

10.6 CORE CONCEPTS

Organizational lever

Culture

Alignment of molecules

Directionality

Business analyst of old and business analyst of the future

Fit

Degrees of alignment (perfect, partial)

Iron bar metaphor

Core architecture of culture, people, process, information, and learning

Cultural manifestations: tacit assumptions, espoused values, and explicit behaviors

CHAPTER 11

PROCESS FORMULATION

11.1 THE COMPETITIVE ADVANTAGE OF PROCESS

In the previous chapter, we discussed the advantage afforded an organization with a strong culture and high level of directionality. In this chapter, we discuss a second source of competitive advantage—business processes.

Peter Keen (1997) has identified four enabling reasons why process improvement is a source of competitive advantage: organizational plasticity (the ability of an organization to change radically), the changing nature of change (the value of transformation over incrementalism), dynamic capabilities (the role of distinctive competencies in providing competitive advantage), and the reduction in coordination costs attributed to IT (Malone and Rockart 1993).

Process is an organizational component that is particularly important in an era where discontinuities are the norm. Processes represent much more than an organization's "operations." They may include not only workflows but also management and cultural practices. Processes may be robust and dynamic, or frozen and unresponsive. Thus, they give an organization its depth and means for handling change and turbulence. In contrast, strategy and structure are more like superficial wrappers that function to give processes a particular context.

Toyota, for example, maintains its competitive advantage in a turbulent market through its assembly process and its corresponding reputation for reliability. It does not matter whether the process is building a van or sedan—its ability to rapidly deploy different strategies in a turbulent environment (and thus be successful) is premised on its process capabilities.

*****

Process formulation is the architecture-driven *shaping* of an organization's processes, and is thus at the center of business transformation. The process molecule contains a rich assortment of concepts and properties with which to formulate processes. The key attributes we shall consider in our approach to formulation are: characterization, transformation, specification, design, and implementation.

While there are endless techniques and methodologies associated with process change, each may be given rigor if included in an architectural construct such as the process molecule. In this chapter, we discuss several techniques and

169

their application with a variety of management approaches. We thus integrate various well-known process philosophies into a single, architectural framework.

11.2 PROCESS CHARACTERIZATION

Characterization involves classifying a process according to some management or organizational paradigm. This may include such constructs as the value chain or the technology models associated with organization theory (OT). Characterization serves to identify the larger organizational context of a process as well as the unit of analysis for the designer. Characterization provides insight into design options, and is therefore a necessary early stage of process formulation.

STRATEGIC ALIGNMENT

THE VALUE CHAIN AND PROCESS

One of the more obvious connections between OM and a popular management concept concerns the relationship between the process molecule and the value chain described by Michael Porter in 1984. The value chain categorizes the generic value-adding activities of an organization and serves as an analysis tool during strategic planning. The critical concept in the value chain is the "value activity" which is part of the infrastructure analysis of an organization.

A value activity *is a* process at some level of abstraction. We may design business processes and describe them in terms of those properties that are used in strategic planning—that is, OM may serve as an architectural basis for strategic alignment between the properties of the process molecule and, for example, Porter's strategic analysis techniques. These characteristics in no way conflict with the specification of the process itself—the value activity affiliation is simply one dimension of process that facilities the alignment of an organization's business processes and change efforts with the strategic analysis of an organization's value activities. This is illustrated in Figure 11–1.

Figure 11–1 is actually a simple representation of an "is-a" (i.e., subtyping) association between the process molecule and the value chain. The process molecule is illustrated in the upper left in Figure 11–1, while the remainder of the figure is essentially a model of the typology associated with a value activity. The key, of course, is the recognition that a value activity is a classification of a process. It is this fact that accounts for the "is-a" association between a process and its subtype value activity, and thereby establishes architectural support for strategic planning and process design.

CAPABILITY, COMPETENCE, AND PROCESS

Traditional models of strategic planning are structural in nature (e.g., positioning as described by Michael Porter (1980) and his five force framework). More recently, a "resource-based" approach has begun to emerge (see Nonaka and Takeuchi 1995). This approach shifts the focus of strategic planning from "where"

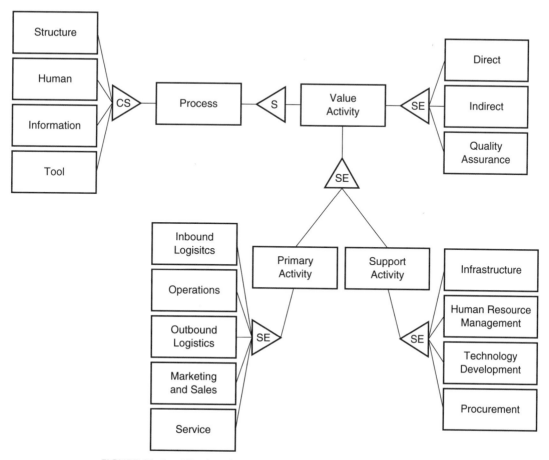

FIGURE 11–1   Aligning the Process Molecule with the Value Chain

to "how." The premise is that behavior-driven strategy is dynamic, and hence more easily accommodates discontinuous change.

At the center of behavior-based strategy are the notions of *capability* and *competence*. Stalk, Evans, and Shulman (1992) see a capability as a set of strategic business processes that span the entire value chain, while a competence is a set of strategic knowledge areas applied to the capability at critical points along its path. Each describes how and with what an organization performs work.

The importance of *process* as a mediator of change is stated by Keen (1997) as follows: "Change was once seen as an issue of organizational structure, and structure and strategy were assumed to be interdependent, with structure following strategy. This view reflected a belief in the possibility of controlling both the firm and its environment, of creating a long-term structure and a strategy that would need only fine-tuning in the future. The language of management was the language of control: span of control, management-control systems, forecasting, synergy, exception reporting, management by objective. The language of business is now about how to plan when you can't predict, how to be adaptable, and how to handle the discontinuities of change. Organizational change is now process rather than structure centered. Managers cannot control their business environments or even predict what they will be like in a few years. Rather than be architects of structure and strategies that may be made irrelevant or even obliterated by the next tidal wave of change, they focus on how work is done, on the process reforms that promise the flexibility needed to meet unforeseen challenges and take advantage of unexpected opportunities."

The raw material for a capability or a competence is the notion of "knowledge," and its devolution throughout the organization. Here the alignment threads are more dynamic and people-focused. In subsequent chapters, we will explore these considerations and their implications.

ABSTRACTION AND PROCESS SUBTYPES

Another form of process abstraction concerns the level of analysis. The notion of a process must support strategic planning (a somewhat high-level of analysis) but also work optimization (a somewhat detailed-level of analysis). At each level, we are referring to transformation and the resources by which it is effected—subtypes of the process molecule. The different abstraction levels are constituents of each other, yet each is a {process} specification. This is illustrated in Figure 11–2.

In this model, we are defining process types to include a firm's interorganizational processes, its organizational level technology, its business processes, work cycles, tasks, and their corresponding work activities. Also, we have found it useful to utilize an intermediate type between a task and a business process: the "work cycle." We define a work cycle as a collection of coordinated tasks. We will revisit coordinated tasks and their specifications later in this chapter.

PROCESS CLASSIFICATION AND TECHNOLOGY MODELS

The process classification hierarchy illustrated in Figure 11–2 is much more than a theoretical exercise in abstraction. Understanding the unit of analysis (i.e., level of process abstraction) enables us to leverage existing models that serve as guides during design. We illustrate the application of process abstraction by mapping process subtypes to various technology models—three classical models from OT as well as a more recent analytical classification that serves to identify processes for improvement. This is illustrated in Figure 11–3.

- Organizational technology has traditionally been classified into two types: service and manufacturing. Joan Woodward (1965) classifies manufacturing technology on the basis of complexity, in effect, subtyping manufacturing technology at the organization level. The classification criterion is *manufacturing complexity (i.e., product standardization/customization, and batch size)*, yielding the following subtypes: *unit production, mass production,* and *continuous production.*

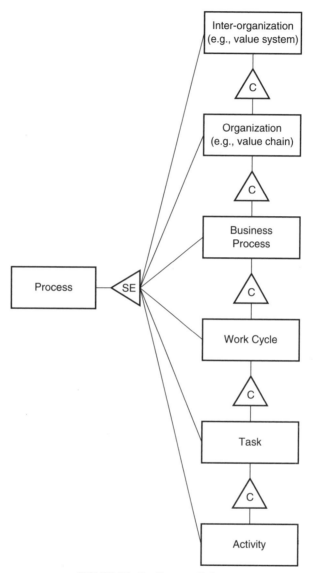

FIGURE 11–2   Process Subtypes

- Peter Keen (1997) classifies business processes on the basis of *salience* (i.e., prominence) and *economic value-added (EVA)*. Classification in terms of salience results in the subtypes (in descending order of EVA) of *identity, priority, background,* and *mandated* business processes.

- James Thompson (1967) classifies technology on the basis of task interdependence; i.e., subtyping business processes or collections of tasks (i.e., work cycles). The classification criterion is *task interdependence,* of which there are three types: *sequential, pooled,* and *reciprocal interdependence.* Each of

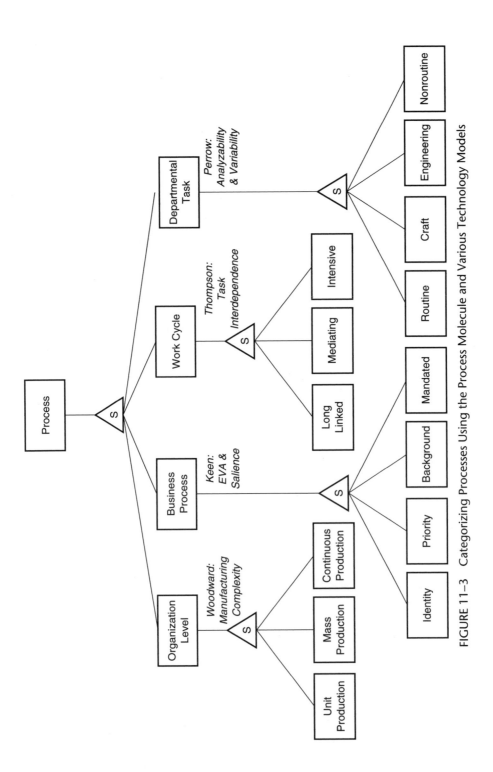

FIGURE 11–3   Categorizing Processes Using the Process Molecule and Various Technology Models

these, in turn, corresponds to the technology subtypes of *long-linked, mediating*, and *intensive* technologies, respectively.

- Charles Perrow (1967) classifies departmental, *knowledge* tasks on the basis of their *analyzability* and *variability* (i.e., number of exceptions). This results in four task subtypes: *craft, routine, engineering*, and *nonroutine*. Tasks that are routine are characterized as analyzable with low variability, craft are unanalyzable with low variability, engineering are analyzable with high variability, and nonroutine are unanalyzable with high variability.

The Woodward, Thompson, and Perrow classification models have received a great deal of discussion and furthered extensive research and, therefore, are well-known to students of management. They have given us insight into the relationship between process (at some level of abstraction) and the structure or strategy of organizations. As such, each serves as a guide during design.

The Keen model serves as a guide in identifying which processes to change. Not all processes have the same value to the organization. It is common practice to choose processes for change on the basis of visibility or customer-focus. Such processes are typically simple workflows and may represent *background* or *mandated* processes in the Keen model—processes with little EVA to the organization. The workflows and complexities of other processes (e.g., acquisition, and management training processes) add as much value, or more, to the organization. These are *identity* and *priority* process types with high EVAs that should be the subject of management attention. Subtyping an organization's business processes on the basis of EVA should be a necessary first step in identifying candidate processes for improvement. By identifying processes in terms of their salience and EVA, organizations may select processes to improve based on their value to shareholders.

11.3 PROCESS TRANSFORMATION

Process transformation and change have taken on an assortment of meanings, the goals of which are to change the way an organization actually does work. Reengineering, continuous improvement, and TQM are examples with which we are all familiar. Creating strategic alignment threads is another model of change, as was discussed in Chapter 7. Routinizing work (a legacy of Scientific Management), and the deployment of new technology are still other views of process change. Each in some way establishes a context in which processes may be formulated.

THE SEPARATION OF SPECIFICATION AND IMPLEMENTATION

The notion of abstraction has several dimensions. Perhaps the most important is the separation of *specification* and *implementation*. In the process molecule, this refers to the specification of an activity {process} and the interaction of organizational resources {human–structure–information–tool} used to implement the activity. Each implementation component (i.e., human, structure, information, or tool) is a *process lever* to be pulled during process change. See Figure 11–4.

Abstraction has important implications for the change process. For example, classical BPR starts with a *tabula rasa* (i.e., "clean sheet of paper")—that is, it is a top-down approach that specifies business processes independent of their implementation. In contrast, continuous improvement is a bottom-up approach that focuses on a process' constituents and their interaction. The difference between radical process transformation (e.g., BPR) and continuous improvement is illustrated in Figure 11–4.

For example, during a BPR effort, desired behavior {process} is specified and serves as the driver; process components {human, structure, information, tool} and their interaction (i.e., the composite-subtyping association) represent an implementation of the specified {process}.

With continuous improvement, we proceed the other way around. The implementation components, in particular their interaction, are adjusted so that some emergent dimension of {process}, such as cycle time, is changed. In this way the process itself is said to improve *incrementally*. Also, establishing component interactions where none existed before, particularly with the information component, often has the same effect as a BPR effort, but over a longer period of time. This was at least one important reason for the success of Japanese organizations in effecting process change, even across business processes, emulating a radical rather than a gradual change (Porter 1985).

Frequently, during a modeling effort, the two dimensions of process specification and implementation are confused. For example, a recent insurance industry workflow analysis mistakenly identified implementation activities, such as "submitted to supervisor" or "assigned to adjuster," as process specifications. The effective designer knows the difference between specification and implementation, and how to design each in light of the other. Modeling the implementation

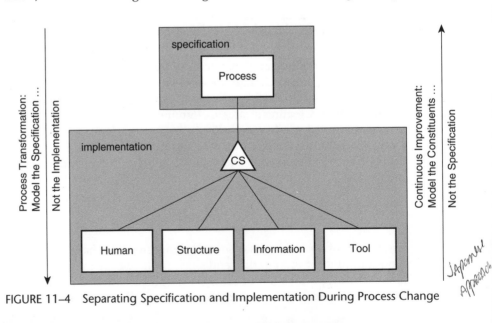

FIGURE 11–4   Separating Specification and Implementation During Process Change

(e.g., "submitted to supervisor") rather than the desired behavior (e.g., "submitted for approval") serves to prematurely constrain rather than liberate the analysis.

ROUTINIZING WORK

A key goal of management is to analyze and refine what have been *craft* and *nonroutine* tasks, and thereby *routinize* them into *routine* and *engineering* tasks. Recall from our discussion of the Perrow model that *craft* and *nonroutine* tasks are characterized by their high level of unanalyzability, while *routine* and *engineering* tasks are characterized as being analyzable. Management constantly seeks to reduce *ambiguity* and *uncertainty* by routinizing work and the business rules governing that work. This means making unanalyzable tasks analyzable. This is illustrated in Figure 11–5.

One technique employed in routinizing work is decomposition. Historically, this required decomposing a craft task into several simpler routine tasks (e.g., Taylor's Scientific Management). Decomposition makes the overall composite task as explicit as possible by breaking it into a series of simpler, component tasks. This same principle may be applied to nonroutine tasks where, as a consequence of task decomposition and explicit specification, the once composite nonroutine task is replaced with several routine and/or engineering tasks. In both cases, routinization requires explicit task specification.

Routinization is thus characterized by process explicitness. Explicitness lowers ambiguity, lowers costs, promotes measurement, and leads to machine-like operations. In contrast, unanalyzable work (i.e., a craft or nonroutine task) is more unclear, and is typically dependent on people with extensive experience who command higher salaries, and who work in less hierarchical structures than otherwise.

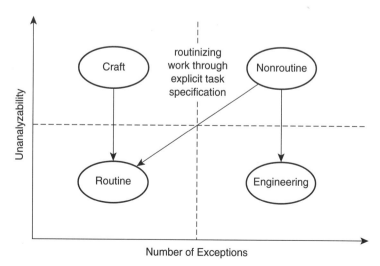

FIGURE 11–5   Routinizing Work Using the Perrow Model

Finally, routinization is successful with administrative or operational processes—those with clearly definable specifications. True "knowledge work," by contrast, is not easily definable, and hence is not subject to process explicitness. Improving knowledge processes requires a human-centered paradigm, as opposed to a process one. We will explore knowledge and knowledge work in Chapters 12 and 13.

ROUTINIZING NEW TECHNOLOGY

The *process* of routinizing work need not be confined to existing processes, but may be used as a vehicle to promote and leverage new technology. For instance, a new paradigm (e.g., object-orientation) or a new application (e.g., data warehousing) is typically first implemented on a small scale. In essence, it is implemented as a *craft* technology. This is because the practice associated with the new technology has yet to be fully understood and systematized (i.e., it is unanalyzable). Over time, as a result of organizational learning, the tasks become more explicit (i.e., analyzable) as software and project management disciplines take form. Eventually, the new technology "scales up" and becomes an *engineering* task. We refer to this development of organization-wide technologies, through the application of organizing disciplines, as *architected scaling*. This is illustrated in Figure 11–6(a).

At the stage that technology has been routinized, it is analyzable and subject to measurement and improvement. Moreover, because it is analyzable (i.e., routinized) it may be implemented on an organization-wide basis.

Observe in Figure 11–6(a) that we have illustrated an alternative direction to producing organization-wide technologies. Unarchitected scaling is characterized by a lack of analyzable disciplines, the result of which is usually chaos. In such a state, there is little pattern formation in the development of a new technology.

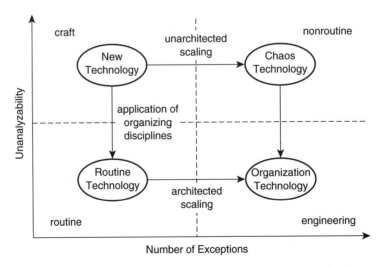

FIGURE 11–6(a)   The Process of Distributing New Technology Using the Perrow Model

For example, an investment bank recently developed a data warehouse for a single department, but in keeping with the culture of the organization, it did so without software disciplines. After an initial success, and despite the pressure to derive organization-wide benefits from the effort, today the warehousing paradigm remains a craft implementation that produces only local benefit. Without the resources or cultural support needed to develop the disciplines necessary for an architected solution, the data warehousing paradigm cannot scale up to the organization level, nor even grow at the local level. It is simply withering away.

This notion of applying disciplines to new technology—paving the way for architected scaling—is almost always difficult to implement. There is always pressure in organizations to quickly reap the rewards associated with some new technology or paradigm. Bertrand Meyer (1995), for example, points out that software managers are demanding "business objects" from developers of the object paradigm. Meyer rightly states that it is better first to develop "stacks" before "business objects"—i.e., "learning before jumping." And this story has been repeated in other domains—random team development, restructuring, BPR efforts, and so on. Each in some way is important, but, if implemented across the organization in an unarchitected way, will lead to less than the expected results, or simply become shelfware. The lesson is the same across all domains—if the *impact* of a change process is to be *real, positive,* and *sustainable,* an architected approach is far superior to jumping!

SYSTEMATIZING NONROUTINE AND KNOWLEDGE WORK

The underlying premise behind Figure 11–6(a) is that the design of technology is an engineering one—an issue of task definition and coordination. The constituents of the tasks themselves may have different characteristics, but may be prescribed in the same manner as the tasks. This has given rise to "human resources," not very different in principle from the resources of the motor pool.

With the advent of knowledge work, all of this changes. The "human constituent" of a task *is* the task. His or her requirements assume an equal footing with the work itself; if well-designed, the two become one! That is the motivation behind Figure 11–6(b). The 21st century will be characterized by nonroutine and knowledge work. The organization need not stumble into chaos, but may design, systematize, and become a knowledge organization. However, the path is as nonroutine as the work!

The process of creating a knowledge technology does not have to start from scratch. Rather, we start with existing craft and engineering frameworks, and apply collaborative structures and informal contracts targeted at candidate knowledge workers (as opposed to the tasks themselves). Recall that we have already seen one type of informal contract, the relational contract described by John Kay.

The process of building a knowledge technology brings forth techniques for its integration into the larger firm. Existing routine and engineering technologies do not go away, but complement, and are complemented by, the new knowledge technology. Naturally, the appropriate alignment threads, particularly with an

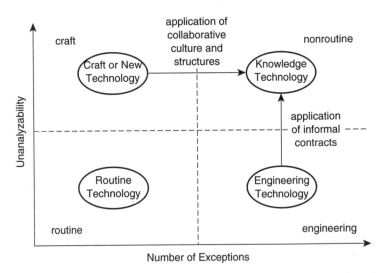

FIGURE 11–6(b)   The Process of Building a Knowledge Technology Using the Perrow Model

organization's culture, need to be established. A knowledge technology is premised on people, and their willingness to share what they know and learn. This will not happen in traditional organizational cultures, nor in updated patchworks of "teams."

11.4 PROCESS SPECIFICATION

As we have discussed throughout this book, organizational domains (e.g., process) may be formulated on the basis of their behaviors. In our approach, we use the notion of a contract to specify behavior. For example, the process *hire an employee* is specified in the contract illustrated in Figure 11–7 (copied from Figure 6–4).

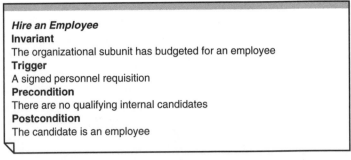

FIGURE 11–7   Contract Specification for Hire an Employee

The process contract *hire an employee* is simple and high-level, yet is associated with several dimensions. For example, it may be decomposed into several constituent process tasks, each of which may be specified in a corresponding contract. Alternatively, it may be inherited by other process specifications or linked to other processes in a network of specifications. And so on and so forth.

In this section we describe these additional dimensions, add to our repertoire of specification techniques, and thereby enrich the manner of process formulation.

PROCESS COMPOSITION AND DECOMPOSITION

A process specification may decompose into other sub-processes or may be assembled from sub-process components. This is depicted in Figure 11–8.

This illustration says that a given process may contain other processes, may be a component sub-process in another process, or both. Note that sufficient decomposition spans types, so that, for example, tasks eventually decompose into activities. This diagram then is similar to Figure 11–2, process subtypes: Figure 11–2 shows that processes may be of different types (e.g., work cycle, task), each of which is a composite or component of another, while Figure 11–8 shows that any process specification, whether or not they span types, may decompose into other process specifications. Also, since we are using the notion of a contract to specify {process}, it is no accident that Figure 11–8 corresponds with Figure A–3 in the Appendix, the contract hierarchy.

As an example, the business process *hire an employee* is composed of other processes, such as establishing a business need, determining skill, education, and experience requirements, soliciting candidates, selecting possible candidates, a series of interviews, a drug test, a formal job offer, an update to an employee database, an update to a benefits database, and many others. A partial representation appears in Figure 11–9.

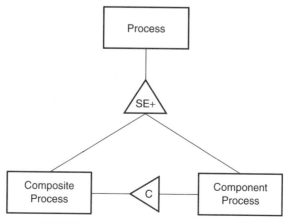

FIGURE 11–8   Process Decomposition

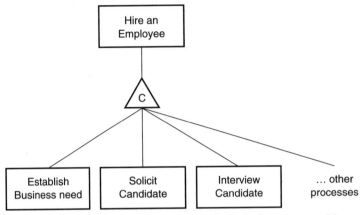

FIGURE 11–9   Hire an Employee Work Cycle Decomposition

The decomposition itself reveals nothing of the semantic dependencies or triggers among the decomposed processes, only that the process *hire an employee* is a composite specification composed of several constituent processes.

Decomposition is a critical activity during process analysis. It is the technique by which we refine business processes and work cycles into tasks. The task is typically considered the basic unit of analysis, specified and designed in conjunction with its corresponding work cycles. In the above example, *hire an employee* is a work cycle, while its constituents are tasks. Decomposition uncovers constituents, and thus makes their specification easier, more precise, and subject to reconfiguration. Reconfiguring constituent tasks transforms the composite work cycle, and is critical to process change.

DECOMPOSITION AND ROUTINIZATION

Decomposition facilitates the routinization of work. Many process work cycles often appear to be complex—craft or nonroutine—but in fact are composites composed of several, simpler routine tasks that lend themselves to straightforward improvement. In the example above, *hire an employee* may be considered a craft work cycle, but its component tasks are varied: *soliciting a candidate* is routine, while *interviewing a candidate* is a craft task. The routine task (*soliciting a candidate*) may be implemented with unskilled people, even outsourced, while the craft task (*interviewing a candidate*) would most likely be implemented through skilled employees. Decomposition, then, permits us to separate tasks, and consequently, apply *different* design solutions to each, according to their respective characterization.

PROCESS INHERITANCE

One strength of the contract is that it is a *single* schema, which facilitates its reuse. One dimension of reuse is *inheritance*: A process specification may inherit assertions from other process specifications.

For example, the specification for *hire an engineer* may be configured by inheriting the assertions in the contract *hire an employee* and conjoining to it the *as-*

sertions that are specific for hiring an engineer. That is, the specification of a local contract for hiring an engineer inherits the general, organization-wide specification for hiring any employee, and adds to it assertions that are unique to hiring an engineer. Local assertions may include experience (a specific requirement for a particular employee requisition), as well as professional certification (a *business rule* that may be local to the hiring department, the firm, or even a legal requirement). This is illustrated in Figure 11–10.

In this example, the contract *hire an engineer* is composed of assertions in the organization-wide contract *hire an employee* and assertions in the local contract *hire an engineer*. The contract *hire an engineer* inherits all assertions—invariants, triggers, preconditions, and postcondition—from the supertype contract, *hire an employee*, to which are conjoined engineer-specific precondition assertions.

Note that specification inheritance implies that, in object technology terms, the contract itself is an "object," and therefore participates in various behaviors, such as inheritance. This is in keeping with the OM philosophy expressed throughout this book—behavior is the *specification construct* on which we are focused, and not the structural properties to which it refers. Ideally, structural properties manifest themselves during realization.

TASK COORDINATION AND COMPLEX PROCESS SPECIFICATIONS

We previously made reference to the fact that in a process decomposition there would typically be an assortment of constraints among the components. For example, a task may have two varieties—a "normal" operating task for expected

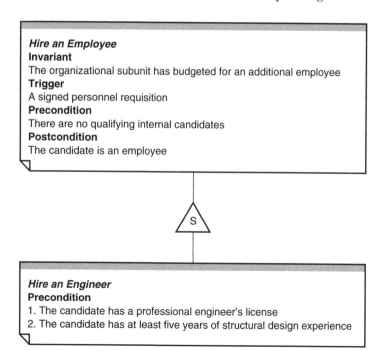

FIGURE 11–10   Process Inheritance: Contract Specification for Hire an Engineer

inputs and an "exception" for unexpected inputs. How can we prescribe each without resorting to the imprecision of commentary or pictures?

Existing BPR techniques illustrate workflows—a representation of an existing implementation ("IS") or a desired one ("SHOULD"). How do we distinguish specification from implementation? How do we create a new business specification, and implement it? How do we identify process tasks that are implemented sequentially because of implementation constraints? How do we create a formal specification that reveals *semantic* cross-dependencies? And what of the somewhat vague, but high EVA cultural and managerial processes? If we could successfully answer each of the above questions, we would have sufficient design artifacts to transform the business. We would be able, say, to identify processes that are implemented sequentially, but have interdependencies, and completely redesign the collection into a single, *reciprocal* composite task (this will become clearer below). We would be able to redesign the organization based on new business semantics! And so on and so forth.

The point is that a rich modeling paradigm is required to transform a high-level management intention into something concrete. Such detailed *semantic* design of processes usually is avoided by most organizations—it requires a modeling paradigm that addresses much more than simple workflows and hand-offs.

GENERIC INTERDEPENDENCE AMONG TASKS

In this section, we develop the common patterns by which tasks are coordinated. We refer to the generic coordinating patterns as *complex molecules*. In the same manner that information objects do not exist in isolation, but form molecules (Kilov and Ross 1994), process tasks also combine to form complex molecules. A *complex process molecule* is a managed collection of process task specifications with semantic constraints between participating task assertions. *A complex process molecule specifies corresponding task interdependencies, and thereby defines coordination constraints between tasks.*

More than 30 years ago, Thompson classified "technology" (i.e., process tasks) into three groups: long-linked, mediating, and intensive (Robbins 1990). Each technology group characterizes a particular type of task coordination: respectively, sequential, pooled, and reciprocal task interdependence. We can leverage this early work and define a series of generic, complex process molecules that are commonly found in most organizational processes.

The following is a description of several complex process molecules. We include the precise specifying mechanism that defines the molecule, and thus the coordination constraints among associated tasks. Note that with each complex molecule, we illustrate the association among constituent "simple" molecules in a diagram. This is for ease of understanding—the semantic that characterizes a complex molecule is found in the correspondence between pre- and postconditions among participating molecules. This may include several such semantic associations in each molecule.

1. SEQUENTIAL MOLECULE

This is the most elementary complex molecule and simply represents a sequence of process tasks. The specification of a sequence is that the precondition of a target process molecule is equal to the postcondition of a source

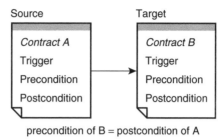

precondition of B = postcondition of A

FIGURE 11–11   Sequential Molecule

molecule. This represents a precise specification of *sequential interdependence* described by Thompson as a long-linked technology. This is shown in Figure 11–11.

Please note that it is only necessary that there be equality between a source postcondition and a target precondition. It is *not* necessary that the target trigger be included in the equality statement. The reason is that the concept of a sequence indicates a sequencing relationship between the "after" and "before" states of source and target tasks, respectively. Of course, a trigger must be fired before a target may be executed, but only if the target's precondition is satisfied. If the target precondition is satisfied as a consequence of the source postcondition, the criterion for sequencing has been established.

For example, for an employee to receive a paycheck at the end of the month, there is a sequence of process tasks, such as *charging time*. The last task in the sequence may be *produce paycheck*. This task may be preceded by a task called *calculate salary*. The sequence of *calculate salary* to *produce paycheck* is established by the postcondition of *calculate salary* equaling the precondition of *produce paycheck*. However, the fact that a salary has been calculated permits a paycheck to be produced but does not trigger it. The trigger for *produce paycheck* is a calendar event, in this case the last day of the month. This is illustrated in Figure 11–12.

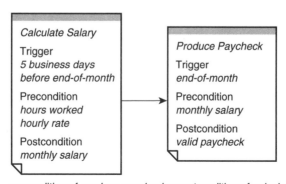

precondition of *produce paycheck* = postcondition of *calculate salary*

FIGURE 11–12   Sequence for Producing a Paycheck

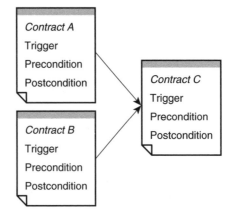

precondition of C = postcondition of A AND postcondition of B

FIGURE 11–13   Mediation Molecule

2. MEDIATION MOLECULE

In this molecule, the precondition of a target process molecule is equal to the conjunction of the postcondition of several source molecules. This is a precise specification of *pooled interdependence* described by Thompson as a mediating technology. This is illustrated in Figure 11–13.

For example, most purchase contracts in firms require pooled interdependence among several tasks, such as budget, allocation, and approval contracts.

3. RECIPROCAL MOLECULE (AND ITS IMPORTANCE IN BUSINESS PROCESS TRANSFORMATION

In this molecule, the notion of target and source molecules breaks down: the precondition of one process molecule is equal to the postcondition of another, and vice versa. This is an example of *reciprocal interdependence*, which Thompson refers to as an intensive technology. This is illustrated in Figure 11–14.

Consider, for example, the process of registration at a college. Certain classes require the approval of the instructor. The tasks of (1) obtaining instructor approval and (2) ascertaining whether the class is open are examples of two re-

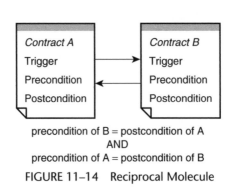

precondition of B = postcondition of A
AND
precondition of A = postcondition of B

FIGURE 11–14   Reciprocal Molecule

ciprocal tasks. The order of the tasks does not matter; both are interdependent and must be completed before the student may register for the class. Prior to the exploitation of IT, this reciprocal process molecule was realized by having a "registration day." This is a controlled environment where the *reciprocal specification is implemented sequentially*—by having the student cycle back-and-forth between tasks, until finally the precondition of one equals the postcondition of the other, and vice versa. Today, of course, IT permits the equality (or inequality) to be established concurrently—*a reciprocal implementation that corresponds to the specification.*

The specification and implementation of reciprocal molecules is at the heart of radical process change, such as BPR. If we were to specify existing business processes, we would discover many instances where reciprocal interdependence has been implemented as a cycle—i.e., a repeated sequence—much like the registration example above. Significant benefit in a BPR effort is usually derived by first discovering reciprocal task interdependence (that has been implemented sequentially), and then using IT to implement them concurrently (rather than as a cycle of sequential tasks).

The use of contracts facilitates the discovery of all such semantics, reciprocal and otherwise. Note that the popular IS- and SHOULD-maps are actually implementation diagrams rather than specifications. Such process flow diagrams are useful, but they may mask the actual business rules. Only during the formulation of task contracts can all implementation constraints be removed and the underlying semantics be revealed. Once the actual specifications are discovered, they may be reconfigured, and implemented in a radically more efficient and effective manner than the mere manipulation of workflows.

One word of caution. Reciprocal interdependences may be discovered, but it may not be possible or desirable to implement them. That is, we may uncover or develop a set of reciprocal specifications, but decide to implement them sequentially, even if it were possible to use IT to implement each of them concurrently. To do otherwise may be another example of failing to address how people actually use information. If people are not factored into the implementation of a redesigned business process, the novelty will eventually wear off and may lead to "caseworker burnout." An implementation that is fully aligned with a specification may not be as beneficial to the organization as a certain amount of measured misalignment.

4. DECISION MOLECULE

This is one of the most common situations in process modeling, and illustrates the inadequacy of graphical techniques. A "decision" is typically shown with a diamond branching to several different paths. The graph itself often becomes the "specification" with decision criteria often hidden as text in a comment.

The key to successfully designing decisions is to realize that decision criteria are actually assertions in the contracts of participating process tasks. In fact, a decision is nothing more than a task with several possible outcomes, each of which is associated with a possibly different target task. The specifying mechanism, therefore, is to *subtype the postcondition of the source molecule by all outcome criteria*,

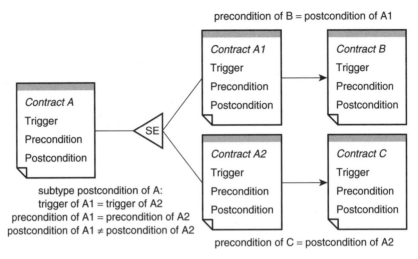

precondition of B = postcondition of A1

Contract A1
Trigger
Precondition
Postcondition

Contract B
Trigger
Precondition
Postcondition

Contract A
Trigger
Precondition
Postcondition

SE

Contract A2
Trigger
Precondition
Postcondition

Contract C
Trigger
Precondition
Postcondition

subtype postcondition of A:
trigger of A1 = trigger of A2
precondition of A1 = precondition of A2
postcondition of A1 ≠ postcondition of A2

precondition of C = postcondition of A2

FIGURE 11–15   Decision Molecule

and associate each with the precondition of each possible target molecule. This is illustrated in Figure 11–15.

5. FEEDBACK MOLECULE

This situation is similar to the decision molecule in that it highlights the imprecision of graphical or textual techniques. Figure 11–16(a) is a graphical representation of a feedback, from process C to process B.

In contrast, Figure 11–16(b) illustrates the relevant assertions and their relationships. Although the reader may find Figure 11–16(a) much easier to read than Figure 11–16(b), the former is not a specification and, as such, is not very useful to actually designing (or reengineering) a business process. Note that we do not actually need to draw Figure 11–16(b); we do so only for the purpose of exposition. What is important is an understanding of the relationships between the assertions that constitute a feedback. The essential points are as follows:

- The feedback process is characterized by the return of output from a target process C to a source process B, based on a prescribed deviation.
- The specifying mechanism for the source process is to subtype the precondition of the source molecule B by the deviation criteria. In this illustration, the source subtype that represents the deviation criteria is B2.

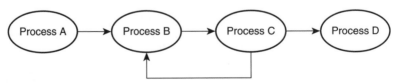

FIGURE 11–16(a)   Feedback Molecule—A Graphical Representation

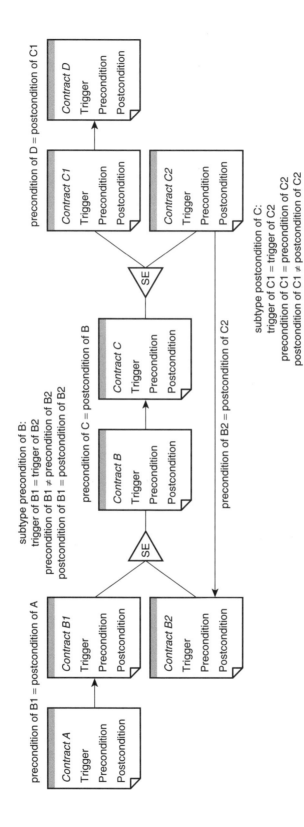

FIGURE 11–16(b) Feedback Molecule—A Contract Specification

precondition of D = postcondition of C1

subtype postcondition of C:
trigger of C1 = trigger of C2
precondition of C1 = precondition of C2
postcondition of C1 ≠ postcondition of C2

precondition of C = postcondition of B

precondition of B2 = postcondition of C2

subtype precondition of B:
trigger of B1 = trigger of B2
precondition of B1 ≠ precondition of B2
postcondition of B1 = postcondition of B2

precondition of B1 = postcondition of A

Contract D
Trigger
Precondition
Postcondition

Contract C1
Trigger
Precondition
Postcondition

Contract C2
Trigger
Precondition
Postcondition

Contract C
Trigger
Precondition
Postcondition

Contract B
Trigger
Precondition
Postcondition

Contract B1
Trigger
Precondition
Postcondition

Contract B2
Trigger
Precondition
Postcondition

Contract A
Trigger
Precondition
Postcondition

SE

189

- The specifying mechanism for the target process is to subtype the postcondition of the target molecule C by the deviation criteria. The target subtype that represents the deviation criteria is C2.
- The feedback is established when the precondition of the source B2 is equal to the postcondition of the target C2.
- The feedback is broken when there is no longer an equality between the precondition of the source B2 and the postcondition of the target C2. At that time, equality is established between the postcondition of another subtype of the target molecule C1 and the precondition of some other process task D, and the sequence continues.

6. EXCLUSIVE OR SEQUENCING MOLECULE

In this example, the molecule C is a target in two sequences with corresponding source molecules, A and B. Either source (A or B) may establish correspondence with target C. Naturally, there may be any number of sequences with corresponding source molecules. The specifying mechanism, therefore, is to *subtype the precondition of the target molecule by all sequencing criteria*, and associate each with the postcondition of each possible source molecule. This is illustrated in Figure 11–17.

11.5 PROCESS DESIGN & IMPLEMENTATION

Design is a term that is applied to a wide variety of efforts. In information systems development, there is "logical" and "physical" design, with the former sometimes called analysis. In process innovation, there are the "IS" and "SHOULD" maps that are said to portray a process design.

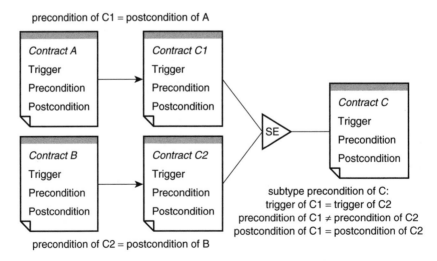

FIGURE 11–17   Exclusive OR Sequencing Molecule

It is usually convenient to think of a specification as "analysis" and the identification of a process' constituents as "design." But the constituents themselves are subject to specification and yet represent the implementation of the process! In practice, then, design is intertwined with process analysis and implementation.

For example, *hubbing* is a term used to describe a consolidated implementation among tasks that heretofore have been implemented across multiple departments, functions, or physical locations (see Keen 1997). Hubbing is most effective if applied to tasks that are logically linked, such as sequential, reciprocal, or some other coordinated specification. Hubbing is typically realized through IT and "case workers" using powerful workstations. The key to hubbing, then, is to use *common* process constituents to consolidate and implement a complex, coordinated set of task specifications (i.e., complex molecule).

PROCESS TASK AS THE BASIC UNIT OF ANALYSIS AND DESIGN

The building block of process design is typically at the task level, and consequently models such as the Perrow model may be used with the process molecule to both specify and implement process tasks. Daft (1998) has suggested possible designs for certain components that fit well with the process molecule. Building on this work, Table 11–1 summarizes possible process component instantiations that are aligned with each other for a particular task classification (i.e., subtype). Consequently, each set of implementation components is aligned with its corresponding process classification, and thereby maximizes the desirable emergent properties associated with a given process task specification.

Table 11–1 illustrates a *generic* component design for each task classification in the Perrow model. This table suggests several generalizations that we will discuss in subsequent sections or chapters. For example, routine tasks (i.e., analyzable, low variability) require low amounts of quantitative data, little or no knowledge or skills, hierarchical structures, and consequently utilize unskilled people and transaction data in computer systems.

Generally, as tasks become more unanalyzable (i.e., craft, nonroutine), the level of ambiguity (i.e., equivocality) increases and requires people with relatively more experience and tacit knowledge, and a certain level of rich information. Note that *skill* is a function of experience that historically has been developed through an apprenticeship (aside: As we will see in subsequent chapters, skill is a form of tacit knowledge). Similarly, as tasks become more variable (i.e., engineering and nonroutine), the level of uncertainty increases, thereby requiring people with more training, formal education and explicit knowledge, high quantities of information, and decision support computer systems.

Also, though we list "task-specific" tools for each task classification, in practice the task-specific tool used in most nonroutine and engineering tasks is computer hardware. For now, it is important to see that the process molecule may be used with an existing task classification model as a guide to actually designing specific task components.

TABLE 11–1   Generic Task Component Design Using the Perrow Classification Model—
Adapted from Daft (1998)

Perrow Task Classification	Process Task Components			
	Structure	Human	Information	Tool
Craft	Lateral	Skilled —high experience —low training —high tacit knowledge	Low rich —process relationships (e.g., observation)	Task-specific (e.g., hand-tools, machinery, instruments)
Routine	Hierarchical	Unskilled —low experience —low training	Low quantitative —transaction data —operational guidelines —functional relationships (hierarchical referral)	Operational computer systems Documents (procedural) Task-specific

Non-routine	Lateral	Knowledge &
		Skilled
		—high experience
		—high training
		—high tacit and
		  explicit kwldg
			High rich
			—process relationships
			  (e.g., meetings)
			High quantitative
			—decision support data
				Decision support
				computer systems
				(e.g., expert systems,
				data warehouses)
				Task specific

Engineering	Matrix	Knowledge &
		Technical
		—high education
		—high explicit,
		  low to moderate
		  tacit knowledge
			Moderate rich
			—functional and process
			  relationships (e.g.,
			  project teams)
			High quantitative
			—decision support data
			—technical reference data
				Decision support
				computer systems
				(e.g., expert systems,
				data warehouses)
				Technical reference
				documents & procs
				Task-specific

MODULAR/COMPONENT DESIGN

Modular design is a broad area that includes a wide variety of approaches and techniques. Throughout this book we have been discussing various constructs and techniques that facilitate component-based organizational design. Among them are the following:

- A schema that separates specification from implementation. This is effected with the *organization molecule* construct where the composite represents a domain specification, while the components represent its implementation. This separation of concerns leads to the potential reuse of either the composite or components. Thus, a composite specification may be implemented with a variety of constituents, while components may be *shared* and used to implement any number of specifications.

- Reuse of a specification through inheritance. Inheritance is the reuse of an existing specification to which additional assertions are added, thereby producing a new specification.

- Reuse of a specification through composition. This is the creation of a new "composite" specification through the conjunction of existing "component" specifications. As with the above, we can compose specifications (composite or component) from existing ones.

For example, a simple process such as registering for a course at a college may have two very different implementation scenarios, i.e., different sets of component instances used to implement the same process specification. Table 11–2 is a summary of the differences in two possible scenarios: registration day and IT/web.

Observe that there is correspondence among the components in each implementation scenario—what we have referred to as consistent alignment. This ensures optimized implementation in either scenario.

EMERGENT CHARACTERISTICS OF PROCESSES

The introduction of a different mix of implementation components, such as in the IT/web scenario, should not change the essential specification of a process (e.g., registering for a class), but it may have a huge impact on its emergent properties. It is these properties that are often visible to clients. In the simple example above, an IT/web implementation reduces costs (an emergent property important to the college), and extends the period of registration from one day to some broader time period, such as one month (an emergent property important to the student).

TABLE 11–2   TWO IMPLEMENTATION SCENARIOS FOR CLASS REGISTRATION

Process	Process Task Components			
	Structure	Human	Information	Tool
Class: registration (registration day scenario)	Lateral: registration day team	Skilled: —administrators Unskilled: —clerks —student help Client: —student	Low quantitative data: —course listing and offering —hierarchical referral Low rich information: —student and registration team interaction	Document systems (often hardcopy, sometimes computer): —listing of course offering and availability —course catalog
Class: registration (IT/web scenario)	None	Client: —student	Moderate quantitative data: —course listing and offering —some decision support software	Computer systems operational: —active web interface —course databases —offering/availability databases decision support: —student study plan documents —financial aid and student loan databases

REDESIGNING PROCESSES AND THE SHARING OF COMPONENTS

In addition to improving "traditional" emergent characteristics of processes (e.g., cycle time, costs), we see that the IT/web scenario *extends* the process specification. In so doing, the new IT/web implementation is satisfying the original *class registration* process, as well as other process tasks associated with financial aid and students' study plans. In effect, we are integrating several, separate process tasks into a single, *reciprocal* process work cycle.

For example, observe in Table 11–2 that the IT/web scenario changes the information and tool constituents of the registration process. It *extends* the information content to include decision support databases as well as the traditional course listing and offering. The IT/web scenario thus permits the student to ask (and get answers) to questions associated with other (but related) process tasks, such as, "Can I take an additional class this semester?" "Can I afford it?" "What is the impact on my study plan in subsequent semesters?" "Can I accelerate my date of graduation?"

This simple example illustrates the following:

1. The use of enriched IT—a specialized tool component (i.e., a dynamic web browser) and the addition of decision support data—*replaces* both the human and structure components in the original registration day scenario, while increasing the service level to the student.

2. The decision support database may already exist to support other related tasks, such as determining student loan availability, projecting and rearranging study plans, etc. In such a case, we are simply *reusing* a *common* information component to reconfigure several, related tasks into a single reciprocal set of tasks. If the decision support database does not exist, its development may be viewed as a mechanism to redesign and integrate several operational and decision support process tasks—class registration, determining loan availability, what/if analysis on a projected study plan, etc.

3. Generally, the reuse of process components facilitates process task consolidation and integration, generally known as hubbing. Such reuse may extend to any component but is particularly effective if applied to people, IT, or both. Powerful workstations or web browsers are examples of how tools, databases, and people may be brought together to implement a collection of related process tasks specifications. It is "networking" technologies that facilitate hubbing.

4. Component sharing should consolidate the implementation of task specifications within a work cycle, or any logical task collection (e.g., complex molecules). In the example above, we integrate several heretofore separately implemented process tasks into a single, reciprocal process work cycle.

5. Radical process redesign is more likely with a vision and strategy, not only for the process itself, but also for its components. An IT strategy for data (as well as knowledge) may serve as an *information infrastructure* that facilitates both process reconfiguration and integration.

Management Intent and Pulling Process Levers

The constituents of a process (i.e., components in the process molecule) serve as change levers during process change. The sequence in which the levers are pulled converges with management intentions to reveal the elaborated, final design.

For example, in implementing the IT/web scenario, the flow of process change is unidirectional: from *technology*, which is used to broaden access to increasing amounts of *information*, to the need for fewer *people* from the organization to assist the client (student), to the elimination of *structure*. Choosing a particular lever as a driver determines the nature of subsequent constituents. However, the full process context and management intent must be understood to realize a successful design. Using technology as a driver for information, for example, is most effective if there are process tasks available for coordination or hubbing.

The selection of a process change lever, then, complements a management philosophy and change strategy. This is particularly true if the drivers are technology and information:

1. IT may be used to build vertical information linkages, and thus complement machine strategies and structures; the essential goal of the design is to minimize behavioral variance and induce strict uniformity.
2. A second application of IT is to coordinate process tasks by building horizontal information linkages. This may be used to facilitate hubbing, and also to empower workers or customers with analytical tools and thus facilitate decision making.
3. A more recent paradigm on the organizational landscape is the development of knowledge work. A third utility for IT, then, is to provide opportunities for *people* to create and apply knowledge. *Collaboration* is an example of a design technique, realized through team structures and work group software, where the intent is to coordinate workers, and thus facilitate knowledge sharing. *With knowledge work, process constituents are designed to coordinate people, as opposed to tasks.* We will discuss knowledge work in subsequent chapters.

Design Diagrams and Maps

The "maps" sometimes used during process design represent process flows that map a task to a functional department. These design diagrams represent workflows, and are popular with managers and consultants alike. An IS map represents a current workflow, while a SHOULD map represents a desired flow. Note that maps do not easily correspond to other forms of processes, such as those associated with culture or management. (See Rummler and Brache 1995 for an excellent discussion of process design maps.)

A map is a representation of process tasks and their corresponding functional structures—a picture of {process} and {structure} elements from the process molecule. A map identifies connection points among process components between functional departments. Such cross-functional hand-offs, then, identify areas for coordination between departmental functions.

EXTENDED MAPS

A traditional map associates process flows and functional departments. We can extend the current notion of a map by including *each* process constituent, separately (one-dimensional) or collectively (multi-dimensional). Listed below are examples of *one-dimensional maps* that we have found useful. In so doing, we identify areas of coordination within each component of a process:

- *Process X structure (functional)*. The commonly used map that serves to identify functional departments and the processes each stewards.
- *Process X structure (team)*. This is also a *process X structure* map, but one that identifies work structures, which, of course, may be cross-functional. Recall that organizational molecules contain many-to-many associations. Consequently, it is straightforward to associate a given process task with *all* corresponding structures, both functional and work.
- *Process X human*. This serves to optimize the deployment of human skills and knowledge, as well as identify opportunities for "case" workers. Individual people, job categories, and skills may thus be optimized across collections of interdependent tasks.
- *Process X information*. This identifies data elements and operations for development of process-driven information systems. Note that this is in contrast to information engineering, which tends to organize information systems around functions, or traditional applications which support isolated tasks. It is thus possible to develop an IS development paradigm around business processes, as opposed to functions or applications.
- *Process X tool*. This serves to optimize the deployment of both standard and unique tools. It is important in process design to identify and compensate for tool disconnects across process links. Computer hardware, for example, may be selected on the basis of tasks in a common work cycle or business process.

MULTI-DIMENSIONAL MAPS

While one-dimensional maps identify areas of coordination and integration within a component domain (e.g., information), another approach is to combine process component maps and create *multi-dimensional maps*. Such maps facilitate our understanding of the relationships *between* process constituents.

For example, a *process X people X structure (functional)* map serves to identify candidate people for participation in cross-functional teams (along one axis), and the functional departments from which each person will be obtained (along the other axis).

As another example, a *process X people X information* map serves to identify the appropriate mix of process tasks, data and their operations, and people that can be integrated on a given person's desk-top. This is particularly important in identifying candidate processes for reconfiguration, data to be integrated, and knowledge to be shared.

A variation on this theme is to create multi-dimensional maps relating components, or components at different levels of abstraction. For example, a *process X system X information (data)* map serves to identify common data elements across different systems. This is a systems integration issue: Most systems have been developed along functional application lines, but we are designing cross-functional processes. Each link between tasks that crosses systems serves to identify areas for coordination, or even integration, between those systems. This is important since we know that integrating all of an organization's data may have negative business value (Goodhue, Wybo, and Kirsch 1992). A *process X system X information (data)* map, identifies those data elements that have a business rationale for integration, and the context (process tasks) to which integration should conform.

SIMULATION AND THE EFFECT OF TIME

Queuing flows and cause-and-effect relationships in design maps add the dimensions of accumulations and casualty to process flows. This was reviewed in Chapter 8. In practice, this necessitates identifying, for each process task, such measures as cycle time (e.g., average, minimum, maximum, discrete values), queue length, wait time, probability of event occurrences, the number of process task occurrences, and so on.

Observe that we believe the time function is generally a design and implementation issue, and not one of specification. For example, the specifications associated with financial services in a bank (e.g., deposits, withdrawals, etc.) are independent of how long you will be on line waiting for those services. That is determined by design—the average cycle time for each service occurrence, the number of people queued, the expected wait time, and the number of task occurrences (i.e., teller stations). Naturally, changing process constituents to effect a time change during realization may effect the specification. In practice, then, time is intertwined with specification and implementation.

Although time is usually associated with realization, it may be part of a specification. For example, time is part of the specification for the requirement for synchronization of a new product release.

11.6 FORMULATING INFORMATION-RICH PROCESSES

Most of the process change literature usually centers on routine or engineering tasks that can be easily modeled by workflows. This is where most consultants operate (the modeling is trivial with high throughput). However, we note that workflows may include nonroutine as well as routine tasks; in fact, typical workflows contain a mix of tasks, though they may concentrate on routine or engineering tasks.

Peter Keen (1997) points out that many processes, particularly those with a high EVA, are more than workflows. The workflow paradigm derives from industrial engineering and characterizes processes with clearly defined inputs, outputs, and flows. However, there are many processes with less clearly defined assertions that affect the success of an organization as much as workflows, e.g., acquisitions, those related to culture, incentives and promotions, etc. Moreover, John Kay has described several imprecise behaviors, based on assumptions rather than explicit specifications, known as relational contracts.

As we move to a more knowledge-intensive society, much of our work is increasingly nonroutine. Many organizations operate with *engineering* tasks (analyzable with a large number of exceptions). This includes most of the traditional information-rich processes, such as designing a bridge, performing surgery, or developing software. This form of process design is complex but straightforward (because the tasks are analyzable), provided we have a sufficiently rich modeling paradigm (because the tasks have a high number of exceptions). The complex process molecules described previously, as well as the process molecule itself with its alignment threads, are ideal for designing engineering tasks.

But what of *craft* processes, such as teaching a class in management, or *nonroutine* processes, such as formulating a new direction for a department? And how about relational contracts, and management processes with unclear assertions (i.e., rules, inputs, and outputs)? And what of knowledge-based tasks? Many such processes have a high EVA, are culture-based, and do not lend themselves to workflows. Here traditional, and not so traditional, modeling paradigms have a problem. With such processes or tasks, we depend on the information molecule and various knowledge models—the subjects of Chapters 12 and 13.

11.7 CORE CONCEPTS

Process formulation	Process characterization
Competence	Capability
Abstraction (i.e., process subtypes)	Routinization
Decomposition (e.g., process)	Inheritance (e.g., process)
Complex process molecule	Task interdependence and coordination
Generic task component design	
Component reuse and sharing	Modular/component design
Hubbing	Simulation
Information-rich processes	Collaboration

One- and multi-dimensional process design maps

Strategic alignment between the process molecule and the value chain

Separation of specification and implementation

Business process transformation (top-down)

Continuous improvement (bottom-up)

CHAPTER 12

DATA, KNOWLEDGE, AND INFORMATION

12.1 REVOLUTION OR RENAISSANCE?

It is hard to overstate the impact which information technology is having on modern organizations. It is common to hear a management guru describe how information technology is transforming our lives, work environments, opportunities, and so on.

One way to understand the effect of information on the organization is to use the value chain as a tool to compare the transformations resulting from the Information Revolution to those resulting from the Industrial Revolution. The Industrial Revolution was driven by the introduction of two technologies: power and transportation. In a firm's value chain, the technology of power primarily effects the *operations* value activities, while transportation technology primarily effects *inbound* and *outbound logistics*. In comparison, information technology (IT) effects every value activity: *inbound logistics, operations, outbound logistics, marketing and sales, service, infrastructure, human resources management, technology development*, and *procurement*. When we consider that the Industrial Revolution thoroughly transformed three of nine value activities and had a profound impact on organizations and societies, we can begin to understand the changes in the modern world caused by IT. As significant as the transformations caused by the Industrial Revolution have been, we can only conclude that the transformations caused by the Information Revolution will be far more pervasive.

THE INFORMATION TECHNOLOGY RENAISSANCE

Revolutions are turbulent. They are also highly destructive. Information technology may be causing turmoil, but its wake has produced mostly positive change. A rising standard of living, a shift of power from the few to the many, greater economic freedom and job satisfaction, and so on, are all examples of beneficial change, not signs of a violent revolution.

Charles Handy (1997) has suggested a different metaphor—a kind of information renaissance. In Medieval Europe, information was in the hands of the few—the monarchy and the Church. The invention of the printing press triggered the European Renaissance. People were able to read the Bible in their native languages. They were able to interpret for themselves, and make their own decisions. The availability of information shifted power from the few to the many. With that shift, of course, came greater responsibility and stress to those with the newly discovered source of power.

Today, the desk-top computer is the equivalent of the printing press. Workers now have access to information long unavailable, even hidden. Information anytime, everywhere, has given knowledge workers greater control over their lives and careers than previously. The organization that uses information for either control or enablement is in revolutionary mode and will surely be at a disadvantage over the long-term. In contrast, the organization that uses information as a vehicle to inspire and create knowledge among its workers will itself be inspired and become a valuable repository of knowledge.

THE INFORMATION VALUE CHAIN

Tom Davenport (1997) has proposed an information value chain. Typically, an information chain starts with determining *business requirements*, proceeds to *capturing* information, *distributing* information, and finally, *using* information. But the essential questions remain: What are we analyzing, collecting, distributing, and using? Can we distinguish, for example, between business requirements for data and those for knowledge? As Peter Drucker (1993) states: "Now that knowledge is taking the place of capital as the driving force in organizations worldwide, it is too easy to confuse data with knowledge and information technology with information." Are the differences important? Do they depend on the type of work being performed? Do they depend on the type of people performing the work? Is there a difference between a data system and a knowledge system? How do we build such systems and associate them with people? And how do we relate it all to business processes? And so on and so forth.

THE INFORMATION CONTINUUM

In order to answer these questions, it is necessary to explore the schemes that classify and operationalize these concepts. Characterization is important. We cannot hope to design the full range of that which is called data, information, or knowledge, unless we understand the characteristics of each, and how each is implemented. Only then can we create a fully expressive architecture that captures the richness of each of these concepts.

Davenport (1997) has advanced the notion of a continuum to help us visualize these concepts. Typically captured in computer systems, data at one end, represents easily structured "states of the world." Information, on the continuum, is "data endowed with relevance and purpose" (a quote from Peter Drucker 1988). Information requires a unit of analysis and human intervention—"relevance and purpose" are provided by people. Knowledge, at the other end of the continuum, is "information with the most value," difficult to structure or implement in computers, and usually requires some period of time for synthesis. There is the implication that the continuum reflects a dependency: information is some form of endowed data while knowledge is a synthesis of information. This increasing "rich-ness" is a function of human intervention—human involvement increases as one moves along the continuum from data to information to knowledge.

*****

Each of these areas—data, information, and knowledge—has an assortment of specific design frameworks, the success of which often depends on the appropriate application. For example, information engineering appears to fail at structuring *information* (i.e., human endowed data in applications), but appears to succeed if the focus is restricted to *data* (i.e., subject area database design).

Data, information, and knowledge have similar, but different definitions and perspectives. For example, both Nonaka and Takeuchi (1995) and Davenport and Prusak (1998) view information as "messages" that elicit or create knowledge, anchored in the existing beliefs and commitment of the person in question. Sveiby (1997) views knowledge as exclusively tacit, while information is explicit. Peter Drucker (1992, 1993) writes about the need to improve the productivity of knowledge workers, and the requirement for a business process context. And so on and so forth. There is certainly no dearth of ideas when it comes to these subjects.

In lieu of embracing any particular perspective, we present an architectural framework around which these perspectual concepts may be given structure and utility. As such, we deliberately emphasize certain concepts and not others. All concepts are important, but only a few may be used to construct an architecture. With architecture, a management concept becomes a *managed construct* in the broader context of organizational design.

Our goal is clear: to answer the questions posed above with useful and easy-to-use constructs that may be successfully implemented. This is particularly important from the perspective of the "business analyst of the future" who will help create the core architecture. Data, information, and knowledge are inevitably intertwined with culture, people, processes, and learning.

12.2 INFORMATION CHARACTERIZATION

Recall from Chapter 3 that uncertainty is defined as the absence of information. Recall also that uncertainty is reduced by sufficient quantities of information. Low levels of uncertainty, as would be found in tasks that are low in variability (i.e., routine, craft), are typically satisfied by standardized work procedures, handbooks, reports, and hierarchical referral. In contrast, tasks high in variability (i.e., engineering, nonroutine) are characterized by high levels of uncertainty that can only be reduced with large amounts of quantitative information, such as those provided by computer information systems, and technical manuals and references.

Recall, too, that equivocality is the presence of multiple, conflicting interpretations of a situation, and is reduced by sufficiently rich information. We described rich information as that which is beyond manifest data, usually associated with an intimate understanding that is a consequence of human experience, learning, and interactive communications. Tasks high in unanalyzability (i.e., craft, nonroutine) are characterized by equivocality and thus require rich sources of information.

Therefore, we can say that the set of information requirements associated with a process task is a function of task characterization, which in turn, determines information sources. The components illustrated in the information molecule represent information sources, and therefore the *character* of the information specification. In Figure 12–1, we have *refined* the information molecule to make the information constituents more apparent. Observe that we have classified the tool component in terms of computer and document constituents, classified structure into hierarchical and lateral relations, and created a composite association between structure and human components. Figure 12–1 shows the characterization of information in terms of these components.

Quantitative information is easily structured, and is normally associated with simple hierarchical relationships, and computer and document systems. In contrast, *rich* information is difficult to structure, and is associated with people and the structures in which they work, particularly structures that facilitate lateral relationships (e.g., teams, matrix structures, task forces, etc.). Rich information is closely associated with learning and may include the acquisition of skills or knowledge.

It is sometimes difficult to distinguish between quantitative and rich information by looking at a source. For example, an expert system is a computer source of information, but are its contents quantitative or rich? Some would say

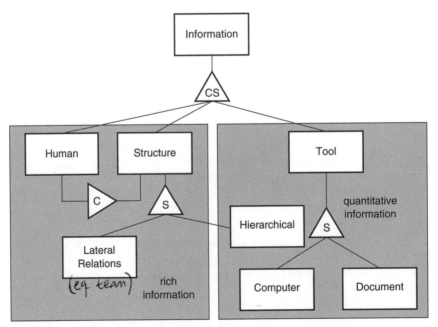

FIGURE 12–1   Characterizing Information in a Refined Information Molecule

rich; but then, can computers be sources of rich information? This leads us to Peter Drucker, and his call to more precisely distinguish data, information, and knowledge.

12.3 DATA, KNOWLEDGE, AND INFORMATION

Consider the following assertion: A manual of technical specifications is "data," and becomes "information" only in a particular "process" context, such as designing a bridge, and when "processed" by an engineer designing a bridge. Similarly, "knowledge" of how to design a bridge resides in the head of an engineer, or a team of engineers, and becomes "information" only when there is a bridge to design and data to process.

As another example, a stockbroker and a client may interact in a *business process* known as financial consulting. As part of the process, the broker may gather *information* concerning investment goals and current positions from a client. The broker will access a computer to read *data* about various financial securities, and drawing on *knowledge* acquired through education, experience, and foresight, make a recommendation (*information*) back to the client. Moreover, the separate process tasks comprising information, data, and knowledge are reciprocal and dynamic.

These concepts—the intermingling, often in real time, of data, knowledge, information, and business processes—are illustrated in Figure 12–2.

Observe that the refined information molecule has connections to two other molecules: a process molecule to establish a process context for information, and a learning molecule to establish a context for knowledge formulation. *Data, knowledge, and information can thus be characterized only through interconnectivity among the information, process, and learning domains.* The rationale behind this architecture is as follows:

- We adopt Drucker's definition that information is "data endowed with relevance and purpose." Data represents states of the world, to which knowledge is applied to determine relevance and purpose. Information is thus characterized by data and knowledge interaction.

- An information continuum is characterized by its poles—data and knowledge archetypes. There is not one intermediate point, but an infinite number of such points, each representing information distinguished by some "mix" of data and knowledge characteristics.

- We do not attempt to identify the "substance" or "nature" of data or knowledge. That is neither practical nor useful during design—knowledge, for example, contains many intrinsic elements yet to be elucidated by science or philosophy, such as thinking or consciousness. Rather, we *characterize* data and knowledge *properties* in terms of what distinguishes one from the other—the form each is likely to assume during implementation.

- Human involvement, and therefore behavior complexity, increase as the information mix shifts from the data to the knowledge pole.

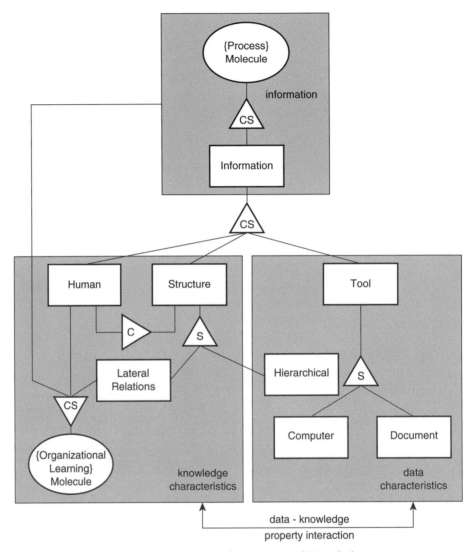

FIGURE 12–2   Data, Information, and Knowledge

- Utility in an organization is a function of context, that is, the interconnectivity of information (i.e., some "mix" of data and knowledge properties) within a business process. Hence, our depiction of information includes interconnectivity with the process molecule (as shown in Figure 12–2). A context may be established through interconnectivity to business processes, or other organizational constructs, such as strategy or culture.

- Data is an observed or measured state of the world, and in an organization, it is typically captured in business events, such as sales or service tasks. Data is easily structured, comparatively static, and closely associated with lean communications (i.e., static, one-way). Its implementation components are thus characterized by simple human relationships, and physical things, like machines or paper.

- Knowledge is related to experience, judgment, and the passing of time, and is therefore not easily structured, is very dynamic, and associated with rich forms of communication (i.e., interactive, two-way). Its operationalized components are thus characterized by people, their complex work relationships, and their learning experiences.

- Information (data and knowledge interaction) makes visible heretofore invisible patterns that give meaning to a particular context, such as a business event. Such patterns elicit and create new perspectives and knowledge.

- A context for learning is established through interconnectivity between the information and process molecules. As we will subsequently see, not all learning is organizational, and not all knowledge is shared. In such a case, only the individual learns, and knowledge resides fully within the human component. In either case (individual or organizational), knowledge is associated with learning.

- Learning creates recursive relationships. Learning extends the notion of knowledge development to information, which includes interconnectivity back to process, data, and knowledge.

Information, then, is that which is a constituent of an organizational construct, such as a business process. That constituent, in turn, is characterized by two dimensions—easily structured things called data, and very complex and dynamic things called knowledge. Data is normally implemented in physical media, like machines or paper, or through simple reporting relationships. If implemented in machines, data may be voluminous. Knowledge, by contrast, is implemented through people, their work structures (e.g., lateral relations), and is intertwined with learning. Knowledge is something human!

> In summary, we can visualize data as record-specific, knowledge as thinking-specific, and information as context-specific.

12.4 DATA CHARACTERIZATION

In our experience, we have observed a certain confusion between *characterizing* data, and *analyzing and structuring* data. The former concerns a particular business context, while the latter addresses software development. For example, most data in organizations has been characterized for routine, operational workflows, and consequently analyzed and structured to support transaction systems. IT professionals have established paradigms and artifacts to structure data for such an operational context.

There are other characterizations of data, however, such as data for decision support or culture change. Unfortunately some of these data forms have been operationalized with the same structuring paradigms that have been applied to operational systems. While successful in the operational arena, IT has had less than dramatic effects in other organizational contexts, such as culture change or learning.

Data management for a 21st century organization must address each of the domains in an organization, particularly its core architecture: data for business processes, data for culture, data for knowledge, and data for learning.

Below are several examples of data characterizations that support several organizational domains. While a short list, it serves to illustrate the challenge the 21st century presents to the IT profession. No doubt, this list will grow even longer.

1. *Data for operational business processes*—specific data that is essentially atomic. The process task contexts are primarily routine, and thus the sources of data include operational computer systems, manuals describing work procedures, policies governing the execution of the task, etc. Such systems may, though not necessarily, support task coordination, what is said to represent *horizontal* information linkages. (Note that if information is sufficiently rich and therefore contains a large knowledge component, such horizontal linkages may be implemented through people.)

2. *Data for analytical and decision support business processes*—specific data for "soft" process tasks, in particular, those that are managerial, analytical, or involve decision making. These process contexts are essentially nonroutine. The data sources are primarily MIS, internal and external data, as well as policy guidelines and standard procedures. Since the information component of these tasks includes a large knowledge constituent (usually in the head of a business analyst or decision maker using the system), the data component must be structured to harmonize with the type and form of knowledge required or possessed by the user.

   Traditionally, such systems have been used for control (e.g., monitoring and management reporting), and are said to represent *vertical* information linkages. However, another class of such systems exists for market exploitation and strategic planning—data mining, for example.

3. *Data for learning and knowledge development*—data that facilitates knowledge transfer. For example, a simulation system may be used to internalize knowledge about the quality dimensions of a new product and its production tasks. It is a framework that intertwines process, data, and explicit knowledge, the goal of which is to transfer and convert specific knowledge into mental models in people. As another example, a CASE tool may be used as a learning system: It facilitates and guides the development of a data model, *and* promotes application and modeling knowledge in the head of an analyst.

4. *Data for behavior and culture change*—this is data, often intertwined with highly structured explicit knowledge, that is intended to shape the behavior

of people, and thereby effect an organization's culture. A common example is an employee handbook which seeks to prescribe the behavior of individual employees. This behavior is process independent, and may be considered data in support of an organization's culture.

Most such data and explicit knowledge is currently designed for control—defining penalties for inappropriate behavior. To facilitate positive cultural enrichment and change, architecting "data for culture- and knowledge-interconnectivity," we will have to structure and deliver data with a very different paradigm than is currently the case. Such data will have to promote positive mental models as well as desirable overt behaviors.

As we can see, data is intertwined with knowledge and a variety of processes, including "soft" business processes (e.g., nonroutine, analytical, managerial, decision making, cultural, or learning). In effect, there is a *cooperative* interaction among data, knowledge, and business processes. There is a *continuum of information systems*, each of which contains some mix of data and knowledge constituents. Until recently, most IT development has concentrated on systems close to the data archetype—data and highly routinized knowledge (e.g., create, read, update, and delete operations on data). Increasingly, however, data has to be formulated to support systems with a significant, non-routinized knowledge component—data for business analysis, data for learning, etc.

ANALYZING AND STRUCTURING DATA

Most data analysis or structuring techniques have usually focused on "data for operational processing." Accordingly, many analysts have defined "correct" data models in terms of operational requirements—a consequence of the characterization of the data and the process tasks they support. These include specific techniques associated with "logical" and "physical" design, waterfall and object-oriented development methodologies, and so on. They have long received the exclusive attention of IT professionals, so much so that the application of these techniques has become a commodity while other forms of data structuring in support of different characterizations of data (e.g., data for learning) are barely acknowledged.

For example, old forms of decision support systems (DSS) are accorded the same data structuring as transactional data, and hence DSS has been little more than "management reporting." This is not exactly support for management decisions in a knowledge era! With the advent of data warehousing, however, new forms of analysis and structuring have begun to take shape, e.g., "multidimensional" models of data. These, too, may be "logical" and define new instrumentalities for DSS—defined in a technology independent manner.

The following is a brief listing of the standard artifacts by which IT professionals analyze and structure data. While these techniques have been effective in operationalizing data for transaction processing, it is not clear how effective they will be for operationalizing other data characterizations.

- Two design dimensions: logical and physical models.
- Logical data models: entities, attributes, and their associations (e.g., an entity-relationship model).

- Extensions to "data" models include the addition of operations. These extensions are data-related operations, and are typically primitive create, read, update, and delete (CRUD) operations on data. Note that the operations associated with data are governed by the characterization of the underlying data. It is not to be assumed that operations for something other than transaction data, say decision support or learning characterizations, include the same operations that are used for transaction processing. Primitive operations may be defined and stored in a library, or in separate "process models," such as data flow diagrams.

  Processing variation has given rise to the notion of a *conceptual model*—a generalized data model with several sets of views and processing operations—each set of which operates on data requirements for a particular set of process tasks.

- Complex processes (e.g., computing algorithms) may also be defined in process models. Generally, a complex process—a specific sequence of particular operations and the invariants governing those operations—move the information content of the process away from the data archetype, and more toward the knowledge pole. Indeed, a complex process contains a certain business logic (i.e., knowledge) applied to data. Such business logic may be dictated by law, industry practice, or an organization's culture. It may be a straightforward process, such as one governing the hiring of a new employee, or be very complex, such as the logic governing risk management. As we will see later in this chapter, such logic represents *explicit knowledge*—knowledge sufficiently well-understood and agreed upon, and thus implementable in computer systems. Even here, however, a person usually mediates the results—in turbulent environments, business logic constantly changes. Again, relevance and purpose are always determined by people, not machines.

- Physical design—tables and columns (for relational databases) by which integrity constraints defined in the logical model are enforced at the physical level. For example, referential integrity is a DBMS level extension that enforces primitive CRUD operations on data.

- Domains—a construct for defining the "lawful state space" of attributes (i.e., data element values), which, combined with primitive CRUD operations, defines the consistency and integrity of a data model. This, too, represents a certain application of explicit knowledge to data: the attribute and attribute *value* combinations that are valid for a particular characterization of data.

Each characterization of data is a function of its business process context, and requires a unique data analysis and structuring philosophy. In the same way that new forms of decision support (e.g., data warehousing) changed standard IT structuring techniques, we believe that each form of data characterization will require its own analysis and structuring techniques. These will most likely be extensions to existing techniques, but may include new model forms to establish a proper business context.

12.5 KNOWLEDGE CHARACTERIZATION

In this section, we introduce several knowledge characterizations that help us structure and facilitate knowledge implementation and interconnectivity. You will notice that these characterizations often overlap, and reflect several perspectives: psychological, social, scientific, industry, and organizational. Each gives insight into how we may characterize, and thereby design, align, and operationalize knowledge in an organization.

DEFINING KNOWLEDGE

As we previously indicated, we will not attempt to formally define the nature or essence of knowledge. Existing definitions span the range of complexity and intellectual richness, from Plato's "justified true belief" (Nonaka and Takeuchi 1995) to a more mundane "the capacity to act" (Sveiby 1997).

This struggle to define knowledge is somewhat analogous to the challenge biologists face as they seek to define "intelligence" across species. A biologist typically defines intelligence as something like "the ability to be successful in one's environment." Unfortunately, this Darwinian view of adaptation fails to distinguish between the intelligence of, say, bacteria (arguably, the most successful life form that has ever lived on earth) and human beings. Yet, even biologists recognize that humans have something very special: They may manipulate and change the environment, in effect, changing the direction of their evolution and adaptation. This ability to change context and goals, the rules of relevance and adaptation, is what distinguishes the intelligence of humans from other species, and, in fact, is not a bad working definition of knowledge.

The point is that knowledge is a slippery concept. How it is characterized, used, and even created within an organization is very complicated. On the other hand, we believe that knowledge, as with other soft constructs such as culture, is subject to some level of modeling, and thus may be architected, integrated, and designed into an organization. We do so with some uncertainty, but with informed discretion.

AN IMPORTANT EAST–WEST DISTINCTION

Nonaka and Takeuchi (1995) describe an important difference in perspective between Western and Japanese intellectual traditions. With respect to knowledge as "justified true belief," Western thought emphasizes the "true" while Japanese tradition places greater emphasis on "justified belief." The Western focus is on a static, nonhuman, absolute notion of knowledge, expressed as propositions or formal logic. The Japanese focus is on knowledge as a "dynamic human process of justifying personal belief toward the 'truth'."

The Western emphasis leads to an orientation where knowledge is something *discrete, external,* and *explicit*, while the Japanese orientation is one where knowledge is *fluid, personal,* and *tacit*. The different orientations lead to divergent work structures and management practices, each with its strengths and weaknesses.

Let us illustrate the difference with a simple example. Suppose Tom has two friends, one Western and one Japanese. Each sees Tom sitting in a room, and is asked, "Is Tom in the room?" Each would answer, "Yes." In a closed environment where uncertainty is minimal, their differing perspectives are inconsequential and lead each to the same answer.

We now inform Tom's friends that Tom has an identical twin who they have never met, and repeat the question, "Is Tom in the room?" The archetypical Westerner would answer, "I need more information." The archetype Japanese person would answer, "Yes." Each would also ask to meet the person in the room, but with different purposes: The Western person is seeking a thread of explicit evidence in order to make a decision in the first place, while the Japanese person is seeking personal engagement and experiential input in order to make a second decision.

The Western perspective is to look outward for discrete pieces of information that would identify the truth, while the Japanese perspective is to turn inward and engage the issue on a personal level, in the expectation that it would move him or her closer to what is true.

RISKS ASSOCIATED WITH KNOWLEDGE PERSPECTIVES

The East-West perspectives give rise to differing managerial and operational risks. Nonaka and Takeuchi (1995) describe the Western risk with a term well-known to IT professionals—*analysis paralysis*. Whether it is an IT analyst building a data model for an IT project, or a senior manager making a decision on a merger, there never seems to enough information. The existence of e-mail and the Internet does not satisfy this cultural flaw. Just look around your office.

Similarly, the risk associated with the Japanese perspective is *overadaptation*, a term sometimes used to describe the failure of a formerly successful species (e.g., dinosaurs) to adapt to a changing environment. The essence of overadaptation is that past success leads to a repetition of past behaviors and rigidities, even if they are no longer successful.

Finally, before we jump to the conclusion that these flaws are solely cultural, consider AT&T and IBM. We may make the argument that each is a captive of its culture and past success, and is struggling to adapt to its new context. Each of these Western firms is an example of organization level overadaptation.

INFORMAL OBSERVATIONS

Experience has given each of us a perspective of knowledge that is not without merit. Below is a brief listing by which most people characterize knowledge. Observe that there is a common dimension to knowledge—its *dynamicity*. Reflection and evidence suggest that knowledge:

- is constantly changing.
- takes time to assimilate.
- is open to interpretation.
- is synthesized over time.

- is about beliefs and commitment.
- underlies creativity and paradigm shifts.
- is a function of experience and its assessment.
- is a function and cause of doing (i.e., "action").
- is the foundation of organizational competence.
- is always associated with people, their feelings and sensitivities, and value judgments.
- is intertwined with "rules" that are constantly changing.
- as with information, knowledge is about meaning and context. Unlike information, knowledge may be non-deterministic and paradoxical.
- is responsible for changing its own context, such as the environment, a product strategy, an organization's markets, or a process task specification it presumably is implementing. In real time, knowledge changes its own rules, goals, and *raison d'être*.

EXPLICIT AND TACIT KNOWLEDGE

Building on an initial paper by Nonaka in 1991, Nonaka and Takeuchi (1995) describe a framework for creating knowledge in an organization. Knowledge is categorized as *explicit* or *tacit*. Western culture and institutions emphasize explicit knowledge, while Japanese culture gives greater importance to tacit knowledge. The levers an organization may pull to promote each form of knowledge are different, and, accordingly, we see these differences in Western and Japanese organizations—IT in the U.S. and social interaction in Japan. However, each knowledge form is intertwined—so tightly that the successful 21st century organization will learn to leverage both.

1. *Explicit knowledge* is formalized knowledge that is easy to express. It is usually represented as principles, procedures, facts, figures, rules, or formulas. Explicit knowledge has both a data- and knowledge-like implementation character. It may be stored and retrieved from computers—everything from easily structured formulas to very complex expert systems.

    The fact that explicit knowledge may be operationalized in a computer is a clear example of the intermediate character of explicit knowledge. Peter Drucker (1997) has observed that "knowledge constantly makes itself obsolete, with the result that today's advanced knowledge is tomorrow's ignorance." As knowledge becomes routinized (i.e., tomorrow's ignorance), it assumes some of the implementation characteristics of data (e.g., static). It remains, however, knowledge and subject to interpretation and change, though infrequently.

    As knowledge becomes more explicit, it becomes more stable, more routinized, and thus less complex in terms of its observed behavior. On the information continuum, explicitness moves knowledge away from the knowledge pole and toward the data pole. However, it is not an observed state (as with data), but a function of analysis, testing, and systematization. All knowledge, including commonly accepted explicit knowledge, has its origins in the heads of people. We should never confuse data with explicit knowledge.

Generally, explicit knowledge is associated with data through business processes. Explicit knowledge that is widely accepted within the organization is closely associated with the data archetype, and in an IS may be implemented through primitive operations (CRUD). As operations become more complex and subject to interpretation, however, they move away from the data pole toward the knowledge pole, and include complex processing algorithms. These complex processes may represent the explicit knowledge component of a particular group, such as the marketing or risk management department.

2. *Tacit knowledge* is not easily expressible and visible. It is highly personal and subjective, and intertwined with behavior and time: It includes experience, ideals, emotions, intuitions, and insights.

Tacit knowledge is distinguished by the *practice of knowledge*—the interrelationship between the content of knowledge and its associated behaviors, experiences, and feedback. For example, a physician, after completing his or her education, has a large reservoir of explicit knowledge, yet he or she is not an accomplished physician. Only through the practice of medicine is the "art" of healing realized. Explicit knowledge by itself is not sufficient, it requires a tacit framework in which it may grow. We call this experiential development an "art" because the arts (e.g., painting, music, etc.) are generally considered the most highly developed forms of *practicing knowledge*, so rich that their tacit character can not easily be communicated.

Tacit knowledge has two dimensions: *technical* and *cognitive*. Technical knowledge is best described as a craft-like skill or know-how. Technical knowledge is highly dependent on experience. An apprenticeship between master and apprentice is one example of how such knowledge develops. A characteristic of technical knowledge is that the rules governing its application are usually hidden, even from the master. Knowledge formation is thus dependent on observation and experience—the practice of knowledge.

Cognitive knowledge is composed of schema, values, and beliefs. As with the technical dimension, the cognitive dimension cannot be easily articulated, and its rules may be hidden. Cognitive mental models are constantly changing, a function of the practice of knowledge. In rare cases, the mental models underlying tacit knowledge may be so rich (as with great composers, painters, or scientists) that practice may enrich a mental model, but not create one. Hence, it is said that great artists are "born" with their gift. Their practice of knowledge grows it.

Observe that there is correspondence between the cognitive dimension of tacit knowledge and the tacit assumptions defined in the culture model described by Schein (discussed in Chapter 10). The implicit models that constitute the cognitive dimension of knowledge are analogous to those of culture: Each filters our perceptions of the world, governs overt behavior, shapes our image of reality, and our vision of the future.

Tacit knowledge is the foundation of innovation and creativity—all knowledge originates as tacit knowledge in the heads of people. An idea or inspiration is tacit knowledge not yet crystallized. Tacit knowledge defines the internal models of an individual and controls his or her perceptions and behaviors. Naturally, value extends to the individual, but also to all who come in contact with that individual. Above all else, tacit knowledge is *self-aware* and contains a *consciousness*.

INDIVIDUAL AND SOCIAL KNOWLEDGE

J.C. Spender (1993) has refined the Nonaka explicit-tacit characterization in terms of knowledge socialization and its strategic implications, as follows:

1. *Social knowledge* is shared, and may be either tacit or explicit. The most obvious kind of shared knowledge is explicit knowledge, which Spender refers to as *scientific knowledge*. Scientific knowledge is generally available. But knowledge may be shared *and* tacit. This is known as *communal knowledge;* its social and tacit dimensions arise from the fact that it is "taken for granted" among several members of an organization.
2. *Individual knowledge* is always tacit. The individual may be aware of his or her knowledge, known as *conscious knowledge*, or take it for granted, in which case it is known as *automatic knowledge*.

Spender suggests that competitive advantage arises from the interaction of the four types of knowledge (i.e., scientific, communal, conscious, and automatic). Competitive advantage based on scientific knowledge, for example, is not sustainable; it is easily appropriable, unless there are other "strategic complimentary resources," such as patents. On the other hand, tacit knowledge is not easily imitated and is thus a source of advantage.

An important management imperative, then, is to transform individual tacit knowledge (conscious or automatic) which is hidden from the organization, into social tacit knowledge (i.e., communal). At the communal level it is organizationally available, but not easily appropriated by competitors. Note that another path leading to the development of communal knowledge is along the social dimension: converting scientific knowledge (explicit) into communal knowledge (tacit) through internalization. Examples of communal knowledge include that which is associated with an organization's culture, as well as the shared tacit knowledge of a project team.

INDUSTRY AND ORGANIZATION KNOWLEDGE

Dorothy Leonard-Barton (1995) has identified four dimensions of a core capability: employee knowledge and skills, physical technical systems, managerial systems, and values and norms. The skill and knowledge base of employees are of three types, each increasingly less codified and transferable, respectively, as follows:

1. *Public* or *scientific knowledge* is generally available, and is equivalent to Nonaka's explicit or Spender's scientific knowledge. The content of scientific knowledge is typically *functional*—computer programming, organic chemistry, etc.
2. *Industry-specific knowledge* is that which is associated with a particular industry, such as brokerage or telecommunications. It includes *both* explicit and

tacit knowledge, and is typically codified in the "business rules" associated with that industry. As with scientific knowledge, industry knowledge is also generally available, but restricted to members of an industry—consultants, suppliers, distributors, and employees of organizations within that industry. Also included are the accepted industry practices and standards.

3. *Organization-specific knowledge* is unique to an organization, and includes both its explicit and tacit knowledge. Organization knowledge may be leveraged to establish a distinctive competence.

DISTRIBUTED AND COMMON KNOWLEDGE

Sack and Thalassinidis (1998) have classified knowledge on the basis of its distribution within an organization. They have identified a range dimension, the poles of which are *distributed* and *common*. Distributed knowledge is fragmented and not fully known to any one group. While individuals or subgroups may know and understand a portion or thread of knowledge, no one person or group understands all of the threads. However, the collection of knowledge threads may be exploited by the group. For example, a communications network consists of innumerable threads of widely distributed, explicit knowledge (e.g., hardware, software, architecture, etc.) that, as a whole, is beyond the comprehension of any one person or group, but collectively may represent a core capability of a firm.

Common knowledge, in contrast, is knowledge understood (consciously or unconsciously) by all members of a group. For example, the members of a programming group that maintain a computer system share knowledge of that system that nonmembers do not.

Between distributed and common knowledge, there are varying degrees of strength. The greater the number of group members who share knowledge, the greater is its "strength" of exploitation. There is another interesting dimension to the distributed-common relationship: The common knowledge thread shared by members of a group may actually represent a portion of knowledge that is a fragment of still more complex, distributed knowledge.

Finally, the competitive advantage afforded an organization is not solely a function of knowledge distribution, but a combination of knowledge dimensions. For example, distributed, explicit knowledge (e.g., a communications network) may be architected and leveraged, but is not easily appropriated. In contrast, common, explicit knowledge is easily leveraged, but also easily imitated. Similarly, distributed, tacit knowledge has no architecture and produces only conflict in an organization. However, common, tacit knowledge (e.g., a strong culture) provides a sense of directionality, while not being easily imitated. Competitive advantage, then, is closely associated with both {distributed-explicit} and {common-tacit} knowledge dimensions.

CONVERGENCE OF KNOWLEDGE DIMENSIONS

The {explicit-tacit}, {individual-social}, {industry-organization}, and {distributed-common} dimensions of knowledge often overlap, and collectively impact a wide range of organizational characteristics, such as the ability to cultivate learning, strategic maneuverability, core capabilities, and so on. For example, Edgar Schein (1996) describes the case of a new product development team at a large automaker that worked with MIT to develop a capacity for learning. This new learning ability resulted in improved effectiveness. However, rather than give team members credit for their achievement in developing a new way of solving problems, upper management gave themselves credit for their ability to control the team. They subsequently disbanded the team and encouraged several of its members to take early retirement.

This example illustrates the impact of management decisions on the convergence of several knowledge dimensions. The new product development team had, as had many successful teams, cultivated a high level of common knowledge: individual and communal tacit knowledge, as well as explicit knowledge threads (e.g., procedures). Disbanding a successful team fractures its communal and common knowledge. And when members of such teams leave an organization, they take their individual knowledge and skills, often developed as members of that team, with them. Any threads of explicit knowledge in the form of documentation or an IS rapidly become shelfware. The organization loses organization specific knowledge and competence, and diminishes a core capability.

12.6 ALIGNMENT CONTEXTS: AUTOMATING, INFORMATING, AND KNOWLEDGING

Shoshana Zuboff has written extensively on the interaction of people and IT, and the all-important shift in management thinking from *automating* to *informating*. Automating typically refers to the use of IT during process change where machines and IT are substituted for people. Automating lowers uncertainty and increases management control. Peter Keen (1997) reminds us that even today most IT professionals think of reengineering in terms of automation.

Informating, in contrast, refers to the effect IT may have on the understanding and transparency of a process. Informating makes people more productive through their use of, and process integration with, IT. Moreover, IT increases the capacity of people to understand the entire value-adding business process. Thus, informating concerns itself with the *connection* people have with their specific tasks, as well as the whole flow of work.

While informating concerns IT and task integration, *knowledging* refers to individual and organizational *learning*, and is characterized by the process of *knowledge creation* and the active *involvement* of the individual with his or her work. Knowledging includes a dynamic interaction between the current situation (i.e., data and explicit knowledge), and a vision of the future (i.e., tacit knowledge). (Refer to Chapter 3 for a discussion of automating, informating, and knowledging.)

Each context may be thought of as a stage, a progression requiring additional alignment threads and trade-offs. In particular, the trade-off between individualism and community may impact the movement from informating to knowledging. Individualism drives individual knowledge and rewards and encourages informating, while the community emphasizes sharing and is more closely associated with knowledging. Table 12–1 is a summary of selected differences between automating, informating, and knowledging. There are many additional differences, but we have focused on connectivity and cultural requirements—each of which is successively more difficult to attain.

The steady progression in exploiting the components of information from tools (i.e., automating) to people (i.e., informating), and finally to organizational learning and knowledge creation (i.e., knowledging) is illustrated in Figures 12–3, 12–4, and 12–5, respectively.

Observe that in every case, automating, informating, and knowledging cross boundaries within the information molecule. For example, while knowledge itself is human-centric, knowledging involves people using data in a process context, transferring knowledge and learning.

Note in Figure 12–3 that automating is rather simple—using the tool-computer component as the exclusive source of information. This typically results in the elimination of people, hence the name "automation." Note that Figure 12–3 illustrates the ideal case. This is not always possible. If computer systems alone are not sufficient, the process of routinizing work may also include hierarchical structure, documents, and standardized procedures—the goal of which is to routinize and make "automatic" the behavior of people. In either the ideal or less-than-ideal case, routinizing business rules means redeploying them as data-centric routinized knowledge.

Informating is more complicated than automating, and in fact, is very difficult to implement. As illustrated in Figure 12–4, informating is the integration of computer information systems, people, and a given business process or task. This refers to what we have introduced above: If computer information systems are to provide information with a high degree of process interconnectivity, each of the information components must be integrated with each other, as well as with the process (its context). In practice, this represents a complex interaction of data- and knowledge-based rules within a business process context.

As may be readily observed in Figure 12–4, knowledging is very complicated. It is based on the accumulation of organizational knowledge (meaning

TABLE 12–1   COMPARISON OF AUTOMATING, INFORMATING, AND KNOWLEDGING

	Automating	Informating	Knowledging
Org. perspective	process refinement	process exploitation	competence exploitation
Alignment threads	process-IT	process-IT-human	process-IT-human-culture-learning
Cultural perspective	machine	individualism	community
Change perspective	Taylor's scientific management	radical process change	organizational learning, and knowledge creation
Info perspective	quantitative	primarily quantitative	primarily rich
Data perspective	transactional	analytical support	decision support
Knowledge perspective	automatic	primarily explicit	primarily social: communal, common

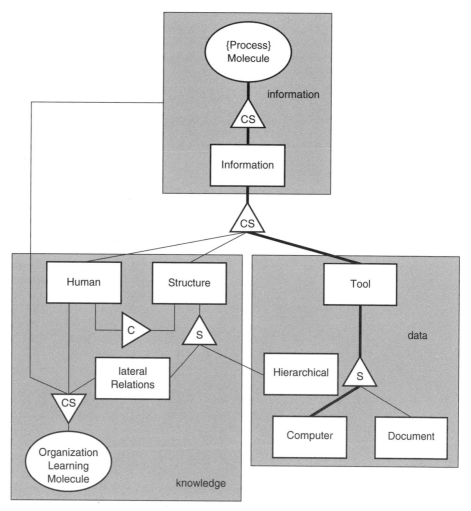

FIGURE 12–3   Automating (Ideal Case)

both collective and personal). Knowledging includes the interaction of computer systems, people, lateral relations, business processes and tasks, and the organizational learning and knowledge creation that integrates, assimilates, and hence, is responsible for an organization's competence. As such, it is highly dependent on alignment threads.

As with automating, knowledging is not an all-or-nothing proposition. Organizations struggle as they successively add the components of knowledge to their business process contexts. For many, learning and knowledge creation seem too slippery as they struggle to first implement teamwork. Of course, this speaks to the importance of directionality—organizations can never embrace learning if they cannot implement cooperative behavior and team structures, each of which has a high directionality with the invariant of community.

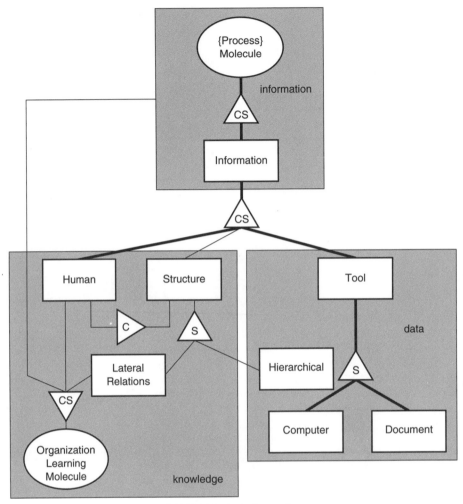

FIGURE 12–4   Informating

12.7 AN UPDATED MODEL OF THE INFORMATION CONTINUUM

Most people recognize an employee record containing an employee's name and social security number as data. Those same people recognize a text of Shakespearean plays as something more. As we see it, the essential difference between an employee record and a Shakespearean play is in the latter's "humanity"—its human-centered creation, context, and interpretation. Explicit knowledge derives from a person's tacit knowledge, a complex process of knowledge conversion. In contrast, data derives from observed states or business events, and need only be gathered, stored, distributed. There is no human content to data.

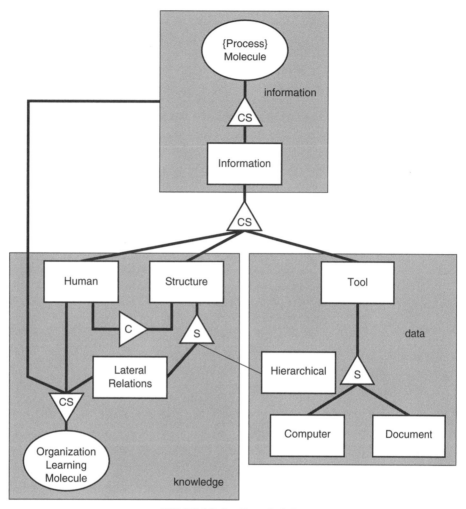

FIGURE 12–5   Knowledging

Separating data and knowledge properties is not very easy. Even a database has a certain structure (e.g., normalization) that represents an application of knowledge by a database administrator. An expert system is a thread of explicit knowledge, typically derived from the tacit knowledge of an expert. The price of an investment security is widely available and may be considered data, but when compared to yesterday's price, may convey information to a particular broker, who, using his or her tacit knowledge, makes a certain judgment as to tomorrow's price. A data mining paradigm may help identify a heretofore hidden pattern among data, but what makes a pattern significant, and therefore information, is human judgment.

Figure 12–6 illustrates an updated model of the information continuum, discussed below.

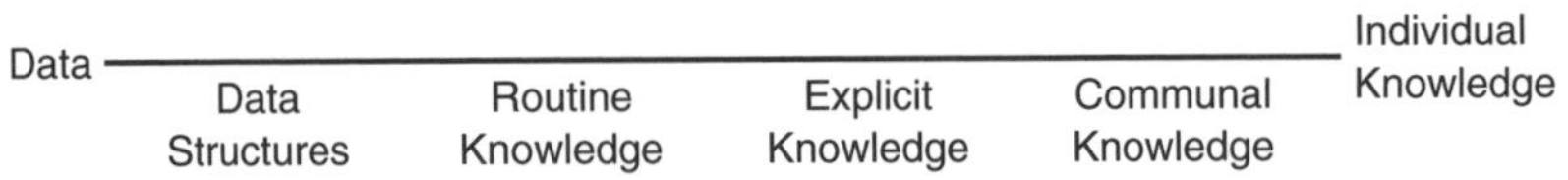

Data					Individual Knowledge
	Data Structures	Routine Knowledge	Explicit Knowledge	Communal Knowledge	

FIGURE 12–6   An Updated Model of the Information Continuum

Form

- At the left pole of the information continuum, the data archetype represents easily defined and structured states associated with business events, while at the right pole the knowledge archetype represents pure, unoperationalized knowledge—i.e., individual tacit knowledge.

- The process of translating from the mental models of the mind to something concrete requires a certain simplification. Explicit knowledge is never as rich as the minds that create it. Tacit knowledge is an inexpressible body language, containing tones and shades of meaning and context.

- Between the two poles, we have information, that is, data endowed with relevance and purpose, defined and constrained by its process context. Relevance and purpose are determined by the application of knowledge, which may change as the context changes.

- While data is static, information and knowledge are dynamic. Information and knowledge have meaning and context.

- Information has a *syntactic* and *semantic* dimension, representing its data and knowledge characteristics, respectively.

Richness

- Information has *varying levels of richness*. Richness is measured by the degree of *common* semantic—the extent to which knowledge has been routinized. Information richness is thus a function of knowledge explicitness. Increasing routinization implies progressively *less* richness: individual tacit, communal (social tacit), explicit, routine, and data structure constructs, respectively.

- Information is transmitted through a "communications channel." According to traditional information processing theory, information richness is associated with the *information carrying capacity of data* and is a function of its *communications channel*. Lean channels (e.g., databases, written documents, reports) are *sufficient* for data with little richness, while rich channels (e.g., face-to-face or group interactions) are *required* for flows of rich information.

- Individual tacit knowledge is information with the most richness. It represents the knowledge archetype, and can be operationalized only through individual people, and includes their relationships and experiences.

- Communal knowledge is information with some richness removed—tacit knowledge shared by groups of people. Shared tacit knowledge is a form of knowledge that has been *coalesced* and functions as a collection (thanks to Keith Morgan for this insight).

- Explicit knowledge is generally available information, and may therefore be operationalized in computers.
- Routine knowledge is information with most, if not all, richness removed (e.g., a financial transaction in an ATM). Routine knowledge constrains transactions governing data values and the existence of logical data records. Examples of routine knowledge include the rules governing create, read, update, and delete (CRUD) operations in databases, and standard operating procedures in routine tasks.
- Data structures are information with the least richness. They represent a specific organization of data elements.

Capturing and Processing Data and Knowledge

- Data is captured by the organization in business events, generally routine tasks designed by the organization to capture very specific data elements. These data elements are stored in physical media (databases or paper forms), and thus made available for processing—the application of knowledge threads that manifest themselves as business logic.
- Knowledge is captured by the organization when it acquires people, through permanent hiring, consultant engagements, or acquisitions. Such acquisitions may include an entire firm, in which case the knowledge acquired includes all its dimensions. Similarly, explicit threads of knowledge may be acquired through a technology or software package. Internally, knowledge may be created and codified into systems, products, or competencies. When codified (through external acquisition or internal development), knowledge may be "reused" if mapped into an appropriate catalog to establish topology and context—interrelated directories of business processes, data, information, and knowledge.
- The business logic of an organization's operations is typically operationalized through the data half of the information continuum—explicit and routine knowledge applied to data structures. Information contracts for operational tasks contain precise assertions corresponding to the data and explicit knowledge half of the information continuum. Process tasks associated with this half of the information continuum are routine.
- The business logic of an organization's innovative activities and processes (e.g., marketing, R&D, concept development) primarily focus on the knowledge half of the information continuum—explicit, communal, and individual knowledge. Information contracts for such tasks correspond to the knowledge half of the information continuum, and are usually formulated implicitly by managers and the people involved in knowledge creation. Process tasks associated with this half of the information continuum are nonroutine.
- The business logic of an organization's core capabilities and competencies usually spans the entire information continuum. Information contracts for a core capability are thus a complex mix of precise explicit knowledge and informal tacit knowledge contracts.

ESTABLISHING CONTEXT

- Abstraction turns information into tacit knowledge, which in turn interacts with, creates, and expands additional threads of both explicit and tacit knowledge. Information and tacit knowledge thus share a complex relationship as each elicits and feeds the other.
- Tacit knowledge is always present, and establishes a context for information. Information references tacit knowledge. Tacit knowledge thus functions as an *invariant* throughout the continuum, determining relevance and purpose in real-time.
- Tacit knowledge rarely becomes explicit knowledge without first becoming communal. Communal knowledge is the foundation of organizational knowledge. Tacit knowledge needs to be socialized (i.e., shared, developed, tested) and transformed into communal knowledge before it can be codified (i.e., made explicit) and leveraged by an organization.
- Flexibility and the capacity to respond to, even dictate, the terms of the environment, can be met only through knowledge creation and amplification: constant streams of tacit knowledge that are mobilized and crystallized into explicit knowledge threads among increasingly larger communities of people.
- Value is created when data is captured and moved to the right on the continuum; the more knowledge applied to data, the greater the value to the organization.
- Explicit knowledge is consciously constructed.
- Routine knowledge is embedded in an organization's information systems.
- Tacit knowledge emerges through work and experience.

12.8 BUSINESS RULES

Business rules correspond in some way to an organization's economic activity. Business rules may manifest themselves in all possible patterns that affect the organization—organizational, business, service, and information patterns. Business rules are typically related across patterns, and are subject to the concepts of alignment and directionality. Consequently, during business design, we select certain business rules in certain patterns and discard the rest.

Rules come in all forms. They may be dynamic or static, atomic or composite. data- or knowledge-based. They may be found in straightforward service patterns, such as the rules governing credit. Or they may be dynamic and intuitive, and correspond, say, to a marketing strategy.

One other important point: the rules we are discussing generally refer to specific behavior(s), not to the requirement for the behavior itself. For example, we consider the government's regulations governing the payment of social security taxes to be a set of business rules. However, the requirement to pay corporate social security taxes is not a rule, but a mandated business process.

ASSERTIONS AND SCOPE

As a manifestation of behavior, business rules may be described with assertions—declarative statements—in a contract governing behavior. Or the rule may be a composite contract describing a sequence of specific behaviors. Depending upon whether the assertion is applied to a local or organization-wide contract, we may be specifying a "department" or "organization" rule. Or, if associated with a professional practice, the rule may apply to members of a profession across organizations.

For example, it may be that for a particular department in an organization, there is a requirement that each engineer in that department be certified with a Professional Engineer's license. This would be a local rule. If the organization were to adopt this rule, it would apply to each engineer in the organization. Similarly, most states now employ this rule as industry practice if an engineer is to review and certify designs. In each case, the same assertion represents the same business rule, but with a different scope and range of effect.

SOURCES

One way to visualize a business rule is in terms of its source. Business rules may derive from industry or professional practice. Government regulations that govern behavior in a given industry, for instance, apply to all organizations in that industry.

Other rules concern professional guidelines and practice, and derive from standards within the profession itself. In this case, these "professional" rules apply to all members of a given profession, and thereby constrain the behavior of organizations who employ members of that profession. The fact that organizations use members of a particular profession transforms professional into business rules.

Business rules may be organization-specific, and derive from the practice and history of the organization, a form of systematized culture. For example, individual knowledge governs the behavior of individuals, but when socialized, heretofore individual heuristics become organizational rules.

THE INFORMATION CONTENT OF BUSINESS RULES

Business rules represent a constraint on a pattern of behavior. The most important dimension of a business rule is its information content. Depending upon whether they have been sufficiently routinized, business rules may take the form of explicit knowledge, and be realized through information systems. If sufficiently rich, they may need to be realized through people. Business rule types follow the same logical categorization as does knowledge in the updated model of the information continuum:

"Knowledge" rules are *dynamic*. According to Sveiby (1997), knowledge rules are of two types: (1) procedural heuristics that are updated as a consequence of knowledge application and feedback, and (2) values, assumptions, and attitudes that serve to filter our perceptions and responses to the environment. Observe that both types correspond to the technical and cognitive dimensions of tacit knowledge, respectively—in effect, Sveiby defines knowledge rules in terms of Nonaka's tacit knowledge dimensions.

Tacit knowledge rules are formed and destroyed dynamically, a consequence of process execution and feedback. Tacit rules are *hidden* and *implicit* in the *practice of the knowledge*. If made explicit, they become *embodied* in the rule itself. Knowledge rules and knowledge are intertwined with each other and with their knowledge dimensions—the *rules* of knowledge, the *practice* of knowledge, and the *content* of knowledge cannot easily be separated.

As we would expect, tacit rules may change in real time, and are therefore ideal in turbulent environments. With explicitness, rules become more stable and resistant to change. If very stable and common, such *routine knowledge* rules may be driven down into code and a data pattern in a database. Such rules of behavior control and record the states of objects in an information system. Knowledge rules thus lead to the development of both explicit and data rules (discussed below), each representing increasing levels of knowledge routinization.

"Relational" rules are *assumptions* within, and hence define, relational contracts. Relational rules come closest to describing the personal arrangements and understandings underlying communal knowledge. Assumptions are premised on human *familiarity*, and may constitute part of an organization's culture—its *shared tacit* assumptions. These assumptions are formed *before* a relational contract is executed, but *reinforced* during execution.

"Explicit" rules are rules related to *explicit threads of knowledge* and data, embodied in the rule itself. For example, the business logic governing the assessment of the credit worthiness of a client seeking a loan at a bank is an example of a complex, but explicit sequence of processes where, at each point along the way, certain combinations of circumstances must exist for a loan to be granted. Whether implemented in computers or people, or both, the rules are merely a set of complex, but explicit algorithms. Such rules abound in organizations, and include everything from simple rules governing vacation time to very complex rules governing risk.

Let us look at another example. The relationship between matter and energy originated as tacit knowledge in the head of Einstein, who then crystallized and quantified it, and made it explicit in an equation. Today, that manifest form of knowledge (i.e., the equation $E = mc^2$) is well-established and accepted, and is an example of an explicit rule describing the behavior of energy and mass. Despite its outward simplicity, we surely would not refer to $E = mc^2$ as a "data" rule. Nor would we mistake $E = mc^2$ for the general theory of relativity itself. An *explicit rule* expressing a specific relationship is very different from, and simpler than, the *knowledge content* underlying the rule. The minds that create explicit threads of knowledge are far richer than their creations.

"Data" rules are *static*, and describe *routine knowledge* operating on data states (i.e., element values in data structures). Operating at a low level of abstraction (i.e., in an information pattern), data rules manifest themselves as operations (1) governing the existence of objects in a database (e.g., CRUD rules) and thus constraining the behavior of its corresponding information system and business process tasks, or (2) constraining the "lawful state space" (domain or domain combinations) of attributes, and hence governing the permitted value combinations of attributes. Data rules may be explicitly defined, and remain *unchanged* before and after process execution—the invariants associated with precise information contracts.

RULE CONVERSION

Rules often coexist in a complex, interactive mixture. As an organization's alignment context shifts to knowledging, business rules become less explicit, more tacit and dynamic, and dependent on real-time execution and people. On the other hand, as knowledge rules become sufficiently routinized they may become more stable, and embedded in an information pattern—the rules in an information model and its corresponding programs and data structures.

For example, organizations often develop standard operating procedures for any number of recurring activities. Business rules that are a consequence of heuristics developed through experience are routinized into a system (i.e., document or computer), and thus made generally available to those without the knowledge of the task, often to employees new to the task.

As another example, an expert system derives from the tacit knowledge of an expert. The inference engine and its rules each derive from people or teams of people, who are the experts. These once-*individual knowledge rules* (i.e., tacit knowledge) have been captured, made explicit, and transferred to an information system (i.e., *explicit rules representing threads of static, explicit knowledge*), thus making them available to people who are not experts.

In each case, tacit knowledge rules, often originating as individual heuristics, are captured and externalized into explicit knowledge. If sufficiently static, well-understood, and accepted, they may be embedded in an information system and widely distributed. In this case, the once-tacit knowledge has not only been externalized into explicit knowledge, but it has been routinized into the organization's systems.

12.9 A WORD ON INTEGRATING INFORMATION

How do we integrate information? It would seem that integrating data and integrating knowledge are different. How do the benefits of integrated information (data or knowledge) translate to organizational value and competitiveness?

INTEGRATING DATA AND ITS VALUE TO THE ORGANIZATION

IT professionals have generally preferred technical approaches to data integration. Consequently, they are torn between approaches to software development that promote data integration and long cycle-time on the one hand, and the business necessity for rapid development on the other.

In Chapter 3, we made reference to the research of Goodhue, Wybo, and Kirsch (1992). In their research, integrated data is defined to be the development and use of data elements with common definitions and code. This study is a synthesis of 35 case studies of large firms over eight years. They find that the *value* of data integration depends on three organizational factors: interdependence of subunits, the need for locally unique or flexible action by subunits, and the difficulty of designing and implementing systems with integrated data. Observe that the value of data integration is tied to organizational concerns, and not to some technology rationale or imperative.

Goodhue *et al.* observed that data integration is not as effective in reducing equivocality (where rich information is required) as in reducing uncertainty (where the *amount* of information is important). Moreover, even in situations where uncertainty is the key ingredient, the cost of implementing and maintaining integrated systems may outweigh the benefit; that is, integration may have *negative business value.*

Data integration is not an all-or-nothing proposition. Organizations may achieve value through partial integration. This may include uniform use of an application, or a database. Another approach is to identify and integrate only data elements deemed critical to the firm.

INTEGRATING DATA AROUND BUSINESS PROCESSES

We propose yet a fourth approach. Rather than integrate around accidents of history (i.e., applications or databases), or elements that may cost more to integrate than value derived, we propose integration around a business process. The integration paradigm would have value to the firm, provided the most appropriate business processes were selected:

1. Integrate data elements across tasks within an identity business process. Recall that in the Keen model, identity processes have the highest economic value-added (EVA) to the organization.
2. Integrate data elements across tasks between different identity business processes.
3. Integrate data elements across tasks between an identity and its corresponding priority business processes. Recall that priority processes have the second highest EVA, and support identity processes.

Even if the systems involved exist (as they surely would), such an integration paradigm would identity data transfers across systems—"hand-offs" that would have demonstrable value to the firm.

KNOWLEDGE SHARING

Knowledge is not so much integrated as it is shared. While explicit knowledge is relatively easy to transmit, tacit knowledge (in both its technical and cognitive dimensions) is more challenging to share.

The term that we use to capture the totality of knowledge is *knowledge world.* Each member of an organization has his or her *own* knowledge world. Organizations have many knowledge worlds—one for *every* member of the organization (not just the folks in R&D).

Organizations have several choices: ignore knowledge worlds, manage separate knowledge worlds, or develop common knowledge worlds—one that develops new forms of knowledge from that which exists among its members, or from what is generally available. If we are to believe Peter Drucker, as the source of wealth shifts from capital to knowledge, it is clear that organizations that actively seek to create their own communal knowledge worlds will have a decided advantage over those who do not. This is elaborated on in the next chapter.

INTEGRATING INFORMATION

If data is to be integrated, and knowledge shared, then how do we converge the two dimensions and integrate "information"? For instance, consider the never-ending pursuit of IT professionals in building a common definition of "what a customer is?" We must ask if this is wise—isn't there a difference between the data and knowledge dimensions of a customer?

At one pole, information is integrated through its data property, but at the other pole it is shared through knowledge worlds. We say that an information *syntax* is mediated through data, while its *semantic* is mediated through knowledge. To integrate information, we need to integrate its syntactic dimension (i.e., data) and share its semantic dimension (i.e., knowledge). Furthermore, as with all knowledge, there are gradations of knowledge sharing that follow the updated model of the information continuum:

- Data is static, and may therefore be *integrated* through common *physical* representations (e.g., length and type) and *values*. For example, it makes sense to define a single storage format and domain for customer numbers. Data represents the *syntax* of information, and may therefore be so constrained through its integration.
- Knowledge represents the *semantic* of information, and thus gives meaning and context to data.
- Knowledge presents the organization with a dilemma. In the example above, does an organization adopt a common definition of customer? This, in effect, would remove richness and turn information about a customer into *routine knowledge*—explicit knowledge with all possible interpretations removed. The organization, therefore, must ask itself if it wants, say, marketing and operations, to share a common understanding of a customer? Or should it permit each to develop a distinctive view?

    If an organization wants to establish a distinctive perspective, it may choose to promote and manage *differentiated* knowledge worlds. A knowledge world represents a semantic perspective, and should therefore be liberated from the syntactic artifacts of data design. The drawback here is that an isolated knowledge world may develop for each member of the organization. That would mean that all knowledge of a customer is *tacit*, open to interpretation, and therefore difficult to leverage.

The best of both worlds may be achieved by building common knowledge worlds among professionals within an organization. The members of the marketing department may have one knowledge perspective of a customer, while those in the service department another. That is to say, there may be differentiated knowledge worlds between professions or functional departments, while members within a group may *share* a common understanding (i.e., a *communal* knowledge world for each department).

- An issue for the organization is whether it wants to make explicit each knowledge perspective, or whether it wants to keep some knowledge tacit. What semantic do we want to share, and how do we want to share it? What should be its level of richness within the organization?

- Therefore, one integrating strategy is to (1) build rich, tacit-knowledge worlds within functional areas, (2) make each functional knowledge world manifest to some level of explicitness through contextualization (e.g., business goals, tasks, and case scenarios), categorization, definition, and derivation, and finally (3) associate each such knowledge world to a corresponding, integrated data syntax.

TECHNOLOGY PACKAGES

Many of our graduate students have reported that their firms' efforts to impose vendor supplied IT solutions in their respective BPR efforts are meeting with mixed results. A technology package may be viewed as an IT-driven process change mechanism, which is fine. Yet we frequently hear from managers across industries that, after purchasing a product, there is a realization that "we don't work this way." What is happening in these organizations? After all, many of these vendors are providing integrated information and business process solutions.

One answer concerns the nature of packaged solutions. There are *software packages* which are low-level IS solutions for a relatively narrow set of specific tasks. An integrated business process and information package, on the other hand, is a *technology package*. This *means* that process, information, and human specifications have been predefined, and, collectively, represent a thread of explicit knowledge for a particular business process or set of processes. Naturally, this technology is generic, and, unfortunately for the organization (but not the package vendor), is available to every other organization.

We ask if it is wise to expect meaningful benefits from such generic components. The answer provided by vendors is usually something such as, "It's *how* you apply a technology or an information system that provides competitive advantage." And we agree. However, the "how" is determined by the design of corresponding business processes, including how people interact with information. Technology packages largely dictate the "how." They *impose* business and information specifications, as well as human interfaces. By definition, a technology package has (1) relevance and purpose defined by the vendor, (2) predefined business process task and information specifications, and (3) predefined explicit knowledge. Finally, (4) all of the above are generally available.

Can an organization derive benefit from technology packages? Of course. If you apply generic components to generic business processes, such as the background processes in the Keen model (e.g., accounts payable, etc.), this may be fine. That is to say, off-the-shelf technology packages may be suitable in the redesign of background or mandated processes. Unfortunately, these are the processes from which the organization derives the least EVA. The processes with the highest EVA, identity or priority processes, are typically not addressed by technology packages. And for good reason. The application of generic components to high EVA processes either do not exist or may cause a firm to lose any differentiating capabilities.

12.10 CORE CONCEPTS

Information renaissance	Quantitative information
Rich information	Uncertainty
Equivocality	Data
Information	Knowledge
Information continuum	Continuum of information systems
Explicit knowledge	Tacit knowledge
Analysis paralysis	Overadaptation
Technical dimension	Cognitive dimension
Individual knowledge	Conscious knowledge
Automatic knowledge	Social knowledge
Scientific knowledge	Communal knowledge
Industry knowledge	Organization knowledge
Distributed knowledge	Common knowledge
Routine knowledge	Business rules
Knowledge rules	Relational rules
Explicit rules	Data rules
Knowledge worlds	Information convergence
Automating	Informating
Knowledging	Practice of knowledge
Syntax of information	Semantic of information
Software packages	Technology packages

Information richness as an inverse function of knowledge explicitness and common purpose

Cooperative interaction among data, knowledge, and business processes

CHAPTER 13

KNOWLEDGE FORMULATION

13.1 KNOWLEDGE WORLDS

Nelson Goodman (1984) has stated: "'How then,' comes the question, 'can we ever establish anything finally and completely and for sure, even the most obvious truism and the most cherished credos?' And the answer is, of course, that we can't, and that is no fault of mine. Neither by logic nor any other means can we prove something from nothing. We have to start with some premises and principles, and there are no absolute and incontrovertible certainties available. But that does not mean that we must start from careless guesses. We follow our confidence and convictions, which are subject to strengthening or weakening or even reversal as we strive to build right versions or worlds on the basis of these. No starting points or ending points or points along the way are either absolute or arbitrary." Thus, each of us creates our own world, a right version of existence. Each right version is as legitimate as the next, though right versions are different from wrong versions. The intent and truthfulness of our quest determine rightness. Rightness cannot be verified through correspondence to a version-independent world—as Goodman states, there are no world-features independent from all versions. We cannot truthfully make a world any way we like. We make versions, and those that are right are real worlds. "Worldmaking" is a matter of mind. Of thinking.

People build knowledge worlds, too—each one different from any other. This is human, a manifestation of our individuality. As in world building, our knowledge worlds are neither absolute nor arbitrary, and right versions are different from wrong versions. *However different "knowledge" may be from right versions, making right versions makes knowledge.*

Organizations have many knowledge worlds—one for every member of the organization. Should an organization develop its own knowledge world—an organizational knowledge world—and if so, from what? Should it rely on the knowledge worlds of only a few of its members? What are the means by which a *common* knowledge world may be built? And how would an organization use it for advantage? Perhaps the most important role for a manager in the 21st century is to answer these and many other such questions.

THE CHALLENGE OF KNOWLEDGING

It is generally acknowledged that the primary sources of advantage are no longer capital, natural resources, or labor. Even IT does not create sustainable advantage: IT-driven advantage is largely determined by "time to market" development, which is increasingly very short. Technology creates an even playing field, producing parity among organizations of otherwise different sizes or resources.

The source of advantage is thus shifting to knowledging. How is knowledge identified, accessed, acquired, mobilized, amplified, distributed, and used in an organization? How is knowledge to be *designed into* an organization's processes, information systems, people, and culture?

Every organization molecule (i.e., organizational domain) contains information. Accordingly, the character, range, and depth of its information contents determine each domain, and ultimately the organization itself. Historically, the data dimension has largely dominated the information continuum. Increasingly, however, 21st century competitive distinctiveness requires a bias toward the knowledge dimension. This is why people are so important: They are reservoirs of continuous flows of what is required for every domain in the organization to be *especially* effective.

In the 21st century, an organization will be defined by its knowledge world. The challenge an organization faces is to create an identifying knowledge world for itself. It must learn to cultivate and crystallize its individual knowledge worlds so that an organizational one emerges. Everything an organization is or wants to become—its systems and products, its culture and values, its vision and aspirations—will be defined by its knowledge world.

> An organization's knowledge world is its signature, its ultimate definition of what it is and where it is going

13.2 LAYERED KNOWLEDGE MODELS

We begin by drawing upon the techniques we have used throughout this book. Organizational constructs have a complex mix of properties and relationships that lead to certain generalities. The layered model of the organization, as well as the organizational molecules, are such examples. Each layered model or molecule is a viewpoint of the organization from a certain perspective.

By extension, we may construct knowledge worlds as layered models. A knowledge world embodies a knowledge perspective. Figure 13–1 illustrates three knowledge worlds that were inspired by the work of well-known philosophers, such as Goodman, Kuhn, and Popper.

A knowledge world contains three layers: *world version, actions,* and *natural world.* The natural world comprises the physical and biotic worlds, including

FIGURE 13–1   Layered Knowledge Worlds

human institutions, such as nations and economic organizations. A world version is composed of tacit models of how the natural world works, and is embodied in the mind in which it resides. The question that naturally arises concerns the role of explicit knowledge. Explicit knowledge—concepts, facts, and formulas—exists only as external manifestations of, and supporting evidence for, an implicit world version. Certainly, explicit threads of knowledge serve as input and thus shape a world version, but similarly, such explicit threads are selected to reinforce a world version, the essence of which is its implicit model, and its associated assumptions and filters. Explicit knowledge arises from interactions between a world version and the natural world.

Actions mediate between the natural world and the models underlying a world version and, as such, create and manipulate threads of knowledge (explicit or tacit). A world version is created and maintained by the continuous actions of people through direct engagement, observation, thinking, or through the behaviors of others, even surrogates such as software agents or robots. Naturally, all such actions are ultimately mediated and interpreted by people, who embody world versions. World versions are necessary to create yet other world versions.

LAYER INTERACTION AND KNOWLEDGE DEVELOPMENT

The interaction of the layers within a knowledge world is the basis of knowledging. Illustrated in Figure 13–1 are three action types: knowledge discovery (KD), knowledge application (KA), and knowledge creation (KC).

1. *Knowledge discovery (KD)* is the discovery of natural world features that serve as input into implicit models. A popular form of KD is the search and discovery of existing threads of knowledge in an area of interest. This may take the form of explicit or tacit knowledge in physical media (e.g., documents, a repository, etc.), or another person who has the desired knowledge.

2. *Knowledge application (KA)* is the application of implicit world version models to the natural world—the use of knowledge to somehow change the world, such as when building a bridge, playing a chess game, or writing a computer program. As part of KA, a person may choose to apply either explicit or tacit threads of knowledge, but this application is always mediated by that person's world version.

3. *Knowledge creation (KC)* comprises both the discovery and application of knowledge, and is key to innovation. For an organization, creating new knowledge means creating a future. KC shapes our implicit world versions (individual or organizational), and often leads to explicit statements of concepts and rules that represent the underlying implicit model of the natural world. Such explicit formulations may become accepted knowledge for a time, until replaced by more suitable ones, a reflection of a new world version. Such new versions arise from action and input from the natural world. KC thus involves an interaction of knowledge discovery and application, and includes tacit or explicit knowledge, or more likely both—a synthesis of world versions and actions.

13.3 KNOWLEDGE CONVERSION AND CREATION

Nonaka and Takeuchi (1995) propose a "spiral" framework for creating organizational knowledge. The underlying premise is that knowledge is created as a result of *knowledge interaction:* Tacit and explicit knowledge interact in a sequence of *knowledge conversion modes* and create "new" knowledge.

Successful knowledge creation, particularly among individuals or groups, does not guarantee wider organizational exploitation. We need only to look at the knowledge innovations of Xerox PARC (e.g., graphical interfaces, including the mouse, graphical icons, and menus), and the failure of Xerox to exploit that knowledge (Davenport and Prusak 1998).

Thus, knowledge must not only be created, but also made manifest and crystallized into explicit knowledge, and distributed throughout the organization. This sequence of *knowledge amplification*—of increasing crystallization and distribution among increasingly larger communities—describes a *knowledge spiral* between knowledge conversion modes, discussed below.

GENERIC KNOWLEDGE CONVERSION MODES

Nonaka and Takeuchi (1995) contend that if an organization is to be successful, knowledge must be created and exploited by that organization. Knowledge creation is a consequence of conversion between explicit or tacit knowledge types. There are four such knowledge conversion modes, which are sequenced to produce a *knowledge spiral* of organizational knowledge creation. Though Nonaka and Takeuchi have described knowledge conversion in terms of new product development in Japanese organizations, all four modes are generic: At least one mode, and possibly all of the modes, characterize all knowledge creating processes. (It is worth stating that "new product development" is generally considered a generic core capability for 21st century firms.)

Listed below is a brief description of each *knowledge conversion mode* in its appropriate knowledge spiral sequence. We describe each mode in terms of its primary *trigger*, and the resulting knowledge *content* that each mode yields. The reader may recall that a "trigger" and content (i.e., "postcondition") are constituents of a contract. Each knowledge conversion mode, then, is a generic process that may be specified with "knowledge contracts."

1. *Socialization:* tacit-to-tacit conversion. Socialization is a process of sharing experiences, usually through observation, imitation, or practice. For example, an apprentice relationship between apprentice and master is a well-known context where tacit knowledge is created in the head of the apprentice from existing tacit knowledge in the head of the master. The essential *trigger* is that which facilitates *personal communication*. The organization, then, must consciously construct "fields" (an organization designed trigger) where sharing experiences is possible. Fields may include formal team structures, office configurations that promote communication, such as "open space office design" where there are few, if any, physical barriers

between people, or "piggybacking" where new employees are made part of a team (Sveiby 1997). Socialization yields a set of shared skills and mental models, known collectively as *sympathized knowledge*.

2. *Externalization:* tacit-to-explicit conversion. This is the conversion from informal to formal models of representation and specification—taking the innovative ideas of individuals and transforming them into specific concepts. Externalization is a process of concept building that employs metaphors, analogies, and models. The essential *trigger* is *dialogue* and *collective reflection*, operationalized through conversations in meetings, or other two-way, rich forms of communications. Externalization produces *conceptual knowledge*.

3. *Combination:* explicit-to-explicit conversion. Combination is the formal aggregation of discrete pieces of information to create larger pieces of information—i.e., combining threads of explicit knowledge to produce new threads of explicit knowledge. This is typically effected through analysis, categorization, and reconfiguration of the specific threads of knowledge. In practice, combination is the process of systematizing explicit concepts into a knowledge system. This may involve linking threads from different parts of the organization, even external sources, and crystallizing them into a new product or management system. The essential *trigger* is the capability to *network* existing or newly created threads of explicit knowledge. This is typically operationalized through IT, documentation, or meetings. Combination yields *systemic knowledge,* such as a new prototype, or a new component technology or method.

4. *Internalization:* explicit-to-tacit conversion. This is the internalization of formalized, explicit knowledge within individuals, which leads to a broadening, extension, or reframing of tacit knowledge. The essential *trigger* is simply *learning by doing*. This may include simulation, role-playing, case studies, or work experience. Internalization develops *operational knowledge,* as explicit knowledge is "absorbed" into tacit knowledge.

As described in Chapter 12, Western tradition is focused on explicit knowledge and assumes a risk of analysis paralysis, while the Japanese tradition is focused on tacit knowledge and may be handicapped by overadaptation. Similarly, the Western and Japanese traditions emphasize different knowledge conversion modes. With its focus on explicitness and IT, Western firms excel at combination and are fairly good at externalization. In contrast, Japanese firms emphasize tacit knowledge and personal relationships, and are therefore adept at socialization and fairly skillful at internalization.

INDIVIDUAL KNOWLEDGE SPIRALS

Though Nonaka and Takeuchi (1995) developed their knowledge creation theory in an organizational context, we believe that their knowledge conversion modes serve as a guide to understanding individual knowledge creation. Individuals and organizations engage in *single-loop* and *double-loop learning*, and thus share certain frameworks for knowledge creation. Recall that tacit knowledge is comprised of two dimensions: technical and cognitive. Single-loop learning refers to the development of the technical dimension (i.e., a craft skill or know-how) in order to solve a specific problem. Double-loop learning involves the cognitive dimension, as new mental models are developed to replace existing ones. In practice, single-loop learning maintains an organization's activities, such as learning a new departmental procedure, while double-loop learning entails a new understanding, such as a department's workings and interfaces. The latter should lead to an understanding of the requirements and characteristics of a new standard procedure. (Since individual and organizational learning are intertwined, both single- and double-loop learning may be applied to organizations. In fact, both interact and facilitate each other. See Kim (1993) for a discussion of the link between individual and organizational learning.)

People engage in knowledge conversion all the time, almost unconsciously. Two people speaking on a telephone about a prospective client are engaged in a form of socialization and externalization, where both tacit and explicit knowledge are created as a result of rich, two-way communication. A student solving a quadratic equation is engaged in a form of combination and internalization as he or she builds a repertoire of equation-solving models and techniques. A chess player, temporarily stymied by an unfamiliar position who suddenly makes a killer move, has gone through the entire knowledge spiral as he adjusts and internalizes his mental model, while externalizing the image through a winning move—the whole cycle may take place in an instant.

Individual and organization knowledge spirals are interrelated; the former is required for the latter. The essence of the knowledge spiral is that all knowledge creation starts with an individual and spirals through successive conversion modes. Each successive spiral, in turn, expands its "communities of interaction" as a larger number of individuals, groups, and ultimately the organization become engaged with the newly created knowledge.

13.4 KNOWLEDGE CONTEXTUALIZATION

Knowledge and information have meaning and context. They have varying levels of richness. They are created in, and applied to, business processes. They embody people and systems. They have specific locations. They have facilitators and triggers. Knowledge may be forthcoming, hidden, or even withheld.

As we have been discussing in this chapter, knowledge may be leveraged through the processes that create it. However, *information about knowledge* may be put into a database and used to support its development and application.

The most common type of "information about knowledge" is a knowledge directory, typically a location finder of people and skills. Such a system is useful in designing training programs, allocating resources, and so on.

If given an "organizational context," a knowledge directory may be integrated into a broader system for organizational design. To establish context, it is necessary to identify knowledge and its interactions: the processes in which knowledge is created, where and how it is being applied, who is applying it, its dimensions, its operationalized form, its level of richness, and so on. Listed below are some of the areas which serve to identify such knowledge interactions:

- Functional knowledge areas.
- People and their physical location.
- People and their skills and education.
- People and their work experience.
- Knowledge and corresponding business process tasks, work groups, and projects.
- People and corresponding business process tasks, work groups, and projects.
- Knowledge categorization.
- Derivation and other computing algorithms.
- Computer and document agents and systems: data and procedures.
- Knowledge richness levels.

13.5 KNOWLEDGE BINDING

The notions of specification and implementation characterize every system ever built. A concept is conceived, formulated to some level of detail, and then implemented. A concept specification may be a simple goal, a complex set of criteria, a formal contract, or an implicit understanding. A specification is typically followed by some corresponding behavior. There may be occasions when it is advantageous, even necessary, to maintain a long lead-time between specification and implementation. At other times, it may be the reverse.

For example, an architectural drawing for a new house is a specification that would normally be developed well before implementation. At other times, it would be prudent to develop a specification just before it is to be realized, such as determining the color of a room only after seeing the room (or a model). And at still other times, a specification may not be fully determined until it is implemented, such as depicting a new house in an oil portrait.

THE GLUE BETWEEN SPECIFICATION AND IMPLEMENTATION

The philosophy underlying the level of separation between the specification and the implementation of a system largely determines its *knowledge binding*. By knowledge binding, we mean at what point along the development process, and by whom, knowledge is applied to a specification.

Knowledge binding largely determines the character of a system or practice. For example, Scientific Management and traditional IS development are each characterized by the application of knowledge early in the process, almost always by senior managers or those designated as domain experts. Hence, they share the characteristics of early and clear separation between desired outcomes (i.e., specifications) and their implementations. In contrast, bottom-up management practice (e.g., decentralization, empowerment) and bottom-up software development share the characteristic of late binding. In late binding, knowledge is applied late in the process, and by a wider variety of people. And finally, tacit knowledge adds the twist of real-time binding where the "designer" and the "doer" are the same person, as specifications both guide and are realized during implementation. Thus, as knowledge is applied increasingly later in the process, there is a corresponding progression of increasing intermingling of specification and implementation, and with it, distinguishing characteristics of each corresponding system.

TOP-DOWN PROCESSES AND EARLY KNOWLEDGE BINDING

Ever since Frederick Winslow Taylor advanced the notion of Scientific Management, and with it the separation of planning from doing, organizations have operated under the premise that virtually all functions and processes may be cleanly divided into specification and implementation constructs. Information systems development has been similarly characterized by this separation—and not without good reason. Early binding facilitates the management of complexity which, in turn, leads to the development of very complex systems: the organization itself, as well as its business processes, computer information systems.

Top-down information planning is no different in principle from top-down business planning. Information engineering is the archetype of a top-down IS development process—an enterprise-wide model is created and successively scoped and refined into business areas and technical systems. There is the implication in traditional IS development, as with all top-down processes, that no one downstream in the process can contribute anything very rich to the specification. Refinement of specifications is an example of early knowledge binding for an IS.

Early knowledge binding is distinguished by the following characteristics:

- Top-down management and development processes.
- Knowledge is applied early in the process, by relatively few people with the necessary authority or expertise. This is an example of centralized decision making.
- A long lead-time between specification and execution.
- A context of comparatively low uncertainty and ambiguity.
- Explicit knowledge refinement and flow as the underlying principle. This is one interpretation of information processing theory: the notion that an organization is an information processing mechanism where "simple and selected information" is passed up the hierarchy, unambiguous concepts and plans (i.e., precise specifications of explicit knowledge) are formulated at the top, and then processed down the hierarchy through the division of labor (Nonaka and Takeuchi). The goal of everyone at every level (other than the top) is to implement decisions (i.e., specifications) already made.

(See Nonaka and Takeuchi 1995 for an in-depth discussion, as well as an extensive list of references.)

- Comparatively long cycle time.
- Optimum effectiveness in non-turbulent environments.
- Typically, an emphasis on explicit knowledge. A long lead-time between concept formulation and implementation favors a *rational* approach to decision making and the systematic development of explicit plans. Information engineering is a classical example of a rational and technical approach to information planning.
- With a long lead-time between specification and execution, and an environment of relatively low uncertainty and ambiguity, there is an opportunity for a full and thorough analysis.
- With an emphasis on explicit knowledge, there is an opportunity to develop a detailed organizational architecture.

Bottom-Up Processes and Late Knowledge Binding

Bottom-up management and IT development incorporate widespread knowledge into the process. This orientation leads to comparatively "late binding" between specification and implementation.

An example of a bottom-up process is Mintzberg's contention that strategy formation is sometimes an emergent process. Emergent strategy is evolutionary, as an organization's processes and management mechanisms constrain and effect future strategic choices. As another example, object-oriented software development is premised on the notion that requirements may be known and articulated by all involved in the process, including downstream programmers and end users.

Most such bottom-up processes incorporate a form of "externalization throughout the division of labor." For example, object development relies on the insights of programmers and users alike, which are then codified into code. It is important to note that specifications are not ignored. Rather, their assertions are determined along the path of development, in addition to those developed early in some formal "analysis phase." In a bottom-up process, specifications are updated with *additional* assertions from those engaged in the process. In practice, this requires the initial development of high-level assumptions, which are then refined and *expanded* during development.

In summary, late knowledge binding is distinguished by the following characteristics:

- Bottom-up management and development processes.
- Knowledge is applied late in the process, by comparatively more people involved in the process than with top-down processes. (This is an example of decentralized decision making.)
- A short lead-time between specification and execution.
- The initial availability of only incomplete information, usually in the form of high-level goals.

- A context of comparatively high uncertainty, and high or low ambiguity.
- Short process cycle time.
- Effective in dealing with turbulent environments.
- Generally, an emphasis on the tacit knowledge of a wide variety of people, eventually externalized into explicit knowledge.
- Little opportunity for a full and thorough analysis, and therefore, a requirement for successive system improvement.
- Little opportunity for the development of a detailed architecture.

KNOWLEDGE REUSE AND BOTTOM-UP SOFTWARE DEVELOPMENT

Two software development features distinguish object-oriented development: (1) downstream externalization and (2) reuse. This is operationalized through a late binding development process. A typical process elicits tacit knowledge through downstream externalization, and codifies it into explicit knowledge in the form of modular code. Unlike traditional software development, object-orientation externalizes requirements from a wide variety of people, even developers. Once externalized, the threads of explicit knowledge are codified and made available for reuse. *The essence of reuse is to reassemble explicit threads of knowledge into new ones, which happens to be the archetype definition of a combination process.*

A specification or its code is more likely to be reused if it is routinized, with as much richness removed as possible. To reuse the resulting code or its corresponding specification (provided there is an appropriate reuse library with suitable navigation and discovery schemes), is to reuse low levels of explicit, primarily routine knowledge. *Object reuse means the assembly and distribution of comparatively routine knowledge, developed through a combination process.*

NON-DETERMINISTIC OUTCOMES AND REAL-TIME KNOWLEDGE BINDING

Systems with large tacit knowledge components are sometimes non-deterministic—their requirements are not fully determined until they are executed. Anyone engaged in creative work knows this to be true. The writing of this book, for instance, is a process conducted within a general framework, but its content took shape only during development, and was determined only when fully executed. The outcome could not be pre-determined. This is a consequence of a constantly changing context, and the characteristic of tacit knowledge to adapt to, and guide, both context and content.

In summary, we may say that real-time knowledge binding is distinguished by the following characteristics:

- An incomplete, initial specification.
- Knowledge applied during process execution, by the person(s) executing the process.
- A context of comparatively high uncertainty and high ambiguity.
- Effective in dealing with turbulent environments.
- An emphasis on tacit knowledge, though explicit knowledge is not excluded.

- Almost no opportunity for the development of an architecture.

Note that non-deterministic outcomes may occur anywhere in the knowledge spiral. There is no guarantee that tacit knowledge may be created and shared during socialization, as there is no guarantee that a programmer may successfully reuse existing code to construct new code.

Also, we note that "real-time" does not necessarily imply speed. For example, R&D is a formal socialization and externalization process that may take years to codify useful concepts or prototypes. Or it may produce nothing.

A QUALIFICATION FOR LATE OR REAL-TIME BINDING

Specification and implementation are not discrete ideas. They are range dimensions—poles on a continuum. The difference between early and late binding is one of comparative weight.

The notion of late or real-time knowledge binding is premised on the late application of knowledge. We must understand that we are speaking of a particular emphasis that distinguishes a system. Most systems start with initial frameworks or concepts. An artist, for example, may develop a portrait in real time, but there is, naturally, an early intent to paint the portrait. The difference, then, between early and late or real-time binding is the location of the predominant knowledge elaboration.

All systems are composed of explicit threads of knowledge. Computer programs must be explicit, but not everything in a system is programmable. Early binding assumes complete understanding, while late binding assumes that business understanding is a learning process. With early binding, specification is an exercise in externalization; with late binding, specification is a learning experience, and includes the development of new mental models. Early binding seeks common ground, late binding seeks differences. Tacit knowledge exists everywhere, all the time, within all forms of binding; the later the binding, the more dynamic is its evolution through learning, the greater the likelihood it reflects the requirements of the system, and the more likely it is to be externalized and realized into something concrete.

13.6 KNOWLEDGE SYSTEM CHARACTERIZATION

As the information continuum illustrates, knowledge has varying levels of richness—routine, explicit, communal, and individual. Hence all systems, in a sense, are knowledge systems. A database is a knowledge system, as is a business process, a procedure, or an entire firm.

We may describe a system in terms of its relative mix of data and knowledge characteristics, its relative importance to the firm as a core capability, or, say, its application of knowledge conversion modes, and so on. There are, then, any number of characterizations. Below, we discuss several characterizations, with the understanding that there are, no doubt, many other such frameworks.

KNOWLEDGE SYSTEM MODELS

System may be described in terms of the various dimensions of knowledge. Recall from Chapter 12 that we have identified four such dimensions: explicit-tacit, individual-social, industry-organization, and distributed-common. We may now include a fifth: early and late knowledge binding. Collectively, they form a five-dimensional model of knowledge systems, as follows:

- Tacit (T) versus explicit (E).
- Individual (I) versus social (S).
- Industry (Y) versus organization (O).
- Distributed (D) versus common (C).
- Early binding (EB) versus late or real-time binding (LB).

Borrowing from the notion of a three-dimensional model of organizational effectiveness from Robbins, these knowledge dimensions combine in any number of combinations to identify knowledge systems in organizations. Naturally, specific combinations correspond to real-world systems, while others do not. Also, certain combinations may not be possible; for example, there is a consensus that all individual knowledge is tacit, and therefore there can be no "explicit-individual" knowledge characterization.

As an example, consider the "TIY" knowledge system model. An example of a system where the prominent knowledge dimensions are {tacit-individual-industry} is that found in the organizations operating on Wall Street. As John Kay (1995) has observed, the firms on Wall Street operate primarily through relational contracts. There is a deep understanding of the business; it is characterized by highly skilled workers who expect long-term relationships within the industry. There is an exclusive, club-like atmosphere on "The Street."

We have found that the E-T and EB-LB dimensions combine to form models that may be used to describe a wide variety of systems. These dimensions combine to form four knowledge system models, as follows:

1. *Relational model (T-EB):* emphasizes tacit knowledge and early knowledge binding. The characteristics of a relational knowledge system include trust, long-term relationships, and a certain ambiguity as to the purpose and functioning of the system. Relational systems are effective where flexibility is at a premium. The relational model is an exception to the expected association of explicit knowledge with early binding. For example, relational contracts are formulated before execution (early binding), and are based on assumptions (tacit knowledge). However, relational contracts and models are validated during execution.

2. *Knowledge model (T-LB):* emphasizes tacit knowledge and late knowledge binding. It emphasizes socialization and the exchange of ideas, but also subsequent validation through direct experience. Such a system is particularly effective where learning or adaptation is required.

3. *Rational model (E-EB):* emphasizes explicit knowledge, and early knowledge binding. Rational systems are highly structured, analytical, and planned.

They are particularly useful where there is a requirement for efficient information processing and routinization.

4. *Network model (E-LB):* emphasizes explicit knowledge and late knowledge binding. High levels of information flows of explicit knowledge characterize network systems, with an emphasis on horizontal information linkages.

Certain models are more likely to represent one organization, functional area, or department than another. For instance, most R&D departments conform to the relational and knowledge models, financial planning to a network system, and so on. Once a department is so classified, it becomes easier to understand and design the necessary alignment threads. Similarly, we may apply our knowledge framework to software or technology packages. For example, the popular packages associated with "enterprise resource planning" (ERP) are examples of a rational system. Though designed for complex, integrated workflows, they are essentially canned, pre-defined threads of explicit knowledge.

Processes with Salient Knowledge Conversion Modes

Certain knowledge creating processes have distinguishing conversion modes. For example, R&D groups are known for their emphasis on concept development, a consequence of both socialization and externalization.

Below, we categorize and describe process types that have a reputation for a specific set of knowledge conversion modes. We draw on several processes that have been identified in the literature as knowledge creating ones. Processes that comprise several knowledge conversion modes generally include modes that are logically contiguous (e.g., socialization and externalization), and would typically be operationalized together, in joined sequence.

1. *Upstream processes.* An upstream process is that which emphasizes socialization and externalization. The most well-known process of this type is Research and Development. Most R&D efforts concentrate on the development of tacit knowledge and explicit concepts. At times, new explicit knowledge is created in the form of a prototype (i.e., combination). However, the salient conversion modes for R&D are socialization and externalization. Other conversion modes may be appended to R&D, particularly combination, but the full knowledge spiral usually involves several other groups in addition to R&D.

2. *Midstream processes.* Midstream processes emphasize combination, with perhaps light externalization and internalization elements.

A well-known midstream process is software development. The essential process includes the development of explicit information and system specifications, which are then transformed and combined into code through combination.

Specifications derive from business or user requirements. Requirements gathering tasks emphasize externalization. Requirements are typically explicit threads of knowledge elicited from users. Analysis and development are essentially combination tasks: Threads of explicit requirements are recombined into a schema suitable for code development, such as an information contract, or a data or process model.

The differing approaches to software development, traditional vs. object-orientation, encompass the same midstream knowledge processes. The essential difference is in their binding. In either case, IS professionals simply facilitate the process; it is the users who externalize *their* internal models into business concepts and IS requirements. Absent extensive experience, IS professionals seldom share the implicit business models of their clients. The differences between the two camps are much less than each supposes.

3. *Downstream processes.* Downstream processes emphasize combination and internalization. Most learning systems fall into this category. For example, a CASE tool may be used as a learning system: An analyst uses it to build a data model (i.e., combination), while its use (i.e., learning by doing) promotes modeling knowledge in the head of the analyst using the tool (i.e., internalization). The knowledge created (i.e., operational knowledge) includes the operations of the CASE tool and the development of modeling as a functional discipline.

4. *Knowledge spiral processes.* These processes include all four conversion modes and thus the entire knowledge spiral. Nonaka and Takeuchi (1995) discuss their theory of knowledge creation in terms of new product development, a knowledge creation process that leverages the entire knowledge spiral. Its importance lies in the fact that new product development is a *generic* knowledge spiral process that exploits knowledge creation and deployment, and is thus a core capability for many organizations in the 21st century.

COMPETENCE AND CAPABILITY

Recall from Chapter 11 that the concepts of competence and capability form part of a behavior-based approach to strategy. Recall, too, that Stalk, Evans, and Shulman (1992) state that a capability is a set of strategic business processes, while a competence is a set of strategic *knowledge* areas applied to a capability at critical points along its path.

Dorothy Leonard-Barton (1995) has elucidated the notion of a core capability. She has defined a *core technological capability* as a system comprising technical competencies. Such a system consists of two knowledge repository dimensions: employee knowledge and skills, and physical technical systems. It also consists of two dimensions that channel and control knowledge: managerial systems, and values and norms. Each of these four dimensions is briefly described below. The reader is referred to Leonard-Barton's book *Wellsprings of Knowledge* for an excellent discussion of knowledge activities and core technological capabilities.

1. *Employee knowledge and skill.* The knowledge and skill of employees include the scientific, industry-specific, and firm-specific dimensions of knowledge discussed in Chapter 12. Each of these is increasingly less codified (i.e., less explicit, more tacit) and transferable, respectively.

2. *Physical technical systems.* This refers to the explicit and routine knowledge codified in accepted procedures and software. Hardware and equipment, as well as the content of databases, may also be considered a constituent of a core capability, depending on the basis of competition in a given industry.

3. *Managerial systems.* This is comprised of a firm's incentive, reward, education, and training systems and policies. For example, Davenport has described the importance of a managerial system that cultivates trust, and, in so doing, dispenses rewards to employees who share knowledge.

4. *Values and norms.* This refers to the tacit assumptions associated with an organization's culture. Included are those values that guide the selection of knowledge and knowledge building activities within an organization.

As we can see from the above listing, the first two dimensions address the knowledge content of an organization, both tacit *(people skills)* and explicit *(technical systems)*. *Managerial systems* refers to the processes that create and control the level of directionality in an organization, while *values and norms* refers to the culture that underlies that directionality.

In a very real sense, the last two dimensions are not specific to a core capability, but refer to an organization's entire fabric and directionality apparatus. All that constitutes an organization—the core capabilities described by Leonard-Barton, and also each of its processes, the commitment of its employees, and so on—are guided by an organization's culture. A major function of its managerial practice is to create sufficient and optimum alignment between those cultural assumptions and the organization's pieces.

13.7 AN EXAMPLE FROM STRATEGIC MANAGEMENT

Strategy is a complex construct. It is a process with content, which serves as an organization's interface with the outside world. Mintzberg, Ahlstrand, and Lampel (1998) have reviewed strategic management, and have been able to discern ten distinct schools. Each school is a glimpse into the entire strategy construct, and reflects a particular point of view or emphasis. The schools represent a somewhat historical progression, from three prescriptive schools (i.e., design, planning, and positioning) that describe how strategy should be made, to six descriptive schools (i.e., entrepreneurial, cognitive, learning, power, cultural, and environmental) that describe how strategy actually gets made, and finally to a tenth school (i.e., configuration) that represents an integrative perspective of the other nine.

Tables 13–1(a) and 13–1(b) are a brief review of the ten schools (adapted from Mintzberg, Ahlstrand, and Lampel), and their corresponding knowledge models in terms of their {E-T} and {EB-LB} dimensions.

Table 13–1(a) reveals certain patterns among the traditional schools of strategy. The positioning school is the (elaborate) heir to the design and planning schools. All three operate best in relatively stable environments where analysis and top-down management processes are particularly effective.

As the environment becomes more turbulent, prescriptive strategy becomes difficult, if not impossible. The complexities of the real world preclude effective information gathering, forecasting, formulation, and deliberate implementation. As the environment becomes more dynamic, and organizations smaller and less formal, the entrepreneurial school gains credibility. But as the environment be-

TABLE 13–1(A) STRATEGY SCHOOLS AND THEIR KNOWLEDGE CHARACTERISTICS, ADAPTED FROM MINTZBERG, AHLSTRAND, AND LAMPEL (1998)

Strategy School	Key Words and Descriptors	Predominant Knowledge Dimensions
Design	Fit; deliberate, simple, informal process; explicit, simple, unique, full blown, strategy; strategy as case study; SWOT analysis; CEO as strategist; stable envir; high centralization Precursor to Planning & Positioning Schools.	Rational knowledge system: explicit, early binding, with emphasis on individual decision maker
Planning	Formalize; formal process; quantitative analyses & techniques; coordinated plans; strategy as programs; planners as strategists; simple & stable envir; machine (high centralization, high formalization), divisional structure.	Rational knowledge system: explicit, early binding, emphasis on information processing
Positioning	Analyze; formal process; value chain, five forces; competitive context; deliberate & full blown, strategy as generic position (Porter); analysts as strategists; simple, stable, mature envir; machine, divisional structure.	Rational knowledge system: explicit, early binding, with emphasis on explicit strategy content
Entrepre-neurial	Envision; Early vision, but real-time adjustment (primarily deliberate, some emergent); strategy as personal vision; leader as strategist; dynamic, simple envir; creative destruction; high experience & intuition; growth-oriented, niche strategy; high centralization, low formalization.	Knowledge system primarily Relational, some Knowledge: individual decision maker, emphasis on tacit strategy vision
Cognitive	Frame; emergent, strategy as concepts and mental maps (mostly individual); thinkers (key individuals) as strategists; information processing (filtered by concepts); high experience; Serves as a precursor to the Learning School.	Knowledge knowledge system: primarily individual, some social; emphasis on tacit concepts

comes very turbulent—dynamic and complex—strategy can no longer be formulated and deliberate. Rather, it forms through learning. The cognitive school, with its focus on thinking and the development of mental models, provides a transition to the emergent strategies that characterize the schools in Table 13–1(b).

Learning is enormously complex, but its rewards are great. Mintzberg *et al.* claim that the success of Japanese firms may be attributed to their learning approach to strategy, and not, as is commonly believed, a cultural approach. Strategic managers manage the learning of their learners—strategies emerge from learners, but are tied together into a coherent whole by managers who understand their integrative role.

Power is defined by Mintzberg *et al.* as the exercise of influence beyond the purely economic, while politics is the exploitation of power in other than purely economic ways. Power is legitimate; politics is illegitimate or alegitimate. Micro power refers to political activity inside an organization, while macro power deals with the use of power by the organization. While the power school promotes self-interest, the culture school promotes common interest; the former fragments, the latter coalesces. Strategy, according to the culture school, is a process of social interaction, premised on common beliefs and values (i.e., tacit assumptions). The culture school is related to the cognition school of strategy, particularly the subjective, interpretative wing (e.g., cognition and culture are premised on tacit assumptions that filters what we perceive, etc.).

TABLE 13–1(B)   STRATEGY SCHOOLS AND THEIR KNOWLEDGE CHARACTERISTICS, ADAPTED FROM MINTZBERG, AHLSTRAND, AND LAMPEL (1998)

Strategy School	Key Words and Descriptors	Predominant Knowledge Dimensions
Learning	Learn; emergent, incremental process and strategy content; strategy as unique patterns, strategic intent, competence; learners as strategists; complex, dynamic, even novel environment; adhocracy, professional structures.	Knowledge knowledge system: communal tacit, with emphasis on late binding.
Power	Grab; conflict, bargaining; micro strategy as emergent position achieved through negotiation, as a map of the existing power structure; interest groups as strategists; macro strategy as deliberate with collective alliances and networks, as ploys and signaling; divisive environment (micro), cooperative environment (macro); adhocracy, professional structures.	Micro: Distributed tacit between contending coalitions, Relational system within a coalition. Macro: Network & Rational systems, emphasis on explicit, cooperative networks.
Cultural	Coalesce; process of social interaction; strategy as a unique, collective perspective, deliberate; strategic stability; passive environment; missionary, machine structures.	Relational knowledge systems: emphasis on communal tacit.
Environment	Cope; passive process as a reaction to the environment, strategy as generic, niche positions, emergent; contingency theory, adaptation, evolution; machine structure.	Primarily Network, some Knowledge systems: emphasis on late binding.
Configuration	Integrate & transform; transformation process yielding quantum shift between stable combination of states (configurations); deliberate and emergent strategies, configuration yielding emergent strategies; any of the above strategies, in context.	Each model, depending on the strategy of school employed.

The environment school considers the environment (more specifically, the environment's forces, such as its stability, complexity, etc.) as the central actor, with the organization's strategy a kind of reactive mirror to that environment. The environment school is related to contingency theory in organizational design, in that certain properties of an organization (e.g., formalization, strategy, etc.) are related to environmental characteristics or forces.

Finally, the configuration school seeks to integrate each of the other nine schools, but not in some all-encompassing composite. Rather, this school assumes that an organization has clustered its "states" around effective combinations, known as a *configuration*. Change is infrequent, but when it comes, it is mediated through a *transformation* process that produces quantum leaps between configurations. (Aside: this view of strategy and organizational change parallels that of many biologists in their view of evolution as short, dramatic shifts between long periods of relatively stable biological states.) Moreover, each configuration is part of an ordered sequence that corresponds to particular patterns, such as the life-cycle of an organization. The transformation process may include that of any of the nine schools, depending on the organization's particular context and time.

COMMENTARY

The three traditional schools of strategy (i.e., design, planning, positioning) emphasize explicit knowledge and its processing through the division of labor. The sequencing of the design, planning, and position schools follows a pattern of increasingly complex explicit knowledge that can be processed only through increasingly elaborate information processing schemes. How successfully its knowledge content is routinized and processed thus largely determines the effectiveness of each strategy.

In contrast to the rational knowledge systems of the prescriptive schools, how successfully its knowledge content is captured and codified largely determines the effectiveness of the descriptive schools with emergent strategies. Of course, this goes to the heart of a knowledge creating firm. Developing an organizational policy of rewards for knowledge sharing, experimentation, prototyping, and so on, is difficult for most traditional firms. We need only to look at the work groups pretending to be "high performance teams" and the failure of many firms to promote sharing, and so on, to realize that knowledge creation may be another unrealized executive slogan.

We have seen how we may use knowledge system characteristics to describe different schools of strategy. As the schools themselves represent mostly historical shifts in approach, we can see how knowledge characteristics also change. As organizational strategies shift from planned and analytical processes to one of learning, so, too, do their knowledge characteristics: from explicit to tacit, from individual to communal, from early to late and real-time binding. Furthermore, the configuration school reminds us that all knowledge system models are with value; like everything else we have been discussing in this book, it is a matter of context.

13.8 CORE CONCEPTS

World building
Layered knowledge world
Layer interactions
Knowledge application (KA)
Knowledge conversion modes
Externalization
Internalization
Double-loop learning
Knowledge binding
Late knowledge binding
Knowledge system characterization
Knowledge model
Network model
Midstream processes
Competence

Knowledge world
World version, actions, natural world
Knowledge discovery (KD)
Knowledge creation (KC)
Socialization
Combination
Single-loop learning
Knowledge contextualization
Early knowledge binding
Real-time knowledge binding
Relational model
Rational model
Upstream processes
Downstream processes
Core (technological) capability

CHAPTER 14

THE 21ST CENTURY LEARNING ORGANIZATION

14.1 CONVERGENCE AND CONFIGURATION

The world is a confusing place. Our organizations move this way and that. The straightforward approaches to design and management—contingency theory (i.e., design to a situation), prescriptive schools (i.e., strategic formulation), management by objectives (i.e., performance appraisals), etc.—seem out of place. The organization's dimensions seem to converge. Everything is related to everything else. In this context, how do organizations learn and change? The answers are not very clear.

STRATEGIC LEARNING AS A METAPHOR FOR CHANGE

We may use strategic learning as a metaphor for coping with this dilemma. Should we develop a prescriptive strategy or an emergent one? Should we seek stability or change? The ten strategy models of Mintzberg *et al.* suggest that organizations are changing all the time, or not at all, and they learn in very specific ways. They have categorized this situation as follows: "Do organizations learn by doing (as in the learning school), by thinking (as in the design school), by programming (as in the planning school), by calculating (as in the positioning school), or by arguing (as in the power school)... the cognitive and cultural schools imply that they learn only with great difficulty. And the environment school suggests that organizations don't learn at all." Mintzberg affirms that the entrepreneurial and configuration schools suggest incremental change with infrequent but quantum shifts in direction.

The same type of questions may be asked about any learning paradigm. Do we concentrate on process or content? Is change planned, emergent, or both? Do we seek stability, constant change, or something in between? What is the best approach to learning: planning, thinking, analyzing, doing, arguing, etc.? Planning and analysis are important, but is it wise to separate them from implementation? Do we compromise and do a little of everything? And so on.

LEARNING AND VALUATION

Another issue associated with organizational learning concerns its value. Figure 14–1 illustrates learning from a knowledge creation perspective: an interaction between people, context, and value generated. The central issue we are depicting

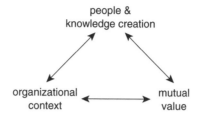

FIGURE 14–1   Learning and Knowledge–Context–Value Interaction

here is the value of the knowledge to the person or persons who generate it, as well as its value to the organization.

Determining value is not easy. We often use measures as indicators of benefit or improvement, such as productivity for a business process. Svieby (1997) asserts that "knowledge assets" require non-financial as well as financial measures. Among the measures Svieby suggests are those associated with employee competence, internal support staff, and external relationships. For example, employee competence includes the number of years in a profession, level of education, "grading," training and education costs, and turnover rate.

These are significant measures to the organization. These measures are, at best, static indicators of potential knowledge creation. However, they do not indicate what is important to the people who create the knowledge, or how well motivated they are to create it. How many managers have asked their employees how they measure the value of their work?

Knowledge is different from other organizational resources—for it depends on people, and is therefore not easily substitutable. Without promoting the individual's sense of value, knowledge work will not be as innovative as otherwise. Individual learning is largely psychological and social, and without individual learning there can be no organizational learning. Successful knowledge creation is more than action—without *individual context* and *individual value* there would be no impetus to act!

Achieving individual context and individual value will be stressful. As with the Renaissance, the knowledge and learning era is bringing forth a shift in power, increasingly, to larger communities of people. People bring with them their values, which are personal, but also social, religious, and political. Ownership of the source of wealth, as always, brings power to those who possess it. In the knowledge era, this means greater democracy, and an overall sense of justice and community. As expressed by Charles Handy (1997) in the *Harvard Business Review:* "The old language of property and ownership no longer serves us in modern society because it no longer describes what a company really is. The old language suggests the wrong priorities, leads to inappropriate policies, and screens out new possibilities. The idea of a corporation as the property of the current holders of its shares is confusing because it does not make clear where power lies. As such, the notion is an affront to natural justice because it gives inadequate recognition to the people who work in the corporation and who are, increasingly, its principal assets. To talk of owning other people, as shareholders implicitly do, might even be considered immoral. Moreover, the language of property and ownership is an insult to democracy. One of the great paradoxes of our time is that it is totalitarian, centrally planned organizations, owned by outsiders, that are providing the material wherewithal of the great democracies. Free people do not relish being instruments of others. The best of them will, increasingly, either refuse to join such institutions or demand a high prices for the sacrifice of their rights."

*****

Nearly every current textbook on organizational design now includes a chapter on learning. Libraries and bookstores have their shelves lined with books dedicated to this subject. Do they say different things, or the same?—it's not clear. That's because learning is perhaps the most complex construct with which organizations must deal. It's a paradigm that captures the organization's convergence and configuration characteristics collectively. Learning is a moving picture of an organization. It includes thinking and analysis, abstraction and conceptualization, development and alignment, trial and error, doing and adjustment, success and failure. It depends on everything coming together, and what comes together has its unique place and its unique time.

14.2 CONTRACT ANALOGS

A contract is a specification—a prescription for outcomes. Its value rests with its explicitness: It is an unambiguous statement of intentions, it can be implemented in any number of ways, and its performance may be tested against the specification. The underlying premise of a contract is early binding; without it, there can be no notion of a specification. Contracts are self-contained and generally avoid problems of time. A contract is an ideal design construct for prescriptive strategies, most computer information systems, routine process tasks, etc. Several exotic techniques, methods, and frameworks have been developed around this paradigm: a SWOT or value chain analysis, information engineering, the capability maturity model, performance appraisals, etc. The contract is the logical end-state for all this—the ultimate design artifact for the culture of the industrial engineering society.

The knowledge society has its own set of distinguishing characteristics. Here, outcomes are not so much formulated as they are formed. The final specification is deferred until implementation, which in turn sets the stage for future outcomes. Specification and implementation are vertically intertwined and have a longitudinal time dimension. What is realized in one instance (i.e., a specific specification-implementation combination) influences the context of subsequent instances. This characteristic is not subject to formal planning, but emerges from execution.

We use the term *contract analog* to refer to all forms of "specification"—traditional contracts as well as those that intertwine specification and implementation. The former characterizes the industrial era while the latter best describes the learning era. This is illustrated in Figure 14–2.

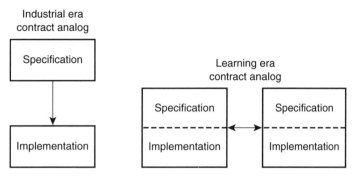

FIGURE 14–2   Industrial and Learning Era Contract Analogs

The contract analogs of the industrial engineering society are *static*: They strive for precision, and isolation and implementation independence. Specification is separate from implementation (i.e., early binding), and isolated from other contracts (temporally as well as statically). This fits in with Scientific Management and traditional software development, as each seeks control over "substitutable" resources. Isolation and implementation independence renders a contract specification *complete*—its success is a function of ascertaining specific requirements and recording them in a suitably formal language.

In contrast, contract analogs of the learning society are *dynamic*: they are dependent on other contract analogs, and on implementation—often the specific individuals and IS implementing the contract. Knowledge workers are not substitutable implementation resources; they are woven into an organization's contract analogs. Implementation dependence renders a contract analog *open*, as each individual determines the character of his or her outcomes. Table 14–1 summarizes the characteristics of complete and open contract analogs.

COMPLETE CONTRACTS

Traditional organizational arrangements—economic, structure, management control processes, software development, etc,—incorporate the notions of information processing and early knowledge binding. *Complete contracts* are those that emphasize explicit knowledge, and early knowledge binding with rules defined before execution. A *precise contract* is the archetype specification construct of the "machine" organization.

For example, a specification for a process task may be precisely defined—provided the task is routine. A routine task is stable and predictable (e.g., as is found in most workflows), and therefore may be reduced to an algorithm. Furthermore, its constituent specifications are similarly precise. For example, information contracts for a routine task have no ambiguity and typically concern data and routine knowledge (e.g., computing operations). Such explicitly defined contracts accurately predict behavior before execution.

As with a precise contract, a *relativized contract* involves explicit knowledge rules. The major difference between them is that in the latter, a person or an IS mediate those rules. Possibilities are determined before execution, but selection of

TABLE 14–1   CHARACTERISTICS OF COMPLETE AND OPEN CONTRACT ANALOGS

| Dimension | Complete Contract | | Open Contract | |
	Precise	Relativized	Relational	Knowledge
Knowledge Characteristic	Explicit, generally routine	Explicit	Tacit, individual and communal	Explicit and tacit
Knowledge binding	Early	Early, and real-time	Early, late, and real-time	Early, late, and real-time
Communication of rules (e.g., invariants)	Before execution, explicitly through assertions	Before and during execution, explicitly through assertions	Before execution, tacitly through assumptions that are reinforced during execution	Before execution: tacitly through assumptions and mental models, and explicitly through assertions, the former of which is reinforced during execution
Longitudinal time dimension	None	During and after execution	Very long, until undermined	Variable, before, during and after execution
Motivation	Satisfy a specification	Satisfy a specification	Arrive at an acceptable agrmt	Satisfy a task requirement
Connotation	Describes states	Describes states	Describes attitudes and expectations	Describes beliefs and justifications
Requirement and Assumption	The central requirement is to reduce uncertainty. Uncertainty may be reduced through the acquisition and processing of information.		The central requirement is for individual and organizational commitment, knowledge creation, and learning. Specific contingencies are unknown, but possibilities are known, and therefore, there is an opportunity for adaptation and reframing.	

which rules to execute are determined during execution. For example, an expert system executes a particular sequence of rules based on input from a user. As another example, a neural network gathers statistics on past executions and determines the appropriate rules during execution. Some consider this an example of machine learning, since the computer determines the best possible solution based on experience. As with a precise contract, specific rules are defined beforehand, but unlike a precise contract, their sequence is determined during execution.

SELECTED ISSUES WITH COMPLETE CONTRACTS

Listed below are selected issues associated with complete contracts.

- *Externalization problem.* There is an assumption with complete contracts (particularly precise contracts) that externalization is sufficient. This is tantamount to saying $E = mc^2$ captures the essence of relativity theory. A contract assertion typically expresses a specific relationship that is codified through some processing of states and, in no way, is equivalent to the underlying knowledge content. Externalization only creates simplistic threads of its underlying implicit model.

    As another example, Earl's work on IS planning demonstrates that the technology and methodology approaches are not as effective as the "soft" organizational approaches. The former two approaches emphasize formal analysis and top-down planning, while the latter emphasizes the development of shared mental models. Also, it is interesting to observe that the technology and methodology approaches to IS are analogous to the positioning and planning strategy schools, respectively, while the organizational IS approach is similar to the learning strategy school. The former share the properties of early binding and explicit knowledge, while the organizational IS and learning strategy approaches emphasize late binding and tacit knowledge.

In each case, the lesson is simple: Externalization is sufficient if the system we are building can be adequately described with states of data and explicit knowledge. To the extent that real-world systems are more complex than the processing of data states, we need something richer than traditional contract specifications—an analog that may leverage mental models and capture all forms of knowledge creation, including socialization.

- *Aggregation problem.* As several writers have observed, important details are lost during aggregation. To capture all important details with explicit assertions requires completeness—an unlikely possibility with modern systems. On the other hand, mental models may capture assumptions about those details, which may be adjusted during real time.

- *Boundary problem.* As Mintzberg *et al.* have observed, you cannot simply put a box around a problem or issue and expect to capture all of its essential properties. There are too many associated, and external, possibilities and contingencies. Yet, the implication with complete contracts is that you can capture everything relevant for a system, or that the environment is sufficiently stable that errors in specification are of little consequence during implementation.

- *Integration and interpretation problem.* Complete contracts are both data and state dependent and operate best with routine knowledge. Though most problems contain a routine component, ambiguity and fuzzy logic characterize modern situations. Explicitness brings rigidity and leads to simplified interpretations. Complete contracts require filtering of those very elements that are responsible for the rich workings of organizations—people, culture, politics, group interactions, etc. Naturally, this problem is related to the externalization problem described above—no system can fully represent its corresponding implicit models. For example, an expert system cannot possibly capture all the rules of an expert. Recall that tacit knowledge is hidden—even the expert is unaware of what he or she knows.

- *Learning.* Complete contracts do not promote learning, at least not very quickly. Isolation, implementation independence, and early binding facilitate the processing of information, not the creation of knowledge. In such an environment, the only mechanism available for adaptation and change is *feedback*, in effect, creating new contract specifications well after their predecessors.

We do not want to leave the impression that complete contracts are without value. To the contrary, they are largely responsible for the development of complex computer systems. A precise contract is a precious tool for an analyst. However, it is one tool in a world that requires a repertoire of tools.

OPEN CONTRACTS

The strength of an open contract is that its inconsistencies and imprecision may be exploited by the organization. It is because of such "vagaries" that people are required for implementation. A dynamic learning environment requires such dependence.

Open contracts are distinguished from complete contracts in several ways:

- *Psychological model.* While complete contracts imply a legal framework, open contracts are largely psychological (a term first used by Chris Argyris in 1960). Complete contracts are static and may be realized through machines, while open contracts are dynamic and require people.
- *Implicitness.* Open contracts are implicit, though they usually contain some listing of specific assertions. Implicit mental models are embodied in open contracts, and address "intentions," even if dynamically generated, and have utility in addressing learning or other dynamic situations. In contrast, complete contracts must deal with static "requirements" articulated with formal assertions.
- *Equivocality.* The ambiguity of an open contract often leads to different interpretations of its meaning, sometimes even its existence. This stands in sharp contrast to complete contracts, which strive for explicitness with all ambiguity removed.
- *Temporality.* Open contracts infer a time dimension; success with a contract analog maintains that contract, while leading to others. Subsequent contract analogs are often not subject to planning.
- *Culture and reciprocity.* An open contract is constrained by the norms and culture of its participants and of the organization. A second constraint is the notion of *reciprocity*—discussed by Argyris, and currently advanced by several writers (e.g., Davenport) as a requirement for knowledge sharing.
- *Engagement.* An open contract may be used as a model that links the requirements (i.e., assumptions and expectations) of people to those of the organization. Implementation dependence embodies engagement and learning, and may thus be used as a template to address the *value requirements* of both parties to the contract (i.e., person-person, person-organization, and organization-organization). In contrast, a complete contract promotes implementation independence and thus ignores human expectations and motivations. Note also that while *feedback* is associated with complete contracts, *engagement* is associated with open contracts. Both are dimensions of change: Feedback is an information processing mechanism, while engagement embodies involvement and learning.

Open contracts are held together because of underlying custom, norms, trust, or at the very least, an expectation of reciprocity. For example, Davenport describes the factors associated with knowledge sharing as reciprocity, repute, altruism, and a culture of trust. They form part of the *informal background* until the actual execution of the contract. Only during implementation do all explicit assertions and implicit assumptions and expectations become visible, the outcome determined, and perhaps most importantly, the informal background of trust and engagement reinforced or undermined.

The first type of open contract is the *relational contract*. Introduced by John Kay (1995), the relational contract embodies the notion of trust between individuals. The primary motivation of a relational contract is to arrive at an acceptable arrangement between participants. In contrast, a *knowledge contract* is focused on work, and through work both the individual and the organization earn and derive value.

RELATIONAL AND KNOWLEDGE CONTRACTS

Relational contracts are foundational. An organization cannot exist without them. Relational contracts are largely responsible for the commitment of people to an organization (and vice versa). Relational contracts are high in nuance, and thus they are open to linkages to other domains, such as culture. Relational contracts contain loosely bound logic, but tight commitment. (In contrast, precise contracts contain a tight logic, but loose commitment.)

A relational contract contains both deliberate and emergent properties—execution reinforces or undermines previous assumptions and expectations. This says nothing of the initial strength of its assumptions and expectations, only that they may strengthen or weaken through successive iterations of the contract. For example, an expectation of a promotion that does not materialize will undermine the relational contract between the employee and employer.

Knowledge contracts are primarily centered on tacit knowledge, though they may contain references to threads of explicit knowledge. In our vocabulary, knowledge contracts refer to tacit knowledge, individual or communal. (Explicit knowledge is captured in an organization's complete contracts.) Knowledge contracts are more narrowly focused than relational, since the former references a task, while the latter embodies a broader social context.

UNFINISHED CONTRACTS VS. OPEN CONTRACTS

Open contracts do not refer to an unfinished specification. A precise contract for a routine workflow, for instance, may initially be a statement of requirements by a strategist that is subsequently refined by an analyst. This situation merely describes an "in-flight" state of a precise contract before its implementation. This is common to all contracts, since intention precedes specification.

However, with open contracts, the intention and its underlying constraints—mental models, assumptions, expectations, task requirements—are all that is required. With open contracts, "refinement" does not really exist; rather, there is simply implementation where actions make the contract *visible*. In the case of a relational contract, the assumptions become clear, such as the trust between the parties to the contract. With a knowledge contract, the final "specification" becomes manifest through action—there is no formalization of assertions.

CONTRACT FORMATION

The four contract types described in Table 14–1 are ideal types. For example, a precise contract for a computer program, or a labor contract between a union and a company, are ideal precise types. In each case, the contract embodies the ideal characteristics of early knowledge binding, analysis, planning, and mechanical implementation. Each assertion is explicitly stated and documented in a contract specification. Subsequent implementation is through code (for the computer program) and the behavior of people (for the labor contract). In each case, adherence to the terms of the agreement is generally easy—it's a function of how explicitly the assertions have been stated in the contract specification.

However, a contract often shares characteristics normally associated with several of the ideal types. For example, software prototyping and object-orientation are examples of software development approaches that produce systems that may be described with precise contracts. Such contracts are not fully developed with early knowledge binding. Rather, certain intentions are prescribed but assertions emerge during development. What materializes, however, is a precise contract—the software (software must be precise or it doesn't work). There may be artifacts of early knowledge binding and specification, such as a use-case scenario, or more traditional artifacts such as a data model. However, these design artifacts are usually left unfinished; the precise specification is implemented in code. What we have, in essence, are contracts whose assertions are developed during development (late knowledge binding), and become fully explicit (i.e., precise) during execution.

CONTRACT ANALOGS AND SAMPLE SYSTEMS

Figure 14–3 illustrates contract types and a sampling of their systems. As shown in the figure, as the knowledge characteristic becomes more tacit, the implementation

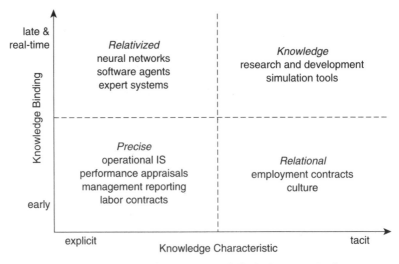

FIGURE 14–3   Sample Systems and Their Contract Analogs

components shift from machines to people. As knowledge binding moves from early to late, the final outcomes becomes more dependent on implementation.

14.3 SYSTEM DYNAMICITY

Figure 14–4 illustrates an assortment of selected systems as a function of organization pattern complexity and information complexity. The position of each type of system is relative and representative of a class. For example, generic technology systems (e.g., accounts payable, materials management, etc.) are integrated, and thus may have a large effect on the performance of several interlocking business processes (i.e., "integrated"); hence they are fairly high as an organization pattern. However, such technology packages are predefined threads of explicit knowledge and generally available (i.e., "generic"), and hence are not very rich on the information continuum.

The reader is cautioned not to interpret positioning as an indicator of importance to an organization. All systems contain threads of knowledge. Knowledge originates in the minds of people, is socialized, externalized, and codified in systems. The central system issues illustrated in Figure 14–4 are the level of knowledge routinization and the level of organizational exploitation.

SELECTED DISCUSSION

DATABASES

A *database system* is a knowledge system. The knowledge content may be highly routine, but the mere act of building a database and, say, associating certain data attributes with each other (while excluding others) to form a data structure (such

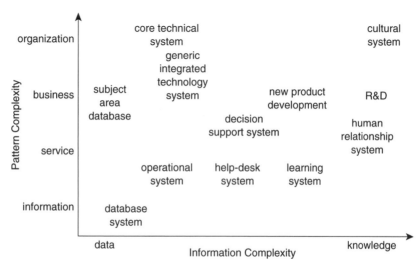

FIGURE 14–4   Systems as a Function of Pattern and Information Complexity

as a table) are examples of applying routine knowledge. Applying referential integrity constraints is yet another layer of routine knowledge. The recent advance of object-relational databases permits the application of still additional layers of explicit knowledge. Such explicit knowledge may take the form of embedded processing methods or may include complex data types (e.g., geo-spatial). A database system is the archetype organization of data in an information pattern.

A *subject area database* is an example of an organization of highly routinized data—so much so that its contents may be made available to the entire organization. Hence, its contents may be embedded in service and business patterns.

In contrast, a specific *operational system* (i.e., an application system) has a narrower scope. It includes a database, with additional threads of application-specific explicit knowledge (i.e., business processing logic), shifting its information complexity to the right in Figure 14–4. Hence, its information is less routinized than that of a stand-alone database. Its contents may be part of a specific service pattern, such as an accounts payable workflow process. In effect, an operational application forms the information constituent for a given business process, which in turn may be represented in a corresponding information and process molecule.

KNOWLEDGE APPLICATION: DEVELOPMENT VS. EXECUTION

The competitive advantage of a system, say, a core technological capability, is a function of applying knowledge along two dimensions—systems *execution*, and systems *development*. The former is associated with the application of tacit knowledge, while the latter is associated with the application of explicit knowledge. For example, a brokerage firm with top-notch brokers may have a natural competitive advantage that is manifest during process execution. In contrast, a network system of a communications firm contains a large knowledge component externalized during decades of development. Hence, applying knowledge confers competitive advantage, either directly through execution (tacit), or through complex and lengthy systems development (codifying tacit into integrated explicit). Naturally, we may combine system characteristics—execution and development. For example, financial consulting is dependent on the advice of specific brokers (execution and the application of tacit knowledge) but is enhanced through broker workstations that access all sorts of applications and market data (development and the application of interrelated explicit knowledge).

Execution and the application of tacit knowledge confer advantage only if there is a strong commitment to trained and experienced workers. Tacit knowledge needs to be cultivated through a commitment to people. The advantage of a system relying on knowledge applied during execution is distinctive human involvement—the mix of culture, training, rewards, and relational and knowledge contracting.

Codifying knowledge during development confers advantage if we build systems sufficiently complex, and if we build them with knowledge externalized and codified into a system. Note that the goal is not to deliberately make software chaotic and expensive to maintain, but to codify knowledge fragments into a larger, more complex framework that emerges through learning. Emergence is a function of people (knowledge codified during development), their training, and the organization's culture. The advantage of a system relying on knowledge applied during development is the extensiveness and complexity of explicit knowledge integration.

VALUE-ADDED DATA AND DECISION SUPPORT SYSTEMS

Nonroutine tasks are associated with sources of rich information—i.e., tacit knowledge. A question that arises concerns the role and design of supporting "data systems."

In the past, management information systems (MIS) have been little more than listings of detailed, operational data elements. Such systems actually represent a patchwork design, where data designed specifically for routine tasks, typically in operational systems, are collected and listed. People performing analytical work (e.g., analysts and managers) have to sift and apply heuristics manually to the data in order to make use of it.

Modern decision support systems organize data differently from their MIS antecedents and serve as a guide in the design of data systems for nonroutine work. In contrast to MIS that rely on data organized to support specific operation criteria (e.g., update consistency leading to normalized tables), a data warehouse or mart organizes data for queries and the application of heuristics (codified knowledge). Such designs and heuristics deliver *value-added data*—decision support systems designed for a *class of problems* (as opposed to specific routine transactions), and include explicit analytical knowledge and multi-dimensional data. Value-added data may include computational algorithms or data visualization logic. If needed, the addition of generalized query tools that facilitate the application of an individual's analytical heuristics provides yet another of level of individualized support for nonroutine work.

APPLICATION DEVELOPMENT

IS managers should expand the traditional midstream emphasis of software development to include both upstream and downstream knowledge conversion modes. Cooperative strategic management between the business and IS communities facilitates the development of shared mental models (i.e., socialization), and therefore increases the likelihood of process interconnectivity (i.e., internalization). As with any product (IT or otherwise), "knowing the customer," asking the customer for likes and dislikes, and so on, is sure to limit product knowledge generation to externalization and combination. This emphasis on explicit knowledge, in the form of externalizing requirements and building code through combination, will not produce long-term customer satisfaction.

Instead, long-term relationships arise from socialization: the development of shared mental models, trust, and rich, personal communications. The goal is to build shared implicit models of the interaction of business processes and IS, and in so doing, both business and IS professionals will share the same learning experiences.

For example, Earl (1993) demonstrated the competitive advantage afforded IS planning characterized by "organizational" approaches over those of "technology." The former includes learning and socialization—the development of shared mental models between business and IS staff—while the latter relies almost exclusively on combination and IS staff. The organizational approaches proved to be far more effective in terms of competitive advantage, demonstrating a certain strength to such "soft" notions as mental models over the "rigor" of analysis.

Prototyping and Evolutionary Software Development

One technique we have found useful in facilitating the development of shared mental models is to initiate projects as prototypes. This forces internalization and socialization, and thus all participants go through the entire knowledge spiral together. When combined with a federated IS and IT structure (discussed subsequently), prototyping and evolutionary development may become the standard approach to software development. Such a systems development practice emphasizes learning and the entire knowledge spiral.

Sustaining Advantage Through Explicit Knowledge Systems

Core technological capabilities and competencies are sources of distinctive advantage. Recall from Chapter 12, that Leonard-Barton described two knowledge content dimensions (people skills and technical systems), and two knowledge-channeling dimensions (managerial systems, and values and norms). To the extent that capabilities and competencies contain large tacit knowledge components, people and values, they will remain core dimensions and advantage may be sustained. Similarly, if the physical technical systems are sufficiently complex, which means that they contain large explicit knowledge components with elaborate interrelationships, the resulting capabilities will also remain core.

This brings to the fore two dimensions for using IT for advantage. The first, as mentioned above, is to build complex and interrelated threads of explicit knowledge into a core technological capability. The second is to apply IT, usually simple threads of explicit knowledge, in an innovative fashion. The development of automated teller machines (ATMs), for example, when first used by relatively few banks, created "value-generating" assets, and these fast "time-to-market" banks achieved a certain advantage for a time. But when all banks quickly followed suit, ATMs became "value-preserving assets," existing only to maintain parity within an industry. (See Peter Keen's *The Process Edge*, 1997.) The lesson is simple, although difficult to apply: The application of IT to a core capability is highly desirable if its explicit knowledge threads are (1) complex and interrelated, and (2) intertwined with the other core tacit dimensions—people and core ideology.

14.4 ORGANIZATIONAL DYNAMICITY

Learning is inextricably coupled with knowledge creation. The knowledge domain may be internally created or externally acquired. In either case, learning involves developing threads of tacit and explicit knowledge, and their amplification throughout the organization. This may be a simple information pattern elevated into a business pattern (e.g., data mining), or something more complex, such as acquiring a firm and incorporating its knowledge with yours.

In this section, we discuss those issues that effect the organization from an architectural perspective, as it transforms itself into a learning organization.

THE EVOLUTION OF ORGANIZATIONAL FORMS

In his text on organizational design, Richard Daft (1998) describes the progression of organizational forms from the classical hierarchy to the modern horizontal form, and finally to a learning organization. Below, we briefly describe each in terms of our architecture:

HIERARCHICAL ORGANIZATION

As a machine, the organization is a deep hierarchy, and management processes are top-down with early knowledge binding. There is an assumption that uncertainty may be reduced through the acquisition and processing of information and, as such, the organization may be sufficiently described with complete contracts. Its information linkages are primarily vertical, and exist to control people and reduce variance in individual behavior. Horizontal information linkages are minimal, and those that exist typically are realized through informal relationships between managers.

HORIZONTAL ORGANIZATION

A horizontal perspective characterizes the second form. The organization remains a hierarchy, though flatter. The major change is in the coordination of work and the requirement for elaborate horizontal information linkages, such as IS, task forces, and cross-functional teams. Moreover, individual workers are empowered for operational decision making, reducing the need for hierarchical referral. While the hierarchical organization was one of control, the horizontal one shifts the emphasis to coordinating work. However, decisions concerning strategy, culture, and other organization-wide domains remain in the hands of the hierarchy. From several perspectives—learning, individual control over careers, etc.—the second wave is not very different from the first. Hence, the horizontal organization may be described with both complete and open contracts, covering the hierarchy and workflow coordination, respectively.

LEARNING ORGANIZATION

A *network* of people or groups of people characterizes a learning organization. Horizontal linkages overshadow vertical. Here, workers are empowered to make strategic as well as workflow decisions. Strategy is emergent, with both late and real-time knowledge binding. Unlike the horizontal organization, we believe the network organization *does* represent a dramatic step in the evolution of organizations. Collaboration is an example of a design technique where the intent is to coordinate workers, and thus facilitate knowledge sharing. Naturally, a culture that facilitates cooperative behavior is required, e.g., rewards, recognition (promotion opportunities, bonuses, etc.), learning opportunities, broader responsibilities, etc.

VIRTUAL ORGANIZING

Venkatraman and Henderson (1998) suggest that a "virtual organization" is optimally realized through *virtual organizing*—a process approach that captures the meaning of architectural dynamicity more so than the notion of a static network organization. This approach may be one method of operationalizing a learning organization, dynamically assembling and disassembling nodes on the network to meet the demands of a particular business context. This further gives rise to the notion of value and ownership raised by Charles Handy. Who owns a network of people assembled for a particular task? The owner of the "organization"? Or perhaps the individuals who participate in the network and who are responsible for its output?

A CULTURE OF ENGAGEMENT

What happens when a *department* employs relational and knowledge models, learns and develops a new paradigm, but the wider organization is frozen in a rational model? The learners, of course, will not be rewarded for their accomplishments, and, after a series of such disappointments, will become disengaged and "retire-in-place." Recall from Chapter 12 the case described by Edgar Schein (1996) of a new product development team at a large automaker that worked with MIT to develop a capacity for learning. Rather than give team members credit for their achievement in developing a new way of solving problems, upper management gave themselves credit for their ability to control the team, which they quickly disbanded.

People disengaged from their work characterize the rational system. The culture of a machine organization promotes separation: management from workers, specification from implementation, people from work. It is designed into an organization's culture and systems.

In the same way that strategy is moving from prescriptive formulas to learning, a challenge for management is similarly to shift the intent of its culture and processes—from separation to engagement. Recall from Chapter 3 that we defined a *culture of engagement* as one that focuses on knowledging. Specifically, a culture of engagement facilitates the process of *knowledge creation*, individual *motivation*, and the active *involvement* of the individual with his or her work. It is only through engagement that learning can take place, and new strategies and knowledge can emerge.

CONTENT VS. PROCESS

Is it necessary to possess knowledge of a process' content in order to effectively manage it? If work is about information processing, designed into the organization through the hierarchy (i.e., top-down, early binding processes), the answer is clearly no. The complete contract, whether for an information system or a business process, is ideally suited to prescribe such systems.

But if the business is evolving, if the business needs to be learned and re-learned, then late binding and bottom-up processes require a different management style and organizational fit. Force fitting these systems into complete contracts is somewhat contrived.

For example, project management and leadership are two areas where there seems to be a never-ending battle over the level of subject area knowledge required for management. Traditional management presumes that leading or managing may be broken down into well-defined pieces—generic, and function- or use-specific. It is further assumed that commanding (e.g., leading, managing, guiding, etc.) the process is somehow separate and sufficient from the content of the process. If we follow the logic, we are forced to conclude, say, that the tacit classical music knowledge of a pianist is of no consequence as he or she plays a Mozart work—knowing the keyboard is sufficient.

This is a question that can never be adequately answered. Generally, for routine tasks using explicit, even routine knowledge, it is likely that one can manage the process independent of its content. But if the work requires a certain amount of tacit knowledge, or if the output itself is emergent, then content knowledge (mostly tacit) and process are intertwined. The manager need not have the same depth of understanding, but some mental model approximating the knowledge content of the process is desirable.

MERGING EARLY AND LATE KNOWLEDGE BINDING

The top-down and bottom-up schools differ primarily in the locus of knowledge application. While it appears that these schools are incompatible, Nonaka and Takeuchi state that for an organization to systematically create knowledge, the organization should configure its structure and management processes along both top-down and bottom-up lines, in effect, intermingling early and late binding. This may be effected through a *synthesis structure* and a *middle-up-down* management process. The *federated structure* is one example of a synthesis structure designed to leverage the advantages of centralization and decentralization.

With middle-up-down management processes, the notion of an organization as an information processing mechanism is discarded, and with it, its concomitant notion that middle managers are "information relays" between the knowledge created at the top and its execution at the bottom. Instead, middle managers are given the role of *knowledge engineers,* who mediate strategic intentions from the top with the knowledge of practitioners on the front line.

KNOWLEDGE LEVERS

The emphasis which an organization places on a particular dimension of knowledge manifests itself in a distinctive organizational form and management practice. Core ideology, culture, systems, and so on follow directly from a particular orientation.

The levers that an organization needs to pull for creating each type of knowledge are different. We can therefore expect to see very different approaches to knowledge creation and exploitation in "explicit" and "tacit" organizations. For example, an organization that emphasizes explicit knowledge may construct complex, interrelated threads of distributed, explicit knowledge. In contrast, an organization that emphasizes tacit knowledge should pursue the coalescence of individual, mental models into common, communal threads. Whereas the levers for explicit knowledge revolve around technology, particularly IT, those of tacit knowledge leverage human relationships, group dynamics, and core values.

Thus, diverse knowledge forms give rise to different organizational forms, ideologies, cultures, management philosophies, and strategies. The challenge to management is to reconcile both paradigms—to realize that Plato was right, knowledge *is* "justified true belief."

SOURCES OF INERTIA

Organizations have traditionally believed that their inertia derives primarily from their people and culture. Their systems—management and operational processes, structure, and information systems—have long been viewed as things that can "easily" be changed.

The knowledge paradigm suggests a different model. Those constructs with significant stores of tacit knowledge—people, culture, and groups—are able to dynamically change. The ability to adapt to, and create a new context, is inherent in individual and collective mental models. Naturally, culture, which is a form of communal knowledge among a large number of people, is less adaptable than a project group, which in turn is less adaptable than a single individual.

In contrast, those constructs with large stores of explicit knowledge are comparatively inflexible. A system is a prisoner of its very explicitness. Experience with IT has demonstrated that, once implemented, an IS rarely is discarded or dramatically changed—it is merely enhanced or interfaces are built to yet other explicit systems. Experience with the Y2K problem has reinforced this perspective.

Thus, the nature of organizational change has changed: The primary change mechanisms—as both drivers and targets of change—are tacit knowledge dependent. This means people and their relationships, to each other, and to their organization.

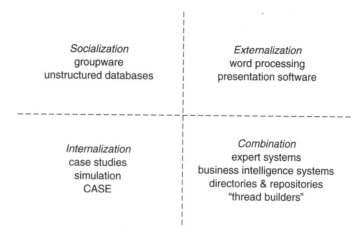

FIGURE 14–5   Knowledge Management Systems and Knowledge Creating Modes

Knowledge Management Systems

Knowledge management systems are specifically designed to support knowledge generation. Such systems may be stand-alone systems, such as tutorials. Others, such as CASE, may serve several purposes—support for operational tasks (combination: building a data model for a specific application), and learning (internalization: learning how to model data, and the application domain). Figure 14–5 illustrates several such systems.

The systems illustrated in Figure 14–5 are categorized on the basis of their predominant knowledge conversion modes. Note that "thread builder" is a generic term we have coined to identify a knowledge management system that permits a user to identify and associate threads of explicit and tacit knowledge in other systems (e.g., application system logic, notes in an unstructured database, presentations, etc.), thus creating a new thread of knowledge. Most such thread builders permit the user to name and categorize the new knowledge thread, thus making it available to others for additional thread building.

14.5 DESIGNING A FEDERATED STRUCTURE FOR IS AND IT

A federated structure is one that leverages the benefits of centralized and decentralized decision making. For IS and IT, the core concept is to build centralized architecture and standards, while developing decentralized applications. This is held together through joint strategic management: business strategy for line businesses, and IT planning for IS and IT. (See Rockart, Earl, and Ross 1996.)

The approach we have chosen to employ in our design is to first identify the IS and IT value chain, and then align it with the broader organization. We aggregate the IS and IT process tasks and functions (e.g., database administration) into corresponding value activities: IT planning, HR for IT, infrastructure, operations, customer service, and application development. They collectively form one view of an IS and IT value chain. Alignment is realized through the first (IT planning) and last (application development) value activities, thus forming a cycle of information flows between the business and IS & IT areas. This is illustrated in Figure 14–6.

At the beginning of the value chain, business strategy and IS & IT planning are collaborative exercises between equals whose members are part of a matrix structure between their respective departments and thus form a *joint strategic team*. We envision such a team to be permanent, with two sets of outputs: (1) the long-term development of shared mental models, and (2) periodic frameworks and project portfolios. The former includes models of both business and IS/IT interactions and requirements, while the latter includes integrated project plans.

At the other end of the IS and IT value chain, these same joint projects are implemented through similar matrix structures, with members reporting to business units and the application development areas, and the *joint implementation team*.

It should be noted that within each team (strategic and implementation), its members function in a collaborative mode as peers. We believe the notion that business is a "customer" of IT rather than a partner will reduce IT to an enabler role. In contrast, among partners, IT is likely to be used as a direction setter as well as an enabler.

Within IS and IT, IS/IT architecture and standards are established. This includes everything from managing emerging technologies, software libraries, repositories, data standards and models, hardware purchases, data integration, relationship management (internal and external), and many other such efforts. Coordination is achieved through internal collaborative arrangements, such as cross-departmental teams, learning groups, liaisons, and shared information systems (e.g., CASE, repositories, etc.).

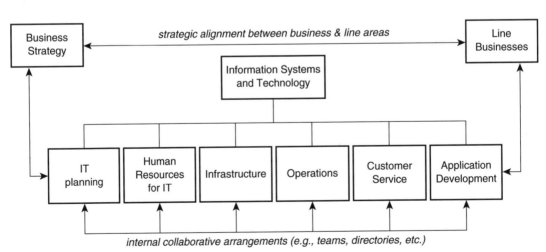

FIGURE 14–6   A Sample Federated Structure for Information Systems and Technology

14.6 KNOWLEDGE MANAGEMENT

Knowledge management is a broad and emerging field. It has come to mean everything from enterprise resource planning systems (ERP) and the development of integrated technology systems, knowledge directories (i.e., people locators), business process reengineering efforts, "data anywhere, any time" through the Internet, and so on.

Briefly, we may think of knowledge management as anything that effects people, the systems they have created, organizational enablers (e.g., knowledge management systems, and technology infrastructure), a knowledge sharing culture, etc. From an architectural perspective, this includes elements of the process and information molecules that have been codified into directories, repositories, procedures, business processes, and systems. These may include the following:

- *Process*. Business process models, and their integration linkages: from service to business and organizational patterns (e.g., ERP systems).
- *Data*. Logical and physical data models.
- *Knowledge directory (tacit knowledge)*. A people directory with cross-references to their training history, education, skills, awards, certifications, licenses, performance appraisals, project experience, application and systems experience, location, functional responsibilities, team and group memberships, etc. In effect, this represents a mapping of an organization's hidden tacit knowledge content to its context cues (experience, education, etc.) that facilitate planning.
- *Systems and documentation (explicit knowledge)*. A directory (or repository) of an organization's information systems. This may include process models, data flow diagrams, information contracts, function and process decompositions, derivation and computing algorithms, programs, etc. This also includes written information, such as reports, procedures, employee handbooks, etc. This represents a mapping of an organization's explicit knowledge.
- *Tools*. A directory of an organization's technology architectures, including hardware type and distribution, network architecture, etc. This also should include a mapping to the organization's systems and documentation models mentioned in the previous item.
- *Organizational enablers*. This includes those systems, policies, and design principles that facilitate knowledge creation, for example, knowledge management systems, rewards for knowledge sharing, and redundant information systems, respectively.
- *Knowledge creating processes*. These are business process formulations (process molecule instantiations) of specific processes designed for knowledge creation. For example, Nonaka and Takeuchi advance a five-phase generic process that, in essence, proceduralizes the knowledge spiral: *sharing tacit knowledge, creating concepts, justifying concepts, building an archetype,* and *cross-leveling of knowledge*. These process stages implement the knowl-

edge spiral conversion modes, justify the knowledge to be created, and amplify the newly created knowledge among increasingly larger communities of people, internal and external to the organization.

- *Knowledge repository.* A repository of knowledge artifacts captured during the execution of knowledge-rich processes. These artifacts include largely unstructured information, such as opinions, slides, graphics, articles, free-form text, etc.

BUILDING A KNOWLEDGE ARCHITECTURE

A *knowledge architecture* enables an organization to leverage its separate knowledge initiatives and projects, knowledge infrastructure (e.g., enablers), and specific knowledge creating processes, as well as existing IT architectures and models. Knowledge and information, whether explicit or tacit, require meaning and context. A knowledge architecture establishes that context for the organization as a whole. *A knowledge architecture may be used to capture or design the distribution of data and knowledge throughout an organization.*

Our approach is to develop a system that operationalizes the information molecule and a particular context (domain), such as a process molecule. In so doing, we may link the output of the various knowledge management efforts, model the distribution of information (i.e., data, explicit knowledge, and tacit individual and communal knowledge) through and among an organization's processes, people, systems, documentation, functional and work groups, and thereby develop context and meaning. A high-level model of such a system is illustrated in Figure 14–7.

Information actors are those elements of a process context that originate, mediate, or receive information. Information actors are of four types: *human, organization, system,* and *document.* Each actor is derived from a process component in the process molecule. *System* is a composite of information and a computer tool, while *document* corresponds to information and paper records. Each includes data and explicit threads of knowledge. *Human* corresponds to the process component human and represents the tacit knowledge required for the corresponding process. *Organization* corresponds to the process component organization, and represents both functional departments and work groups or teams. Naturally, a given actor instance may participate in any number of process instances.

A knowledge architecture may be used for both prescriptive and descriptive activities in an organization. Each information actor includes information derived from the knowledge management efforts described above. For example, the *human* actor represents a specific person, his or her location, competencies, skills, etc. This represents what a particular person is doing or has done in the past. Alternatively, the *human* actor may represent a set of *requirements* for a person in the context of a specific process. In that case, we would identify the location, competence and skill level, experience, etc., required for a particular process, which, in turn, forms a template for an employment opportunity.

Also, each object in the model in Figure 14–7 is subject to abstraction. For example, a process instance may be an entire business process, and this business

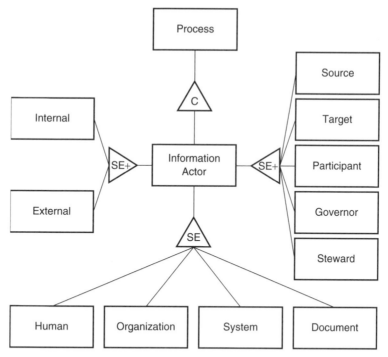

FIGURE 14–7   A Framework for Establishing a Knowledge Context

process instance will contain several work cycle instances, each of which, in turn, will contain several task instances.

The other two hierarchies represent the roles a given actor (i.e., human, organization, system, and document) may play. They are as follows:

- *Source*. A source of information (i.e., data, knowledge) transfer.
- *Target*. A target of information transfer.
- *Participant*. An enabler of information transfer.
- *Governing*. Authorization for information transfer.
- *Steward*. An information owner.
- *Internal*. An actor internal to an organization.
- *External*. An actor external to an organization.

A process may have any number of actors, playing many of the same or different roles. However, those roles are specific to a process instance. For example, a firm's financial *system* may be a *target* of information in a *process* that receives information from a *system* belonging to an *external organization*. That *external organization* and its *system* are both *sources* of information in this process.

As with all molecules, vertical and horizontal threads should be consistent. If *process* represents a specific business process (and its respective formulation constructs discussed in Chapter 11), then information actors such as *system* may include several applications (and their respective data and codified knowledge (code)), *organization* may correspond to several departments, and so on.

On the other hand, if *process* represents a specific task, then information actors such as *system* may include a specific operation with specific data, *organization* may be a particular team, *human* may be a specific employee, etc. Naturally, each instance of this more granular model should correspond to a higher level instance—task to work cycle *(process)*, operation to application *(system)*, employee to department *(department to functional structure)*, team to project organization *(structure)*, etc.

One final word: In the example above, we have operationalized the process and information molecules. In this case, we have established a knowledge context with process. However, we may choose to establish a knowledge context with some other organizational domain, such as culture. This would be advantageous if we are to understand the role of an organization's collection of knowledge threads on its culture. This requires operationalizing the information and culture molecules.

Generally, then, *operationalizing* the information molecule and a particular domain molecule (e.g., process, culture) is a useful mechanism to build a knowledge architecture for a specific domain of an organization.

14.7 THE BUSINESS DESIGNER OF THE 21ST CENTURY

Systems analysis and development are no longer in terms of database or application systems in support of "simple" information and service patterns (e.g., workflows). The business analyst of the future is expected to capture information requirements for complex systems in terms of their corresponding data and knowledge contents.

Why does one analyst fail at a task, and his or her successor succeed? How is it that the second, with the same staff and the same level of understanding, is more successful than the first? Could the problem be a failure to develop sufficient business interconnectivity and context? This is a particular problem within the IT department, whose responsibility is to steward the organization's information, which, by definition, serves to establish a business context for data and knowledge.

We have observed, for example, that several IT departments establish interconnectivity only within the data domain itself. This is where information engineering has been fairly successful. Unfortunately, designing and delivering data, as critical as it may be, is now a commodity, affording little advantage to the organization in the 21st century.

It is no secret that most success with "IT" has been with respect to the "T" and not the "I." Architecting information has changed little—it is the technology of implementation that has improved and is largely responsible for the transformational impact of IT on the organization.

The current focus in IT departments is to build on data and establish better interconnectivity with process tasks. It is not clear how process interconnectivity is being established, particularly since most organizations do not design process tasks, even their straightforward workflows, with any formality. The data-centric approaches are not very useful in this regard. We believe data cannot be ignored, since rich information ("data endowed with relevance and purpose") builds on data. The primary problem with traditional approaches to software development has been data exclusiveness, as opposed to data itself.

It is important to realize that the information and implementation architectures as we understand them today represent the infancy of the information renaissance. The transition path from a business analyst of the past to one of the future should build on data, and extend interconnectivity to the domains of knowledge and culture. In an era where knowledge is the information component which often determines success, IT departments will always get minimal results unless they broaden their horizons to include the entire set of process and information constructs—knowledge and learning, as well as data and process.

To architect and manage information is to architect and manage data (which IT professionals do fairly well), business processes (which management consultants do fairly well if the processes are workflows), knowledge (which few do well), and their respective interconnectivity (which few understand). This is going to require IT managers with radically different perspectives from the current sort.

Establishing Mutual Context and Value

To design one domain is to design the mutual context of every other domain. This is the essential task of a designer. We must ask, then, does an individual business designer ask the right questions? Do the senior managers structure the organization's culture to permit the asking of such questions? A sampling of questions that facilitate mutual context may include the following:

1. *Implicit models, intentions, and requirements.* Is there an opportunity to develop mental models of the associated business theory, or is there someone available to participate in its socialization? Can we build business process and information simulations to facilitate the development of such shared models? When we externalize our communal models of the theory of the business, what are the corresponding process and task requirements?

2. *Process formulation and characterization.* How are we formulating the process? This gives rise to a large body of questions concerning the issues discussed in Chapter 11, such as strategic alignment, change context, process characterization, specification, and design. Each of these areas must be fully developed if we are to establish interconnectivity within the business. We may, for example, identify process work cycles in terms of their task interdependencies (e.g., sequential, reciprocal, etc.), and identify task constituents in terms of the Perrow classification model, as described in Table 12–1. This will lead to such questions as, "Do the processes have a large knowledge or human component?"

3. *Contract analog characterization.* How can we best describe the appropriate contract analogs for the system (e.g., the business process and its constituents)? Can the system be described with precise contracts? Are we developing a system with fuzzy logic? Do we need relational or knowledge contracting?

4. *Information characterization.* How do we characterize the information requirements for the process? Is it primarily quantitative, or is it rich? What are the likely implementation components? How do we envision their interaction?

5. *Pattern and information complexity.* Where on the pattern-information complexity chart (Figure 14–4) does this system or process fall? As a consequence, what are my design options and risks? What level of *information penetration* is likely—where on the information continuum does this system fall? What is the level of *pattern penetration*—is there an opportunity to raise the pattern level so that other areas of the organization may leverage the system?

6. *Data.* What are the data requirements associated with the system? Can we distinguish between data requirements that are task-specific (e.g., today's stock quote) and data that may elicit knowledge (e.g., a history of closing stock prices and possible trends)?

7. *Knowledge and learning.* What is the knowledge characterization of the process (e.g., tacit or explicit, individual or social, scientific or communal, distributed or common)? What knowledge system model characterizes the wider organization, as well as the system being developed? Does the system in question require knowledge creation, and, if so, which knowledge conversion mode(s) seems appropriate, and what is its likely trigger? What is the likely content of the knowledge being created? What (e.g., existing information systems) and who are my knowledge sources? Where are they found? What are the individual value requirements of the people who possess and develop the required knowledge (e.g., autonomy)? What are the optimum work structures to satisfy their knowledge value requirements? What are the requirements for data imposed by the knowledge requirements? Do we need to access or create knowledge? How do we develop a learning environment in the context of this business process? Is this system a constituent of a core capability? Does it utilize a core technology? Are there additional learning and value requirements for the people performing the work—this may be broader than the learning required for the task itself, such as the desire of people to pursue a formal education, specialized training, certification, etc.

8. *Culture.* What are the *value requirements* of the people performing the work, as well as those of the organization? What are their constraints? This covers a broad area, and may include social and salary requirements, growth opportunities, flexible work hours, etc. Can we push the cultural envelope, and where?

9. *Organizational Context.* What are the requirements imposed by the organization's culture and formal structure, in particular, existing management processes, reward policies, and knowledge binding characteristics? Is there an organizational environment for learning? How do we develop the appropriate process and knowledge structures while conforming to the constraints of the formal organization? What are the Type 1 and Type 2 organization invariants?

10. *Communal knowledge.* What are the opportunities to integrate or share knowledge worlds? Can we develop a larger organizational framework in which such integration has value? Are there opportunities to access individual knowledge and socialize it within groups?

And so on. These are some of the questions a business analyst of the future may ask. Competitive advantage in the 21st century will depend on asking and getting answers to these questions, and on delivering solutions based on innovative organizational architectures.

14.8 CORE CONCEPTS

Convergence	Configuration
Strategic learning	Value and context (individual, mutual)
Contract analog	Complete contract
Open contract	Precise contract
Relativized contract	Relational contract
Knowledge contract	System dynamicity
Organizational dynamicity	Engagement
Prototyping	Hierarchical form
Horizontal form	Learning form
Synthesis structure	Middle-up-down management process
Federated structure	Virtual organizing
Organizational inertia	Knowledge management systems
Knowledge management	Pattern and information complexity
Knowledge architecture	Information actors

Operationalizing process and information molecules

Business design in the 21st century

A Brief Review of Information Modeling

The OM architecture uses an approach to analysis known as information modeling. Information modeling employs generic modeling concepts and the notion of a contract for the precise specification of behavior.

Below is a brief overview of information modeling, taken largely from Morabito and Singh (1993). For an in-depth discussion, the reader is referred to Kilov and Ross (1994), and Kilov (1999).

Abstraction

Abstraction is "the process of suppressing irrelevant details to establish a simplified model" (ODP 1994). That is, abstraction is the process of hiding what you are not interested in so that you may focus on what you are interested in.

The purpose of abstraction is to promote understanding so that, as Dijkstra has said, one can "be absolutely precise." It is through abstraction that we manage complexity. For example, if we want to travel between two points in a city, the model of our trip would be very different if we were to travel by taxi rather than by subway. Both models are correct; each is a representation of the real world that represents a different map of a different trip. What is common to both models, however, is the specification of the trip between two points—the manner of travel is irrelevant to the specification.

Abstraction has three dimensions. Through *information hiding*, we discard irrelevant information by enforcing a barrier so that implementation is hidden. *Encapsulation* is characterized by a not-so-rigid separation of specification and implementation. Encapsulation means that information is understood in terms of its external behavior—it is not necessary to know its internal structure (though, unlike information hiding, we may be aware of the internal structure). Good analysts use both concepts to *separate concerns*. That is, by deliberately ignoring implementation we ensure semantic correctness. Information modeling is characterized by the explicit use of abstraction.

Objects and Associations

Using objects and their associations, we may specify information systems. Good analysts know that there are "generic" associations—business rules—that are application, or even enterprise independent. Information modelers "reuse" these associations to improve their productivity and quality of output, much as programmers reuse tested subroutines.

Kilov and Ross (1994) have identified "generic" associations. Generic associations are precisely defined by means of their invariants—properties that remain true no matter which operations are applied to these associations and their participants. Furthermore, these generic associations have operations (create, read, update, delete) specified in the form of contracts for each generic association, and are stored in an information library. The analyst does not have to re-invent specification; he or she may reuse contracts specifications from the information library.

A list of the generic associations and their associated objects is given in Table A-1. Note that several associations are known by other names. For instance, subtyping is also known as a classification hierarchy. A complete specification of the contents of the generic object class library—semantics (i.e., invariant)—and contract specifications for create, read, update and delete (CRUD) operations are described in several publications (see Materials 1992, Kilov and Ross 1994). Using a library of generic, pre-specified concepts promotes specification reusability, as well as improved quality.

Generic information modeling concepts are defined within the context of their associations. For instance, an entity is a *Parent* only in the context of its dependency association with another entity, a *Dependent*. Note also that each generic modeling object (e.g., *Parent*) is defined on the basis of its behavior in a given association. When creating an information model, generic information modeling objects and their specifications (i.e., contracts) from the Generic Object Class Library may be reused. To the generic specifications (i.e., contracts) are added application-specific assertions. This is discussed in more detail below.

Figures A-1 and A-2 illustrate graphical representations of the generic concepts that are used when creating an information model. Note that, in contrast to "traditional" entity-relationship (ER) modeling, a *relationship* is an object to be managed in the same manner as any other object.

Below is a brief description of each generic information modeling concept (i.e., invariant) in the generic object class library:

1. *Dependency.* The existence of a dependent instance implies the existence of a corresponding parent instance(s). Note that a dependent instance may have more than one corresponding parent instance.

2. *Reference association.* The existence of a maintained entity instance implies the existence and property value correspondence of a corresponding refer-

TABLE A–1 REUSABLE GENERIC ASSOCIATIONS AND THEIR ASSOCIATION OBJECTS

Generic Association Name	Associated Objects	
Dependency	Parent	Dependent
Reference Association	Maintained Entity	Reference Entity
Composition	Composite	Component
Subtyping	Supertype	Subtype
Relationship Association	Relationship	Regular Entity

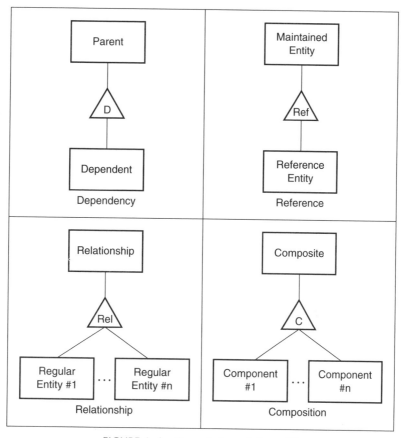

FIGURE A–1   Generic Associations (1)

ence entity instance. Reference entities are *read-only* instances used for creating, updating, or deleting instances of corresponding maintained entity instances. The reference entity, naturally, is itself a regular entity that has been created prior to creation of its corresponding maintained entity instances.

3. *Subtyping (generic).* The existence of a subclass instance implies the existence of a corresponding superclass instance with the same object identifier. Properties of a superclass instance are generally inherited by its corresponding subclass instance(s), though overrides may be specified for behavioral properties. Four subclasses of the generic subtyping association, each with specific semantics, are shown in the Figure A-2.

4. *Composition (generic).* A composite class corresponds to one or more component class, and a composite instance contains zero or more component entity instances of each of these classes. It is assumed that the composite instance contains *deliberate* and *emergent* properties; the former is specific to the composite instance, while the latter corresponds to properties of corresponding component instances. Note that changing the identity of a component instance does not change the identity of the corresponding composite instance. There are several criteria used to organize subclasses of the generic

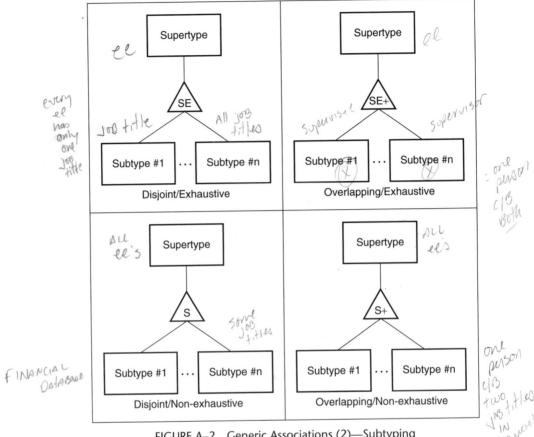

ee

every
ee
has
only
one
job
title

Job title   *All job titles*

ee

supervisor   *supervisor*

= one
person
c/B
Both

All
ee's

some
job
titles

ALL
ee's

one
person
c/B
two
job titles
IN

FINANCIAL
Database

Financial
database

FIGURE A–2   Generic Associations (2)—Subtyping

composition, including serializability (e.g., ordered components), change-ability (e.g., fixed number of components), hierarchy (e.g., a network of compositions), and linkage (e.g., assembly and package).

5. *Relationship association.* The existence of a relationship instance implies the existence of exactly one entity instance for all immediately participating (regular) entities.

CONTRACTS

A major difference between the information modeling approach and "traditional" object-oriented approaches is the notion of jointly owned behavior—behavior may, and usually is, jointly owned by more than one object. Behavior is specified by means of contracts: by invariant, pre-, and postconditions. The specification may be with structured "natural" language, or with formal methods, such as the "Z" specification language (see Potter and Sinclair 1991).

The concept of a contract is used to precisely specify behavior. A contract can be thought of as a formal agreement between a client and a supplier. The client is required to meet certain obligations before a contract can be invoked, but once these have been met, the supplier is required to fulfill its obligations (Henderson-Sellers 1992). How the supplier meets its obligations is hidden (e.g., encapsulated) from the client; in fact, the contract implementor (i.e., supplier) may make use of sub-contracts unknown to the client. This is illustrated in Figure A-3. This shows a contract participating in an exhaustive, overlapping (SE+) subtyping association. A contract may be a general contract, a sub-contract, or both, while a general contract consists of any number of sub-contracts. Also, the same sub-contract may be a component of more than one general contract (i.e., reusability). Note that if a contract does not consist of other contracts, it is merely an atomic contract, i.e., a sub-contract with no corresponding general contract. With this schema, a contract may be used to specify certain types of *business* as well as IT behavior. The contract is a specification schema that may be reused at any level of abstraction.

Behavior is precisely specified in a contract by means of *assertions:* specifically, *invariant*, *preconditions* and *postconditions*. An invariant is a condition that is always true, outside of an operation; it may be applied, and usually is, to several objects. The invariant specifies the semantic context of objects, their associations and their associated objects. A precondition for an operation is a condition that is required to be true prior to the operation (i.e., the obligations of the client) and a postcondition of an operation is that condition that is required to be true after completion of this operation (i.e., the obligations of the supplier). *It is with assertions that business rules (behavior) are specified in a simple, clear and precise way: in a single construct—the contract.* Unlike other approaches, there is no need to correlate several constructs in order to specify behavior. This is illustrated with an example in Figure A-4.

In this example, the required operation is to create an instance of an *accountant*. *Accountant* is one of a set of objects modeled in a classification association as a subclass of *employee*. Illustrated in Figure A-4 is a contract that specifies the create operation for an *accountant*.

There are four points to note in this example:

1. A contract specifies behavior that may be owned by one or more objects. In this case, both *employee* and *accountant* jointly own the contract, create an accountant instance.

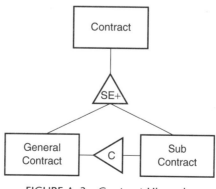

FIGURE A–3   Contract Hierarchy

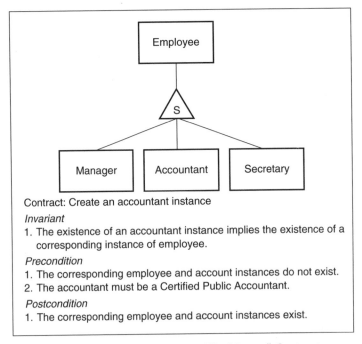

Contract: Create an accountant instance

Invariant
1. The existence of an accountant instance implies the existence of a corresponding instance of employee.

Precondition
1. The corresponding employee and account instances do not exist.
2. The accountant must be a Certified Public Accountant.

Postcondition
1. The corresponding employee and account instances exist.

FIGURE A–4   Application-Specific "Create" Contract

2. The contract uses "structured" natural language to specify behavior; however, a contract may also be specified with formal methods (e.g., "Z" specification language). The specification may be translated from a formal notation into a structured natural language to promote understanding.

3. Each assertion, or set of assertions, represents a business rule. Generally, business rules may be classified as either generic or application-specific. For example, the existence dependencies in the contract shown in Figure A-4 are part of a *generic* create contract for a subtyping association, located in the Generic Object Class Library. The assertion requiring certification as a Certified Public Accountant is *application-specific*. Conjoining generic and application-specific contracts or assertions, therefore, composes the resultant contract.

4. The behavior is fully and precisely specified with a contract; the diagram is for ease of understanding, and is not required for specification. For the given information model, the resultant application-specific contracts and other contracts are integrated into the Corporate Object Library.

BIBLIOGRAPHY

Benjamin, R.I., and Levinson, E. 1993. "A Framework for Managing IT-Enabled Change." *Sloan Management Review,* Summer 1993.

Block, P. 1996. *Stewardship.* San Francisco, CA. Berrett-Koehler Publishers.

Collins, J.C., and Porras, J.I. 1996. "Building Your Company's Vision." *Harvard Business Review,* September-October 1996.

Czech, R., Fjermestad J., and Jonsson, P. 1995. "Object-Oriented Organizational Modeling." *Proceedings of the 28th Annual Hawaii International Conference on System Sciences. IEEE 1995,* pp. 353–362.

Daft, R.L. 1998. *Organization Theory and Design,* Sixth Edition. South-Western College Publishing.

Daft, R.L., and Macintosh, N.B. 1981. "A Tentative Exploration into Amount and Equivocality of Information Processing in Organizational Work Units." *Administrative Science Quarterly,* (26) 1981, pp. 207–224.

Davenport, T.H. 1993. *Process Innovation: Reengineering Work Through Information Technology.* Boston, Mass. Harvard Business School Press.

Davenport, T.H. 1994. "Saving IT's Soul: Human-Centered Information Management." *Harvard Business Review,* March-April 1994, pp. 119–131.

Davenport, T.H. 1997. *Information Ecology: Mastering the Information and Knowledge Environment.* Oxford University Press.

Davenport, T.H., and Prusak, L. 1998. *Working Knowledge: How Organizations Manage What They Know.* Boston, Mass. Harvard Business School Press.

Drucker, P.F. 1988. "The Coming of the New Organization." *Harvard Business Review,* January-February 1988.

Drucker, P.F. 1992. "The New Society of Organizations." *Harvard Business Review,* September-October 1992.

Drucker, P.F. 1993. In Harris, T.G. 1993. "The Post-Capitalist Executive: An Interview with Peter F. Drucker." *Harvard Business Review,* May-June 1993.

Drucker, P.F. 1997. "Looking Ahead: Implications of the Present. The Future That Has Already Happened." *Harvard Business Review,* September-October 1997.

Earl, M.J. 1993. "Experiences in Strategic Information Systems Planning." *MIS Quarterly,* March 1993, pp. 1–24.

Fish, S. 1996. "Professor Sokal's Bad Joke." *The New York Times,* May 21, 1996.

Framework: A Disciplined Approach to Analysis, Bell Communications Research Science and Technology Publication ST-OPT-002008, Issue 1, May 1992.

Galbraith, J. 1973. *Designing Complex Organizations*. Reading, MA. Addison-Wesley.

Galbraith, J. 1995. *Designing Organizations*. San Francisco. Jossey-Bass Publishers.

Goodhue, D.L., Quillard, J.A., and Rockart, J.F. 1988. "Managing The Data Resource: A Contingency Perspective." *MIS Quarterly*, (12:3) September 1988.

Goodhue, D.L., Kirsch, L.J., Quillard, J.A., and Wybo, M.D. 1992. "Strategic Data Planning: Lessons From the Field." *MIS Quarterly*, March 1992.

Goodhue, D.L., Wybo, M.D., and Kirsch, L.J. 1992. "The Impact of Data Integration on the Costs and Benefits of Information Systems." *MIS Quarterly*, September 1992.

Goodman, N. 1984. *Of Mind and Other Matters*. Harvard University Press.

Groenfeldt, T. 1995. "Lehman CIO: Outsourcing Will Dominate Information Technology." *Securities Industry Daily* , December 6, 1995.

Handy, C. 1993. *Understanding Organizations*. Oxford University Press.

Handy, C. 1997. "Looking Ahead: Implications of the Present. The Citizen Corporation." *Harvard Business Review*, September-October 1997.

Henderson, J.C., and Venkatraman, N. 1993. "Strategic Alignment: Leveraging Information Technology for Transforming Organizations." *IBM Systems Journal*, 1993, (32:1), pp. 4–16.

Henderson-Sellers, B. 1992. *A Book of Object-Oriented Knowledge*. Prentice Hall, Inc., Prentice Hall Object-Oriented Series.

Jacobson, I., Christerson, M., Jonsson, P., and Overgaard, G. 1992. *Object-Oriented Software Engineering: A Use Case Driven Approach*, Addison-Wesley Publishing Company.

Kay, J. 1995. *Why Firms Succeed*. Oxford University Press.

Keen, P.G.W. 1997. *The Process Edge: Creating Value Where It Counts*. Harvard Business School Press.

Kepner, C.H., and Tregoe, B.B. 1981. *The New Rational Manager*. Princeton, NJ Princeton Research Press.

Kilov, H. 1999. *Business Specifications: The Key To Successful Software Engineering*. Englewood Cliffs, N.J. Prentice Hall, Inc.

Kilov, H., and Ross, J.M. 1994. *Information Modeling*. Englewood Cliffs, NJ Prentice Hall, Inc. Bertrand Meyer Series.

Kilov, H., and Simmonds, I.D. 1996. "Business Patterns: Reusable Abstract Constructs for Business Specification." In *Implementing Systems for Supporting Management Decisions*. Chapman & Hall, 1996.

Kim D.H. 1993. "The Link Between Individual and Organizational learning." *Sloan Management Review*, Fall 1993.

Kuhn, T.S. 1970. *The Structure of Scientific Revolutions*, Second Edition. University of Chicago Press.

Labovitz, G., and Rosansky, V. 1997. *The Power of Alignment*. New York, NY John Wiley & Sons, Inc.

Lederer A.L., and Sethi, V. 1988. "The Implementation of Strategic Information Systems Planning Methodologies." *MIS Quarterly,* (12:3) September 1988, pp. 445–461.

Leonard-Barton, D. 1995. *Wellsprings of Knowledge,* Harvard Business School Press.

Luftman, J.N., Lewis, P.R., and Oldach, S.H. 1993. "Transforming the Enterprise: The Alignment of Business and Information Technology Strategies." *IBM Systems Journal,* 1993, (32:1), pp. 198–221.

Malone, T.W., and Rockart, J.F. 1993. "How Will Information Technology Reshape Organizations? Computers as Coordination Technology." In *Globalization, Technology, and Technology.* Bradley, S.P., Hausman, J.A., and Nolan, R.L. (eds.) 1993. Harvard Business School Press, pp. 3–32.

Materials: A Generic Object Class Library for Analysis, Bell Communications Research Science and Technology Publication ST-OPT-002010, Issue 1, November 1992.

Meyer, B. 1995. *Object Success.* Englewood Cliffs, NJ Prentice Hall, Inc. Bertrand Meyer Series.

Miles, R.E., and Snow, C.C. 1994. *Fit, Failure & The Hall Of Frame: How Companies Succeed or Fail.* New York, NY The Free Press, A Division of Macmillan, Inc.

Mintzberg, H. 1983. *Structure in Fives: Designing Effective Organizations.* Englewood Cliffs, N.J. Prentice Hall, Inc.

Mintzberg, H., Ahlstrand, B., and Lampel, J. 1998. *Strategy Safari: A Guided Tour Through The Wilds Of Strategic Management.* The Free Press.

Morabito, J. 1993. "OOOM: An Object-Oriented Model of the Organization." Academic Excellence Award (first place). Society for Information Management, 1993.

Morabito, J. 1994. "Business Process Modeling: An Object-Oriented Framework for Business Infrastructure Specification." In *Workshop on Specification of Behavioral Semantics in Object-Oriented Information Modeling,* Ninth Annual Conference on Object-Oriented Programming, Systems, Languages, and Applications (OOPSLA'94), October 1994.

Morabito, J. *Organizational Modeling: An Object-Oriented Approach,* Doctoral Dissertation, Stevens Institute of Technology, April 1995.

Morabito, J., and Bhate, A. 1995. "Organizational Culture: An Object-Oriented Framework." In *Workshop on Specification of Behavioral Semantics in Object-Oriented Information Modeling,* Tenth Annual Conference on Object-Oriented Programming, Systems, Languages, and Applications (OOPSLA'95), October, 1995.

Morabito, J., and Bhate, A. 1997. "The Benefits of Object Orientation in Business Process Design." In *Workshop on Precise Semantics for Object-Oriented Modeling Techniques,* Eleventh European Conference on Object-Oriented Programming (ECOOP'97), June 1997.

Morabito, J., Bhate, A., and Sack, I. 1996. "When to Leave Your Department (for Better Prospects or Worse): A Precise Specification." In *Workshop on Specification of Behavioral Semantics in Object-Oriented Information Modeling,*

Eleventh Annual Conference on Object-Oriented Programming, Systems, Languages, and Applications (OOPSLA'96), October 1996.

Morabito, J., and Singh, M.S. 1993. "A New Approach to Object-Oriented Analysis and Design." In *TOOLS USA 93* (Proceedings of the 11th International Conference on Technology of Object-Oriented Languages and Systems, Santa Barbara, 1993). Prentice-Hall, 1993, pp. 45–55.

Nadler, D.A., Gerstein, M.S., Shaw, R.B., and Associates. 1992. *Organizational Architecture: Designs for Changing Organizations.* San Francisco. Jossey-Bass Publishers.

Nadler, D.A., and Tushman M.L. 1984. "A General Diagnostic Model for Organizational Behavior: Applying a Congruence Perspective." In *Organization Theory: Cases and Applications,* Daft R.L., and Sharfman M.P. (eds.) West Publishing Company.

Newman, D.S. 1996. "Class-based Reengineering." *Object Magazine,* March 1996, pp. 69–74.

Nonaka, I. 1991. "The Knowledge-Creating Company." *Harvard Business Review,* November-December 1991.

Nonaka, I., and Takeuchi, H. 1995. *The Knowledge-Creating Company.* Oxford University Press.

ODP 1994. ISO/IEC JTC1/SC21/WG7, Basic Reference Model of Open Distributed Processing—Part 2: Descriptive Model (DIS 10746–2) February 1994.

Peters, T. 1988. "Restoring American Competitiveness: Looking for New Models of Organizations." *Academy of Management Executive,* May 1988.

Pfeffer, J. 1994. *Competitive Advantage Through People: Unleashing the Power of the Work Force.* Harvard Business School Press.

Porter, M.E. 1980. *Competitive Strategy: Techniques for Analyzing Industries and Competitors.* New York, NY The Free Press.

Porter, M.E. 1985. *Competitive Advantage: Creating and Sustaining Superior Performance.* New York, NY The Free Press, A Division of Macmillan, Inc.

Potter, B., Sinclair, J., and Till, D. 1991. *An Introduction to Formal Specification and Z.* Hertfordshire, UK. Prentice Hall International (UK) Ltd. C.A.R. Hoare Series.

Prahalad C.K., and Hamel, G. 1990. "The Core Competence of the Corporation." *Harvard Business Review,* May-June 1990.

Robbins, S.P. 1990. *Organization Theory: Structure, Design, and Applications,* Third Edition. Englewood Cliffs, NJ Prentice Hall, Inc.

Rockart, J.F., Earl, M.J., and Ross, J.W. 1996. "Eight Imperatives for the New IT Organization." *Sloan Management Review,* Fall 1996.

Rummler, G.A., and Brache, A.P. 1995. *Improving Performance: How to Manage the White Space on the Organization Chart,* Second Edition. San Francisco, CA. Jossey-Bass Inc., Publishers.

Sack, I., and Thalassinidis, A. 1998. "Toward a Comprehensive Specification of Agent and Multi-Agent Knowledge Types in a Globalized Business Environment" In *Proceedings of the Second ECOOP Workshop on Precise Behavioral Semantics,* Brussels, July 24, 1998.

Savage, C.M. 1990. *Fifth Generation Management: Integrating Enterprises Through Human Networking.* Digital Press.

Schein, E.H. 1985. "Defining Organizational Culture." In *Classics of Organization Theory.* Shafritz, J.M., and Ott, J.S. (eds.) 1992.

Schein, E.H. 1994. "Innovative Cultures and Organizations." In *The Information Technology Revolution,* Allen, T.J., and Morton, M.S.S. (eds.) 1994. Oxford University Press.

Schein, E.H. 1996. "Three Cultures of Management: The Key to Organizational Learning." *Sloan Management Review,* Fall 1996.

Seashore, S.E. 1965. "Criteria of Organizational Effectiveness." In *Management and Organizational Behavior Classics.* Matteson, M.T., and Ivancevich, J.M. (eds.) 1989.

Senge, P.M., Kleiner, A., Roberts, C., Ross, R.B., and Smith, B.J. 1994. *The Fifth Discipline Fieldbook: Strategies and Tools for Building a Learning Organization.* New York, N.Y. A Currency Book, Doubleday, Inc.

Shafritz, J.M., and Ott, J.S. 1996. *Classics of Organization Theory.* Pacific Grove, CA. Brooks/Cole Publishing Company.

Smith, Adam. 1776. *The Wealth of Nations.* In *Classics of Organization Theory.* Shafritz, J.M., and Ott, J.S. (eds.) 1992.

Spender, J.C. 1993. "Competitive Advantage From Tacit Knowledge?: Unpacking The Concept And Its Strategic Implications." *Academy of Management Best Papers Proceedings 1993,* 1993, pp. 37–41.

Stalk, Jr., G., Evans, E., and Shulman, L.E 1992. "Competing on Capabilities: The New Rules of Corporate Strategy." *Harvard Business Review,* March-April 1992.

Stahlman, M. 1993. "Creative Destruction at IBM." *The Wall Street Journal,* January 6, 1993.

Sveiby, K.E. 1997. *The New Organizational Wealth,* Berrett-Koehler Publishers, Inc.

Taylor, D.A. 1995. *Business Engineering With Object Technology,* John Wiley & Sons, Inc.

Thurow, L.C. 1992. "Who Owns the Twenty-First Century?" *Sloan Management Review,* Spring 1992.

Thurow, L.C. 1996. *The Future of Capitalism: How Today's Economic Forces Shape Tomorrow's World.* William Morrow and Company, Inc. New York.

Tushman, M., and Nadler, D. 1978. "Information Processing as an Integrating Concept in Organizational Design." *Academy of Management Review,* (3:3) July 1978, pp. 613–624.

Venkatraman, N. 1994. "IT-Enabled Business Transformation: From Automation to Business Scope Redefinition." *Sloan Management Review,* Winter 1994.

Venkatraman, N. and Henderson, J.C. 1998. "Real Strategies for Virtual Organizing." *Sloan Management Review,* Fall 1998, (40:1).

Walden, K., and Nerson, J. 1995. *Seamless Object-Oriented Software Architecture: Analysis and Design of Reliable Systems.* Prentice Hall International (UK), Ltd.

Woodcock, J. C. P., and Loomes, M. 1988. *Software Engineering Mathmatics.* London, England. Pitman Publishing, p. 262.

Zuboff, S. 1988. *In the Age of the Smart Machine: The Future of Work and Power.* New York. Basic Books.

INDEX

A

Abstraction, *See* Process
Ahlstrand, B., 8, 244, 283
Alignment, 7, 11, 26, 48, 43-44, 70, 77, 91,
    94-108 (Chapter 7), 109, 111, 117, 120-121,
    126, 128-130, 136, 139, 141, 143, 147, 150-
    152, 155, 158, 222, 244, 250, 261, 266, 283
    compatible, 99-102, 105, 108
    consistent, 99-101, 105, 108, 193
    context, 8, 105, 215-219, 225. *See also*
        Automating, Informing, Knowledging
    cultural, 7, 98-99, 103-105, 108, 158-168
        (Chapter 10). *See also* Directionality
    degrees of, 107-108, 126, 146-147, 152,
        160-168
    dynamic, 99, 101-105, 108
    pattern, 7, 152
    strategic, 1, 10, 94, 103, 106-108, 156, 170,
        198, 271, 282-283
    thread, 99-102, 105-106, 108, 118-120,
        123, 126, 134, 142, 150-152, 161-168,
        172, 175, 179, 198, 215, 217, 242
Ambiguity, 35-36, 42, 177, 191, 237-239,
    251, 253-254, *See also* Equivocality
Analysis paralysis, 210, 229, 234
Architecture
    organizational, 1-8 (Chapter 1), 13, 41, 44-
        46, 61, 65, 78-79, 89-90, 95, 108, 126-
        133, 140-141, 150, 155-157 (Part 2),
        164, 238, 273, 284
    core 21st century, 155-157 (Part 2
        introduction)
    hard and soft architectures, 7, 91-93, 102-
        103, 105, 129-130, 137, 141, 150-151,
        161
    pattern of patterns, 93, 126, 153
Architecture-in-the-large, 6, 9, 16, 95, 126
Architecture-in-the-small, 6, 9, 16, 95
AT&T, 147, 210
Automating, 8, 30, 215-217, 229

B

Bhate, A., 13, 283
Brache, A., 195, 284

Business

    class, 44, 57-59
    model, 2, 59, 134, 243, *See also* Enterprise
        model
    object, 25, 58-61, 153, 179
    pattern, *See* Organizational pattern
    process, *See* Process
Business rules, 8, 44, 53, 56, 75, 82-83, 86,
    114-116, 123, 134, 139, 177, 183, 187, 214,
    216, 222-225, 229, 275, 279, 280
    data, explicit, knowledge, and relational
        rules, 8, 222-225, 229
Business analyst of old, 156-157, 168
Business analyst of the future, 157, 201, 270-
    273

C

Capability, 42, 91, 98, 146, 170-172, 198
    core technological, 33-34, 42, 213-215,
        221, 233, 240, 243-244, 247, 258, 260,
        272
Chandler, A., 37
Characterization, 8, 169, 200, 271
    contract analog, 271
    data, 205-208
    information, 201-203, 272, *See also*
        Information characterization
    knowledge, 209-215, 272, *See also*
        Knowledge characterization
    knowledge system, 240-244, 247, *See also*
        Knowledge system characterization
    process, 170-175, 182, 198, 207, 271
Collaboration, 157, 195, 198
Collins, J., 38, 162, 281
Communications channel, *See* Information
Competence, 6, 37-38, 42, 99, 106, 170-172,
    198, 211, 215, 217, 243-244, 247, 249, 268,
    284
Competitive advantage, 2, 7, 16, 26, 29, 32,
    41, 43, 72, 90-91, 94-95, 108, 141, 156, 160,
    164, 169, 213-214, 228, 258, 260, 273, 284-
    285
Complex process molecule, 184-190, 198
    decision molecule, 187-188

exclusive OR sequencing molecule, 190
feedback molecule, 188-190
mediation molecule, 186
reciprocal molecule, 186-187
sequential, 184-185
Composite-subtyping, 56-58, 61, 66, 89, 176
Configuration, 118, 120, 149-150, 233-234, 244, 246-248, 250, 254, 273
Continuum of information systems, 207. *See also* Information
Contract, 13, 16, 41, 54-56, 65-66, 74-77, 81-83, 85-86, 110-111, 115-121, 129-132, 136-138, 140, 147-148 151-152, 180-183, 187, 223, 233, 250, 256, 263, 275-276, 278-279, 280
    culture, 103, 105, 108, 136-137, 159-160, 164-168
    information, 12, 110-111, 119-121, 136-138, 221, 225, 242, 251, 267
    precise and imprecise, 7, 12, 16, 89-93, 102-103, 137, 141, 151-152, 179, 236
    process (specification), 12, 16, 54, 139, 169, 180-190, 197-198, 228-229
    reuse, *See* Reuse
Contract analog, 8, 250-257, 271, 273
    complete, 8, 251-254, 261, 263, 273
    knowledge, 6, 8, 12, 221, 252, 255-256, 258, 271, 273
    open, 8, 251-252, 254-255, 261, 273
    precise, 7, 8, 12, 221, 251-252, 255-256, 271, 273
    relational, 7, 8, 12, 91-93, 102-105, 108, 129-131, 137, 152, 160, 179, 198, 224, 241, 252, 255-256, 271, 273
    relativized, 8, 251-252, 256, 273
Convergence, 214-215, 229, 248, 250, 254, 273
Core concepts, 25, 42, 61, 77, 93, 108, 123, 153, 168, 198, 229, 247, 273
Core technological capability, *See* Knowledge system characterization
Crystallization, 5, 7, 8, 76-77, 124-153 (Chapter 9), 233, 213, 222, 224, 231, 233-234
Culture,
    alignment of, *See* Alignment and Directionality

Anglo-American, 49, 52
Continental Europe, 49, 51-52
Eastern, 49, 52-53
engagement, 30, 42, 262-263, 273
eternal triangle, 49-52, 61, 83, 104-105, 112-113, 142, 145. *See also* Organization invariant
manifestation of (model of), 6, 8, 159-160, 168, 212
molecule, *See* Organization molecule

D
Daft, R., 31, 32, 35, 36, 86, 191, 261, 281, 284
Davenport, T., 7, 8, 10, 33, 36, 107, 121, 200, 201, 233, 244, 254, 281
Derivative management philosophies, 24-25 45-46, 57, 79-80
Directionality, 8, 106-107, 158-168 (Chapter 10), 169, 214, 217, 222, 244
Division of labor, 14-15, 18-19, 23, 25-26, 28, 31, 39, 67-68, 72, 237, 238, 247
Drucker, P., 2, 26, 28, 31, 40, 72, 113, 200, 201, 203, 211, 227, 281
Dynamicity, 8, 105, 130, 152, 210
    organizational, *See* Organizational dynamicity
    system, 8, 257-260, 273

E
e-business, 107
Earl, M., 2, 33, 149, 157, 252, 260, 265, 281, 284
Economic value added (EVA), 173-175, 184, 197-198, 226, 229, 264
Engagement, 111, 123, 210, 232, 254-255, *See also* Culture
Enterprise model, 2-4, *See also* Business model
Equivocality, 35-36, 42, 78, 191, 201-202, 226, 229, 254, 281, *See also* Ambiguity
Eternal triangle, *See* Culture
Evans, E., 37, 171, 243, 285

F
Factory system, 14-15, 25, 28, 31-33
    post-factory system, 28-30
    pre-factory system, 27, 34

Federated structure, *See* Organizational
structure
Feedback, 50, 111, 123, 212, 223-224, 253-
254
feedback molecule, *See* Complex process
molecule

G
Galbraith, J., 7, 10, 34, 65, 70, 78, 122, 282
Goodhue, D., 33, 34, 35, 36, 86, 107, 197,
226, 282
Goodman, N., 230, 282

H
Hamel, G., 37, 284
Handy, C., 18, 20, 40, 41, 199, 249, 262, 282
Henderson, J., 10, 94, 262, 282, 285
Henderson-Sellers, B., 157, 279, 282
Hewlett-Packard, 51, 124, 130, 133
Hierarchical referral, 31-32, 70, 201, 261
Hubbing, 191, 194-195, 198

I
IBM, 210
Information
actor, 268-270, 273
carrying capacity of data, 32, 36, 220
communications channel, 18, 32, 34, 220
characterization, *See* Information
characterization
complexity, 257-258, 272-273
continuum (data and knowledge), 8, 200-
201, 203, 207-208, 211, 218-222, 229,
240, 257, 272
continuum of information systems, 207,
229
convergence, *See* Information integration
integration (data, knowledge, information),
225-228
molecule, *See* Organization molecule
modeling, 4-5, 8, 11-13, 39, 44, 53, 56, 64-
65, 157, 163, 275-180 (Appendix)
pattern, *See* Organizational pattern
renaissance, 199-200, 229, 249, 271
reuse, *See* Reuse
semantic (knowledge), 8, 220, 227-229
syntax (data), 8, 220, 227-229

Information characterization
amount, 35-36, 42, 84-86, 110, 191, 201-
203, 226, 281
quantitative, 32, 35-36, 110, 191, 201-203,
227, 272
rich(ness), 32, 35-36, 42, 84-86, 96, 99,
110, 191, 197-198, 201-203, 206, 220-
221, 223, 226-229, 235-236, 239-240,
257, 259, 271-272
Information linkage (horizontal and vertical),
24, 31-32, 35-36, 42, 128, 195, 206, 261
Informating, 8, 29-30, 42, 215-218
Inheritance, *See* Process
Iron bar metaphor, 162-163, 168

K
Kay, J., 7, 10, 12, 16, 41, 51, 91, 103, 105,
106, 109, 143, 145, 152, 160, 179, 198, 241,
255, 282
Keen, P.W.G., 169, 171, 173, 175, 191, 197,
215, 226, 229, 260, 282
Kilov, H., 54, 56, 157, 184, 275, 276, 282
Kirsch, L., 33, 34, 86, 107, 197, 226, 282
Kleiner, A., 285
Knowledge,
architecture, 8, 268-270, 273
binding, *See* Knowledge binding
characterization, *See* Knowledge
characterization
contextualization, 235-236, 247, 267-273
contract, *See* Contract analog
creation, 30, 156-157, 215-217, 221-222,
231-235, 243, 247-249, 253, 261-262,
267, 272. *See also* Knowledge
conversion mode and Knowledge world
directory, 235, 267
layered model of, *See* Knowledge world
management, 1-2, 8, 15, 145, 265, 267-
270, 273
management system, 265, 267, 273
practice of, 212, 224, 229
repository, 243, 268
reuse, *See* Reuse
spiral, *See* Knowledge conversion mode
system characterization, See
Characterization and Knowledge
system characterization

system model, *See* Knowledge system
   characterization
Knowledge binding, 8, 236-241, 244-247,
   251, 256-257, 261-263, 272
   early, 236-238, 240-242, 244-247, 250-
      251, 253, 256, 261, 263
   late, 237-242, 244-247, 253, 256, 263-264
   real-time, 237, 239-241, 247
Knowledge characterization, 209-215, 241,
   272
   automatic, 213, 216, 229
   cognitive dimension of tacit, 212, 224, 226,
      229, 235, 244-245, 248
   common, 8, 214-215, 241
   communal, 213, 215, 220-222, 224, 227-
      229, 240, 247, 255, 264, 268, 271-273
   conscious, 213-214, 229
   distributed, 8, 214, 241
   explicit, 6, 8, 30, 32, 45, 191, 199-273
      (Chapters 12, 13, and 14)
   individual, 8, 213, 215, 220-221, 223, 225,
      229, 231, 234-235, 241, 273
   industry, 214, 229, 241
   organization, 213-214, 229, 235, 241
   routine, 32, 91, 207, 216, 220-229, 239,
      243, 251, 253, 258, 263
   scientific, 213-214, 229
   social, 8, 213, 229, 241
   tacit, 6, 8, 30, 45, 91, 158-168, (Chapter 10),
      191, 199-273 (Chapters 12, 13, and 14)
   technical dimension of tacit, 213-213, 224,
      226, 229, 235
Knowledge conversion mode, 233-235, 240,
   242-243, 247, 259, 265, 267-268, 272
   combination, 234-235, 239, 242-243, 247,
      259-260, 265
   externalization, 234-235, 238-240, 242,
      247, 252-253, 259, 265
   internalization, 213, 234-235, 242-243,
      247, 259-260, 265
   socialization, 213, 233-235, 240-242, 247,
      253, 259-260, 265, 271
   spiral, 8, 233-235, 240, 242-243, 260, 265,
      267-268
Knowledge system characterization, 240-247
   competence, 243-244. *See also*
      Competence

core technological capability, 243-244. *See
   also* Capability
downstream processes, 243
knowledge system model (knowledge,
   network, relational, rational), 241-242,
   245-247, 262
midstream processes, 242-243
upstream processes, 242
Knowledge world, 8, 226-232, 247, 273
   actions, 231-232
   knowledge application (KA), 223, 231-
      232, 247, 258-259, 263
   knowledge creation (KC), 231-232, 247
   knowledge discovery (KD), 231-232, 247
   layered knowledge model of, 8, 231-232,
      247
   worldmaking, 230
   natural world, 231-232
   world version, 230-232
Knowledging, 8, 30, 42, 215-219, 225, 229-
   232, 262

L

Lampel, J., 8, 244, 283
Lateral relation, 19, 34-36, 42, 86, 164, 202,
   205, 217
Lattice, *See* Organization pattern
Learning, 155-273 (Part 2). *See also*
   Organizational formation
   double-loop, 234-235, 247
   individual, 205, 234-235, 248-250
   organizational, 248-273 (Chapter 14)
   single-loop, 234-235, 247
   strategic, 244-250
Leonard-Barton, D., 8, 34, 213, 243, 244, 260,
   283
Lewis, P., 107, 283
Luftman, J., 107, 283

M

Malone, T., 30, 31, 169, 283
Managed collection, 16, 53, 55-58, 61, 69, 79,
   184
Manager-architect, vii, 5
Manifest representation, 127, 124-153
   (Chapter 9), 233

Middle-up-down management process, 263-264, 273
Meyer, B., 59, 179, 282, 283
Miles, R., 37, 124, 283
Mintzberg, H., 7, 8, 11, 12, 38, 39, 72, 76, 77, 84, 128, 145, 238, 244, 245, 248, 253, 283
Morabito, J., 13, 275, 283, 284

N

Nadler, D., 34, 73, 94, 284, 285
Nerson, J., 120, 285
Network organization, *See* Organization
Nonaka, I., 8, 19, 170, 201, 209, 210, 211, 213, 224, 233, 234, 237, 238, 243, 263, 267, 284

O

Oldach, S., 107, 283
Object meta-model, 53-55
Object-orientation, *See* Business class
OM Refinement Model, 7, 48, 85, 110-123, 152
    alignment layer, 117-118, 122-123
    baseline layer, 112-113, 122-123
    engagement, 111-112, 123. *See also* Engagement
    execution layer, 120-123
    feedback, 111-112, 123. *See also* Feedback
    realization layer, 118-120, 122-123. *See also* Realization diagrams
    scoping and elaboration layer, 113-115, 122-123
    specification layer, 116-117, 122-123
Organization,
    designing (existing concepts and approaches), 26-42 (Chapter 3)
    invariant, *See* Organization invariant
    layered model of, 7-9, 48, 62-77 (Chapter 5), 87, 133, 141, 152-153
    modeling (OM), *See* Organization modeling
    molecule, *See* Organization molecule
    network, 27, 34, 262
    pattern, *See* Organizational pattern
    Theory, 14-25 (Chapter 2). *See also* Schools of Organization Theory and Scientific Management
    unified model of, 58-61

    virtual, 15, 27, 31, 262, 273, 285
Organization invariant, 48-53, 61, 82-83, 91-92, 103-106, 112-116, 123, 138-139, 143-145, 150-152, 158-168 (Chapter 10). *See also* Eternal triangle
    Type 1 socio-cultural, 49-51, 61, 152
    Type 2 organization, 49-50, 61, 152
Organization modeling (OM), vii-ix (Preface), 1-8 (Chapter 1),
    Applications of, 155-273 (Part 2 introduction and Chapters 10-14)
    Concepts of, 9-13 (Part 1 introduction), 43-153 (Chapters 4-9)
    Review of existing concepts and techniques, 14-42 (Chapters 2-3)
Organization molecule, 6-7, 9, 13, 48, 62, 64, 78-93 (Chapter 6), 136-137
    culture, 88, 103-105, 113-115. *See also* Directionality and Alignment cultural
    elaborating an, 87-89
    generic, 80-85
    information, 86, 95-98, 119, 199-229 (Chapter 12)
    process, 85-88, 95-100, 116-117, 119, 169-198 (Chapter 11). *See also* Complex process molecule
Organizational architecture, *See* Architecture
Organizational constructs, 23-25, 45-46
Organizational domain, 2-6, 9-11, 24-25
    instantiating, 81-84, 87, 95, 116-117
Organizational dynamicity, 8, 146-147, 153, 261-265, 273
    adaptiveness, 146, 152-153, 162
    maneuverability, 107-108, 146-147, 152-153, 162, 215
    See also Dynamicity
Organizational formation, 8, 48, 83-85, 93
    assumptions and behaviors, 158-160
    contract, 256
    pattern, *See* Organizational pattern
    stages of (conceptualization, learning, operationalizing, adaptation), 84
    strategy, 12, 84, 126, 238
Organizational materials, 23-25, 44-46
Organizational pattern, 8, 30, 41, 124-153 (Chapter 9), 267
adaptive, 146-147

business, 134, 139-140
competitiveness, 141, 143-144
competitive distinctiveness, 142-144
emergent characteristics of, 124-126, 141-145
formation, 127-132. *See also* Crystallization and Manifest representation
information, 135, 138-139
lattice, 141-146
organizational, 133
service, 134
Organizational properties,
    deliberate, 11, 48, 57, 61, 63-64, 71-72, 80-81, 84, 95, 111, 113, 122, 128-129, 131, 152, 244-245, 255, 277
    dynamic, 7-8, 11, 43, 55, 62-63, 78, 84, 89, 99, 101, 105, 146, 152, 169, 171-172, 203, 210, 215, 220, 222-225, 251, 254, 257, 261-262, 264
    emergent, 12, 39, 48, 57, 61, 63-64, 67, 71-72, 77, 80-81, 84-85, 95, 101, 106, 108, 111, 113, 117, 121-122, 124-135, 139, 141-147, 152-153, 162-164, 176, 191, 193-194, 222, 231, 238, 245, 247-248, 250, 255, 259, 262-263, 277
    multidimensional, 88-89, 91, 148, 150-151, 196-197, 207, 259
    single-dimensional, 88, 148, 150-151, 196
    static, 11, 63, 84, 89, 222
Organizational structure, 2-4, 10-11, 19, 28, 30, 36, 45, 53, 65, 74-76, 96, 122, 171
    centralization (dimension), 18, 20-21, 25, 35, 37, 39-40, 145, 149, 263
    complexity (dimension), 20-21, 25, 37, 39, 59
    dimensions of, 20-21
    federated structure, 8, 149, 260, 263, 265-266, 273
    formalization (dimension), 19-22, 25, 35-37, 39-40, 128, 145, 246
    generic components of, 38-39, 42
    generic structures of, 11-12, 39-40, 42
    reuse, *See* Reuse
    synthesis structure, 263, 273
Overadaptation, 210, 229, 234

P
Package,
    software, 221, 228-229
    technology, 221, 228-229, 242, 257
Paradigm shift, 11, 62-65, 77, 211
Perrow, C., 19, 20, 35, 155, 175, 177, 191, 271
Peters, T., 72, 284
Pfeffer, J., 27, 29, 284
Porras, J., 38, 162, 281
Porter, M., 1, 11, 30, 37, 38, 75, 128, 150, 155, 170, 176, 284
Prahalad, C., 37, 284
Process,
    abstraction, 172-173,
    characterization, *See* Characterization
    classification and technology models, 172-175
    decomposition, 181-182
    design and implementation, 190-197, *See also* Realization diagrams (structural)
    inheritance, 182-183
    molecule, *See* Organization molecule
    reuse, *See* Reuse
    specification, 180-190
    transformation, 175-180
Procter & Gamble, 51
Prototyping, 247, 256, 260, 273

Q
Quillard, J., 33, 282

R
Realization diagrams (structural), 139, 118-119, 120
    process, 118, 120
    queuing-process, 118, 120, 139, 197
    causality, 118, 120, 139, 197
    maps (IS SHOULD, extended, multidimensional), 11, 139, 184, 187, 190, 195-197
    simulation, 197
Refinement, 7, 47, 81, 84, 88, 109-111, 137, 237, 155. *See also* OM Refinement Model
    level, *See* Three views of modeling
    path, 84-85, 88, 109-111, 117
Reuse, 65, 71, 74-76, 149
    component, 192-193, 198

contract, 279
information, 275-276
knowledge, 221, 239, 240
process, 75, 182, 194
strategy, 75
structure, 76
Robbins, S., 15, 18, 20, 22, 23, 37, 63, 184, 241, 284
Roberts, C., 285
Rockart, J., 30, 31, 33, 149, 169, 265, 282, 283, 284
Ross, J.M., 54, 56, 157, 184, 275, 276, 282
Ross, J.W., 149, 265, 284
Ross, R.B., 285
Rummler, G., 195, 284

S

Sack, I., 8, 13, 214, 283, 284
Savage, C., 29, 30, 284
Schein, E., 6, 8, 30, 92, 102, 108, 158, 159, 212, 215, 262, 285
Schools of Organization Theory, 17-20
Scientific Management, 18-19, 25, 90, 175, 177, 236-237, 251
Senge, P., 20, 118, 285
Shulman, L., 37, 171, 243, 285
Simmonds, I., 54, 282
Simulation, 46, 197-198, 206, 234, 271
Singh, M., 275, 284
Smith, A., 2, 15, 17, 39, 285
Smith, B., 285
Snow, C., 37, 124, 283
Spender, J.C., 8, 213, 285
Stalk, 37, 171, 243, 285
Strategic intent, 131-132, 152, 264. *See also* Visualization
Strategy-in-the-large, 92-93
Strategy-in-the-small, 92-93
Strategy reuse. *See* Reuse
Structure, *See* Organizational structure
Svieby, K., 249

T

Takeuchi, H., 8, 19, 170, 201, 209, 210, 211, 233, 234, 237, 238, 243, 263, 267, 284
Taylor, F.W., 18, 63, 90, 177, 237
Taylor, D., 44, 285

Team,
fit of, 70
joint strategic, 266
joint implementation, 266
Technology model,
background (EVA), 173-175, 229
continuous process production (manufacturing), 19, 172, 174
craft (knowledge), 19-20, 35, 174-175, 177-180, 182, 191-192, 198, 201-202
engineering (knowledge), 19-20, 35, 174-175, 177-180, 181, 191-192, 197-198, 201
identity (EVA), 173-175, 226, 229
intensive (reciprocal task interdependence), 20, 173-175, 184, 186-187
long-linked (sequential task interdependence), 20, 173-175, 184-185
mandated (EVA), 173-175, 222, 229
mass production (manufacturing), 19, 172, 174
mediating (pooled task interdependence), 20, 173-175, 184, 186
priority (EVA), 173-175, 226, 229
nonroutine (knowledge), 19-20, 34-36, 61, 66, 84, 96, 110, 174-175, 177-180, 182, 191-192, 197-198, 201-202, 206-207, 221, 259
routine (knowledge), 16, 19-20, 35-37, 84, 91-92, 110, 145, 174-175, 177-180, 182, 191-192, 197, 201, 221, 250-251, 255, 259, 263
unit production (manufacturing), 19, 172, 174
Thalassinidis, A., 13, 214, 284
Theory of the business, 2, 271
Three views of modeling, 7, 46-48, 61
richness of ideas, 46-47
modeling granularity, 47
refinement levels (philosophy of organizations, meta-framework, organizational perspective, architectural building blocks, realization, real world), 47-48
Thompson, J., 20, 173, 175, 184, 185, 186
Toyota, 106, 124, 130, 133, 169

U
Uncertainty, 20, 34-37, 42, 78, 177, 191, 201, 210, 215, 226, 229, 237-239, 252, 261

V
Venkatraman, N., 10, 32, 33, 94, 262, 282, 285
Virtual organization, *See* Organization
Visualization, 8, 131-132, 148, 150-153, 162
    strategic intent and, 131-132. *See also*
        Strategic intent
    vision framework, 38, 42, 162-163

W
Walden, K., 120, 285
Woodward, J., 19, 172, 175
Wybo, M., 33, 34, 86, 107, 197, 226, 282

X
Xerox, 147-148, 233

Z
Zuboff, S., 29, 215, 285